Adventure Guide

Florida Keys
&
Everglades National Park

4th Edition

Bruce Morris

HUNTER

HUNTER PUBLISHING, INC,
130 Campus Drive, Edison, NJ 08818
☎ 732-225-1900; ☎ 800-255-0343; fax 732-417-1744
www.hunterpublishing.com

Ulysses Travel Publications
4176 Saint-Denis, Montréal, Québec
Canada H2W 2M5
☎ 514-843-9882, ext. 2232; fax 514-843-9448

Windsor Books
The Boundary, Wheatley Road, Garsington
Oxford, OX44 9EJ England
☎ 01865-361122; fax 01865-361133

ISBN 1-58843-403-6

Printed in the United States

© 2005 Hunter Publishing, Inc.

Cover photo: Roseate spoonbill © Nancy Camel
All other images provided by the author.
Index by Nancy Wolff
Cartoons by Joe Kohl

Maps by Lissa K Dailey & Kim André, © 2005 Hunter Publishing, Inc.

1 2 3 4

www.hunterpublishing.com

 Hunter's full range of guides to all corners of the globe is featured on our exciting website. You'll find guidebooks to suit every type of traveler, no matter what their budget, lifestyle, or idea of fun.

Adventure Guides – There are now over 40 titles in this series, covering destinations from Costa Rica and the Yucatán to Tampa Bay & Florida's West Coast and Belize. Complete with information on what to do, as well as where to stay and eat, *Adventure Guides* are tailor-made for the active traveler, with all the practical travel information you need, as well as details on the best places for hiking, biking, canoeing, horseback riding, trekking, skiing, watersports, and all other kinds of fun.

Alive Guides – This ever-popular line of books takes a unique look at the best each destination offers: fine dining, jazz clubs, first-class hotels and resorts. In-margin icons direct the reader at a glance. Top-sellers include *St. Martin, St. Barts & Anguilla; The Cayman Islands;* and *Aruba, Bonaire & Curaçao.*

Our **Romantic Weekends** guidebooks provide escapes for couples of all ages and lifestyles. Unlike most "romantic" travel books, ours cover more than charming hotels and delightful restaurants, with a host of activities that you and your partner will remember forever.

One-of-a-kind travel books available from Hunter include *The Best Dives of the Bahamas; London A-Z; A Traveler's Guide to the Galapagos; Cruising Alaska* and many more.

Full descriptions are given for each book at www.hunterpublishing.com, along with reviewers' comments and a cover image. You can also view pages and the table of contents. Books can be purchased on-line via our secure transaction facility.

About the Author

Bruce Morris grew up in Miami and has traveled and lived in the US, Europe, Asia and Central America – sampling the food, fishing, diving, music and good life. He received a BA in Journalism from College of the Potomac while working as photographer and designer at the music magazine *Third Ear*. He has written for a wide variety of magazines and newspapers and wrote *HTML in Action* published in 1996 by Microsoft Press and *Costa Rica Alive!* published by Hunter Publishing in 2003. He founded *The Web Developer's Journal*, started and managed the Internet department at computer manufacturer Gateway 2000, served as Director of Technology at Carlton Online in London and COO of OnAir Europe. He is an avid diver and angler. He lives with his wife at their farm in east Tennessee, along with cats, dogs, horses, assorted barnyard animals and other creatures, as well as several guitars.

Acknowledgments

Without the support of my lovely wife I would never have contemplated taking on this project. Thanks also to my mother and Greg Weinstein for checking the manuscript for errors and foolishness. Dr. Paul Kanciruk provided more help than he knows.

Contents

INTRODUCTION

MARATHON & THE MIDDLE KEYS

LOWER KEYS

∎ Maps

Introduction

As a boy growing up in Miami I fell in love with the beauty of the Keys and the wilderness of the Everglades. With a friend, I spent my weekends snorkeling, pole fishing along the Tamiami Trail and sailing in the Keys. When I was a teenager, my family moved to the hills of Tennessee (with its own wilderness charms) and I was unable to visit South Florida for almost 20 years. When I managed to return for a visit I was afraid that the

over-development and urban sprawl I had seen in other parts of Florida had turned the Keys into just another tacky tourist haven. Thankfully, my fears were unfounded. Certainly, there are more hotels and cheesy, tourist-oriented attractions now than when I was a boy, but the minimal change surprised me. Although not totally unspoiled, both the Keys and the Everglades remain beautiful, full of wildlife and adventure. The fishing, diving and beautiful natural vistas I enjoyed as a boy are still there, and the magic of them can be easily appreciated by car, bike, boat or on foot.

To me, the greatest adventures in the Everglades and Keys involve the wonderful diversity of wildlife, plants and life in the sea. Part, if not most, of the fun of fishing is having an excuse to roam around the flats and reefs checking out birds and sea critters. The best part of scuba diving and snorkeling is looking for – and sometimes coming face-to-face with – some of the strangest looking creatures imaginable. On a short walk along any of the trails in Everglades National Park, you might just spot alligators, crocodiles, vultures or snapping turtles. I'm not much of a birder, but this region of Florida helps me to understand how enthusiasms can grow into intensely absorbing hobbies. Even with my casual knowledge of birds, I enjoy seeing anhingas, diving ducks, pelicans and egrets. I don't keep lists of the fish I see when diving, but I do enjoy browsing through reef fish identification

charts after a dive and learning the names and habits of the psy-
chedelically colored fish I encountered.

Adventure is where you find it and what you make it. It can be
observing birds nesting, snorkeling almost motionlessly over
sawgrass flats, watching shrimp do their thing, or scuba diving
at the edge of the Gulf Stream while looking out for bull sharks
and pelagic predators. But then, there is also plenty of adventure
to be found almost any night on Duval Street in Key West.

Why Come?

Leaving the more earthly delights of Key West aside for a moment, the Keys and Everglades are places for people who enjoy
the outdoors, particularly the sea. Because the water here is relatively shallow, calm and accessible, sea life is easily seen and appreciated. Coral reefs – surely one of the wonders of the world –
are still astounding and relatively unspoiled, and the austere
beauty of the Everglades has been preserved by the creation of
the national park, which is now one of the Park Service's crown-
ing jewels.

Birders are drawn to this region.

For the historically curious as well as hard-core party people or laid-back drifters, Key West is a paradise at the end of the road. If you plan to visit briefly for a few nights of fun, or want to stay awhile and gently go to seed (as so many do), Key West has all that lures such ambitions. The smell, flavor and visions of Hemingwayesque Old Key West with its pirates, spongers, quaint homes (many now serving as B&Bs) and historical walks exist in the middle of one of the premier party towns in the US. Key West lures the young, happy partygoers. A popular spring break destination, it has more festivals, street parties and loud, raucous bars and clubs than you'll have time to visit in a week. As a permanent residence for gay living and visits, the tolerant lifestyle and attitudes of the island are renowned.

While one can have a fine time in the Keys or Everglades without ever setting foot in a boat or dipping a toe in the water, the bulk of the area's charms lie offshore on the reefs, flats and in the canals and mangrove estuaries. To get the full Keys or Everglades experience, a boat, canoe, kayak or even an inner tube are required. Drifting over the shallow flats looking in the turtle grass at exotic seahorses is an experience that can't be had elsewhere. Some of the finest coral reefs in the world are hidden just a few miles offshore and are accessibly shallow, well preserved and astounding in their riot of color and unusual formations.

The sportfishing capital of the US, the Keys and Florida Bay offer both delicate fly-fishing for bonefish and pole-busting sailfish and tarpon action. Guides abound. Trips lasting a day or just a few hours can be arranged with little or no advance notice. Some guides even offer "no fish, no pay" guarantees.

The Everglades seem a long way from Key West. There are no neon signs, no blazing bars, no clubs with guitar-strumming comedians. Instead there is profound silence, slow-moving canals, the desolate beauty of swamps and a sky filled with puffy white clouds gliding over endless miles of saw grass. The Everglades have long attracted the adventurous and those who appreciate nature at its wildest. Parks are designed to make it possible for wheelchair-bound travelers to access the wilderness and appreciate the beauty and variety of birds, exotic orchids, and even hissing crocodiles. To truly enjoy the area, one must be in a reflective and observant mood. Sometimes you have to look hard to spot the attractions. Fortunately, help in the form of the Park Service is at hand, with educational tours, guided walks and paddling expeditions on offer.

The balmy climate, tolerant lifestyle and outdoor opportunities attract a goodly share of retirees and snowbirds fleeing the frozen north. I loved playing here when I was growing up, and I plan on spending many years of my retirement doing the same. A small house on the bay with a dock, snorkeling and fishing gear, and a cooler of beer are all I need. Apparently, many others feel the same way.

How this Book is Organized

This book is designed as a complete guide for the adventurous. I don't mention every bar, hotel, sandbar, stretch of swamp or reef, just the best or most noteworthy in each category. The *Introduction* and *Travel Information* chapters should give you a good feel for the region and all that it offers. They provide all the information you need to plan your trip.

The rest of the book is divided into five region – the Upper Keys, Marathon Area, Lower Keys, Key West and the Everglades. Each of those regional chapters has a brief introductory section and a list of the highlights. Then it's on to the available adventures – on land, on water or even in the air – as well as the guides who can help you enjoy them. Sights and attractions are next. My selection of the best hotels and restaurants is just that, a selection. While many guidebook authors visit as many as five or six hotels and several restaurants every day during their research in an attempt to be "complete" or "comprehensive," I have personally stayed in almost all of the hotels listed, most of them for at least two nights. Any that I have not visited come highly recommended by trustworthy friends or family. My recommendations are based on firsthand experience, not a walk through the lobby. Finally, you'll find details about the local party spots and other nightlife, everything from mild to wild.

History

■ Florida Before Columbus

When Europeans "discovered" Florida it was already home to hundreds of thousands of Native Americans who enjoyed a rich culture and reasonably comfortable lifestyle. Although relatively barbarous and violent compared with our conception of civilized behavior today, their lifestyle was as comfortable and safe as that of the average rural European of the time.

Hundreds of archeological sites in the Everglades show signs of **Paleo-Indian** activity from approximately 10,000 BC. Bison, mammoth, saber-toothed tigers and other large beasts shared the area. The pre-glacial period humans were likely **hunter-gatherers** subsisting on small game, fruits of the sea and foraged vegetable foods. But as the glaciers retreated and the sea level rose, the climate changed and the present form of the Everglades began to take shape with cypress and saw grass swamps. The **Archaic Period** (8,000-750 BC) saw indigenous peoples developing basic tools and pottery, shards of which are still found today. During the **Glades Period** (750 BC-AD 1500), some permanent settlements developed and evidence – indicated by finds of ornaments and pottery typical of other regions – reveals there was extensive trade between people here and those in the Caribbean and Central America. During the **Historic Contact Period** (AD 500-1750), tribes that included the Calusa, Tequesta, Jeaga and Mayaimi may have had a combined population of as high as 20,000. As the Spaniards explored the area they spread diseases common in Europe, such as measles and syphilis, but they were new to the Florida region and decimated the population. Slavery and death, the byproducts of Spanish conquest, further contributed to the decline of the indigenous population, and by 1750 few of the original natives remained. European settlers arrived, driving the newer Creek and Cherokee residents deep into the Everglades. Between 1817 and 1858, bands of Indians, feeling from the Seminole Wars and deportation to reservations in Oklahoma, formed the backbone of what is now known as the Seminole tribe. Their descendants still live in Florida, concentrating on the fringes of the Everglades.

■ Explorers & Conquistadors

As Columbus, Ponce de Leon, De Soto and other explorers moved through the area claiming land for European kings and queens, they dispensed violent and casual death. While few (some would call them conquistadors, others would call them invaders) were slaughtered by indignant indigenous warriors, the superior European technology and use of horses pretty much assured the eventual dominance of the new arrivals. Unfortunately, respect for human life was not a widely followed idea and, indeed, many of the explorers did not consider the natives to be "human" at all. Natives died in their thousands at the hands of the explorers and from the deadly diseases brought with them.

Early settlements were tough places for new arrivals in Florida, and violent or unpleasant death was more frequent than long healthy life. Considering the difficult circumstances, hostile natives and unpleasant climate, the courage and audacity of the early explorers is remarkable. Florida would remain sparsely settled until the invention of air-conditioning made life here tolerable.

■ Pirates

The golden age of pirates lasted only about 100 years, but it was such a colorful time that books, movies, theme parks and legends of pirate gold still make Florida a dream destination for children of all ages. The numerous islands and shallow twisting waterways made the area a prime hiding place for rogues of the sea. Caesar's Creek, a winding, tidal channel separating Old Rhodes Key from Elliot Key, got its name from pirate Black Caesar, who used it as a hideout.

PIRATE'S LAIR

Black Caesar was able to escape capture by dashing into the network of unmarked and confusing channels where it was difficult for anyone to follow. It is said his ship was fitted with collapsible masts so that, once deep in the labyrinthine creek, he could lower the masts and not be seen by his pursuers.

Pirates ranged from the Tortugas to St. Augustine, lurking in the shallow coastal waters, hiding from pursuit or waiting for unsuspecting Spanish treasure ships in the Gulf Stream. Rumors of buried treasure persist to this day and Old Rhodes Key, Indian Key and other places have suffered from the pick and shovel attentions of today's treasure-seekers.

AUTHOR TIDBIT: I have it on good authority that there is buried pirate treasure 150 feet due south of MM 102 in the middle of what is now a Kmart parking lot. Good luck. Remember you heard it here first. Yo ho ho and a bottle of rum.

■ Industries

Wrecking

Due to the remote nature of the Keys and Everglades, inhabitants had to be creative to make anything more than a bare living. Who can blame the locals for taking what they could when ships piled themselves up on the treacherous reefs lining the coast? The reefs were mostly unmarked and ran almost 150 miles along the edge of one of the busiest shipping lanes in the world, so wrecks were common. The harvesting of wrecks became a sophisticated business around 1840, with special warehouses and courts set up in Key West specifically to deal with the disposition of salvaged goods. Fortunes were made and lost. Spotting towers were built so clever wreckers could spy ships in distress on the reefs. A system of lighthouses brought the wreckers' ball to a close around 1890.

Sponging

Natural sponges flourish in the shallow, clean waters around the Keys and the northern US market for them was strong throughout the 19th century, leading to the establishment of a large and booming sponge industry centered mostly in Key West. When the market collapsed in the 1890s, the mostly Greek spongers regrouped farther up the coast near Tarpon Springs on the Gulf, where a few spongers still operate. Although natural sponges are sold in tourist shops, most of the ones you'll see are imported.

Plume Hunting

During the 19th and early 20th centuries, the fashion was for ladies to wear hats with long white tail-feather plumes and colorful bird feathers for decoration. To fill the needs of style-conscious women in New York and Boston, hunters blasted away with shotguns at thousands of nesting birds in the mangroves of the Keys and Everglades. Eggs and nestlings, along with their plume-bearing parents, were destroyed. The hunters were used to seeing tens of thousands of egrets, flamingos, roseate spoonbills, herons, ibis and ducks. Extinction seemed impossible, but even the primitive rifles of the day led to the thinning out and extinction of numerous bird species. When belated conservation laws were passed in 1891 and 1901, few resources were allocated to enforcing them. Those agents who tried to enforce the laws were often themselves made extinct by the lawless and independent-minded plume hunters. Today, only a hint of the vast and colorful bird populations remain.

Cigars

With the cigar paradise of Cuba only a few miles south of Key West, it is unsurprising that the manufacture and distribution of cigars grew in the port. Stirred in part by the Spanish-American War, Cuban cigar producers established themselves in Key West in a big way in the late 1800s. Thousands of workers earning as much as $30 per day rolled millions of cigars for export and local consumption. Hurricanes and the power of the unions drove manufacturers to other parts of Florida, including Tampa, in search of cheaper labor. A few cigar makers still ply their trade in Key West, catering to the tourist trade, and it is not uncommon to see young fellows out for a night self-consciously waving around expensive cigars as they disport themselves in the bars and restaurants around Duval Street. Inexperienced cigar smokers rarely manage to finish them.

> **AUTHOR TIDBIT:** If you are not a regular smoker of cigars, take it easy; cigar smoke is much stronger than cigarette smoke and can upset your stomach and make your head spin.

■ Flagler's Railroad & the Overseas Highway

Railroad magnate **Henry Flagler** had a vision of a railroad running from New York to Key West, where it would link up with shipping lines sparking off a new era of trade between northern US cities and Cuba. The railroad was built on causeways and miles of low bridges, an impressive engineering feat at the time. And while Flagler lived to see the railroad completed, the effect it had on trade with Cuba was minimal. In 1936 a hurricane struck, and large parts of the railroad were destroyed. At that time, a road from Miami to Key

Old Bahía Honda Bridge, one of Flagler's originals.

West was under construction. After several years without recon-
struction efforts on either the road or the railway, it was finally
decided to abandon the railroad and carry on with the road.
Many of the railroad bridges were converted for use by cars and
trucks. The Bahía Honda Bridge still stands with the railroad
tracks running underneath and an extension on top for road.
Much of the old Seven Mile Bridge uses railroad tracks as guard-
rails.

■ The Growth of Tourism

Although the railroad initially made Key West accessible to casual visitors, the construction of the Overseas
Highway made it easy for families to load up and head
for the exotic delights of Key West and the Keys. As the area's attractions became known, tourism exploded. As a boy growing up
in Miami in the 50s and 60s, the lure of the Keys drew my family
like a magnet. Although there were few buildings higher than
one story, the motels and tourist traps seemed like intense
overdevelopment. And when I returned to the Keys after a hiatus
of 20 years, I was certain I would find the place ruined by condo
developments and cheesy roadside attractions. Not so. I was
amazed to see how little the solitude and splendor of the Keys
had changed. Some locals I spoke with seemed to feel otherwise
but, even though there are now vastly more inhabitants and visitors, most of the glorious natural heritage of the Keys has been
preserved. Few high-rise condos exist. Certainly, there are more
roadside attractions (and many of them are cheesy), but the reasons I loved the Keys when I was growing up – pristine waters,
good fishing and diving, the pervasive bohemian community in
Key West – are still there.

The Land

Southern Florida is low and flat with lots of pine trees and mangroves near the coast. Most of the Everglades and surrounding
areas are wet about half the year and have groups of cypress and
pine forests spread among huge seas of saw grass. The entire area

is not much more than a thin layer of topsoil or sand over limestone – the remains of enormous coral reefs now dead for eons.

■ Barrier Reefs & How the Keys Were Formed

A 200-mile wall of living coral parallels the coastline of South Florida, running from Miami all the way past the Dry Tortugas. Shallow areas of sand and turtle grass break the reef here and there. This barrier reef sits at the edge of the swift and warm Gulf Stream, which feeds it with microscopic plankton. It is a rich and intense aquatic environment of sponges, large and small fish, and undersea plant life. As shallow and slow-growing coral pushes through the ocean's surface it forms small islands of dead coral and sand. Little by little, vegetation begins to grow, as mangroves take root and seeds wash up or are deposited by passing birds. At times hurricanes blast the new land, causing the process to start all over again. This centuries-long land-formation process continues almost imperceptibly to the human eye.

Most of South Florida and the Keys were formed in this way and you can still see fragments of the old barrier reef as you drive along the waterfront in Coconut Grove. Dig down almost anywhere and you'll encounter coral rock just inches below the recently arrived soil.

■ The Gulf Stream

Circular currents in the Gulf of Mexico form a relatively warm and salty water route, called the Gulf Stream, that spins off and heads north through the narrow passage between Cuba, Florida and the Bahamas, moving within only a few miles of the East Coast and past Maine before circling east towards England and Europe. It maintains its warmth long enough to be one of the major contributors to weather patterns in the north of the Western Hemisphere. Without this warming effect, both New England and Northern Europe would be much colder. Civilization in Europe would not have developed as it has. There would be no tea and crumpets, no Monty Python. There would have been no Napoleon, no fancy French food and perhaps no (groan!) cricket or soccer. The coral reefs fringing the Keys would not exist. There would be no tourism in the Keys with its attendant fishing and diving were it not for the Gulf Stream.

■ Parks & Preserves

Without the many high-quality parks and preserves that have been created in the area, the beauty and unique wildlife of the Keys and Everglades would have been lost to excessive development years ago.

Local, state and national parks cover vast areas of the Keys. Everglades National Park itself is surrounded by other protected areas. Some of the more interesting and important parks, such as John Pennekamp Coral Reef State Park, are entirely or almost entirely underwater.

Cypress hammocks are common in natural areas.

A national park differs from a national preserve in the activities that are allowed. Little is allowed to disturb the natural scheme of nature in a National Park, whereas a National Preserve might allow a variety of activities, such as hunting, fishing, cattle ranching, off-the-road vehicle use, logging and even oil extraction. If you are looking to do more than watch for birds, you're probably best off heading to a National Preserve.

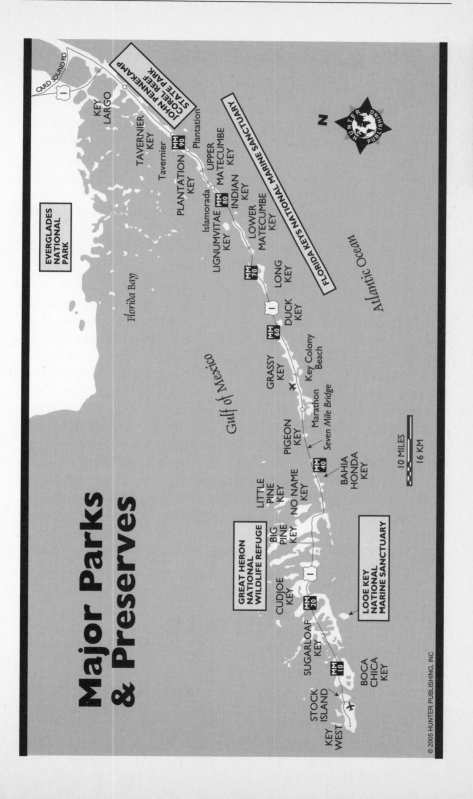

Major Parks & Preserves

© 2005 HUNTER PUBLISHING, INC

■ The River of Grass

Author and conservationist Marjory Stoneman Douglas was perhaps the first person to refer to the saw grass swamps and plains of the Everglades as a "river of grass." And it is a river, only this river's current is excruciatingly slow. It could take years for a molecule of water to move from Lake Okeechobee to the Gulf. Islands in the form of "hammocks," clumps of cypress and other trees and shrubs, dot its surface. This watery ecology is the home and incubation area for many important species: shrimp, various fish species and bird life are dependent on the nutrients and sheltered spawning areas the Everglades offers.

For many years, few people ventured into this river. Saw grass has sharp, saw-like leaves. Snakes, panthers and bears patrol the water's edge. Almost unbearable heat and storm clouds of mosquitoes kept humanity at bay. But the invention of air conditioning made life bearable, providing a new target for suburbia. As a result, development-fueled drainage projects have reduced the river to a piddling stream in many places. The saw grass and other vegetation depending on seasonal moisture is disappearing. In spite of the new awareness of this problem and legislation providing funds for clean up and undoing of drainage projects, powerful forces in favor of continued development remain. Much has been made of the sugar industry's efforts to dilute such legislation so it can continue to allow pollutants and other damaging, nutrient-laden runoff to poison vast areas of this sensitive environment. Some think the destruction is irreversible. Even if it is not, the cost of restoring the Everglades to near-pristine conditions may be prohibitive.

Climate

Florida is a world-famous tourist and retirement destination. It's not just the beaches that have earned this reputation – the climate, although hot at times, is great. Southern Florida rarely sees freezing temperatures and the summer heat is cooled by trade winds and afternoon showers.

■ **Summertime**

Temperatures in the 80s and 90s are normal from May through October, but it's not a dry heat. Humidity adds to the experience, making summertime my favorite season in Florida. The trade wind tends to blow moderately from the east in the afternoon, often accompanied by cooling and spectacular passing thunderstorms. Wear a hat with a broad brim and drink lots of water. Soak in the hotel pool and enjoy tropical fruit drinks in the shade.

■ **Hurricanes**

Hurricane season runs approximately from September through November and, although tourist activity is down a little during this period, it is probably the best time to visit. Smaller crowds, cooler weather and lower prices make it my favorite time for a trip here.

Evacuation procedures for moving people out of the low-lying Keys to the mainland are well developed, so it is unlikely that tourists will be allowed to remain in the area for a serious bout with a hurricane. Still, even the threat of a hurricane moving through the Bahamas or across Cuba can ruin your well-planned vacation. Stormy, rainy weather occurs even when hurricanes are passing at a safe distance. Can you plan for this? Other than simply avoiding hurricane season, no!

■ **Wintertime**

"Winter" is not really winter in South Florida. People expect warm, sunny days in December and January and are rarely disappointed. Still, a mid-winter vacation may see temperatures that hover in the high 60s for weeks at a time. I remember one Christmas season spent with family on Ramrod Key when we felt quite put upon because the temperatures were "too cold" – in the 60s. Locals refuse to go in the water before June or after August, but that's their hang-up. We did plenty of diving and fishing and found the temperature perfect for walking around Key West or playing around in kayaks. A light sweater or windbreaker is likely the only extra equipment you will need if you come in the winter.

Flora & Fauna

South Florida is lush with interesting tropical plants. **Mangroves** line the coasts; **royal palms, cabbage palms, coconut palms** and dozens of other palms grow wild as well as pampered in people's yards. Just outside Everglades National Park in Homestead are dozens of **orchid** and exotic tropical plant nurseries. Krome Avenue, in particular, is lined with commercial nurseries and well worth a visit.

A cormorant watches you, watching him.

Every Everglades visitor wants to see **alligators, crocodiles, panthers** and **bears** in just about that order. I'd like to say there are thousands of them running around everywhere, but the only things you are likely to see in thousands are fellow tourists and other cattle. But even if you only get a half-day or day in Everglades National Park, you'll see plenty of alligators and, probably, crocodiles. Cats and bears are rare and seldom seen even by the park naturalists. Don't bet your bank balance on seeing either.

WILDLIFE WATCH: *Hard to find but of interest to some are the **cotton rat**, found in the Lower Keys, and the **rice rat**, seen only on Cudjoe Key.*

■ Birds

Twitchers get excited about the number of species they can add to their life list during a trip to the Everglades and Keys, and Everglades National Park is one of the top four or five places in the US for birders.

Humble **brown pelicans** and **seagulls** are everywhere. The graceful flight of the pelican is in direct contrast to its landings, which resemble a bag of cement being tossed into the water. Somehow, they come up with fish by diving this way. The **American white pelican** makes an occasional appearance during winter months. Seagulls are great squabblers that like to fight over every scrap. **Fish hawks** are a fairly common sight, often perched menacingly on top of pine trees or floating on the up-drafts as mere specks in the sky. **American bald eagles** are a little bit bigger than hawks. Eagles are rarely seen nesting in the remote mangroves, but look for their dark body and distinctive white head. **Cormorants**, or what I like to call "diving ducks," can be seen sitting on top of pilings and sticks. They swim quite well underwater, looking for fish which they gobble up with their long, thin beaks. They can travel several hundred feet below the

Herons spend many hours poking in the water with their long beaks.

surface without coming up for air. Feathers plucked from dead **roseate spoonbills** were used as hat ornaments in the late 1800s and early 1900s. Since that time, the species has remained scarce. Look for a pink body with a black ring around the neck and an outlandishly long bill with a big flat spoon on the end. A roseate spoonbill is featured on the cover of this book.

PHOTOGRAPHY

Photography opportunities in the Keys are everywhere. The colorful islands themselves along with the many-hued sand flats, coral reefs, turtle grass beds and the blue channels between them make stunning pictures. Add a friend or loved one and a boat or two and you'll be able to bore your friends for hours upon your return to Ardmore, Oklahoma or Carbondale, Illinois.

If you have a telephoto lens, you are bound to get some good bird shots, especially pelicans, but do give serious consideration to buying a tripod, too. Serious birders flock to the Keys to observe waterbirds and subtropical species. Don't forget, Everglades National Park, famous for its wildlife, is only minutes away on the Bay side from most of the Keys. You won't be able to resist the inevitable sunset shots as the golden orb goes down over Florida Bay.

To cope with the extremely bright sun, select film of no more than 200 ASA; 100 ASA is preferable for outdoor shots. In the bright light of the Keys, a polarizing filter will keep the skies from looking washed out and make puffy white clouds look bright and prominent.

One-hour photo developing services are offered at many locations. **Walgreen's** does a fair job at a fair price. **CAM Plus**, MM 83, ☎ 305-664-5475, in Islamorada, is the place to go if you need something you can't find in the big chain stores.

As you drive into the Keys from Homestead, you'll see what look like medieval torture devices – tall poles with small platforms on top. If an **osprey** has taken an interest in these strange bird-houses, the top will be adorned with a huge pile of sticks, passing for a nest. Ospreys build their nests on top of power poles and other high, man-made structures and tall trees. Ospreys look a bit like eagles, but are not as elegant.

Herons are the great big, long-legged, long-winged, long-necked beasts you see flying around and squawking loudly. Both **egrets** and herons are wading birds that spend hours poking their absurd beaks into the mud looking for crustaceans, fish or almost anything else that doesn't get out of the way. **Blue herons**, **Louisiana herons**, **great white herons**, **snowy egrets** and **great egrets** nest in large colonies in areas of dense mangroves. You are sure to see hundreds of them stepping daintily through the mud flats as you drive along.

> **LOCAL LINGO:** Some residents refer to the snowy egret as the **Chokoloskee chicken** due to its fine eating qualities.

Sharp eyes and patience may lead to sightings of **Cape Sable seaside sparrows**, **purple gallinules, wood storks** and **moorhens**. Hard-core birders pursue obscure birds like the **mangrove cuckoo** and **white-crowned pigeon**. Although I would love to see these, I share the joy of birders and sailors everywhere watching the flying ability of the more common **man-o-war** or **frigate bird**. These birds have extremely sharp eyesight and can spot schooling baitfish from thousands of feet up. Fishermen look for them to show the way. Dozens of other flashy and rare bird species lurk in the depths of the Everglades.

■ Big Cats

 The **Florida panther** (more correctly referred to as a puma, *Felis concolor coryi*) is the most endangered animal in Florida. These panthers are large, weighing up to 250 lbs. Their fur is light brown, with spots on the young. Under 100 Florida panthers are believed to live in the whole state. Most of those have been caught by researchers and now wear radio-tracking collars for the edification of science and to determine how we can help them survive. Unfortunately, the population is so small that genetic defects from inbreeding are the most serious obstacle to their continued existence. An unusual whorl of dark hair on their backs and a 90-degree crook at the end of their tails distinguish the Florida panther from their more numerous cousins in the rest of the country. Some biologists say these traits in themselves are evidence of inbreeding. Heart defects and low motility of panther sperm are believed to be the result of inbreeding or of high mercury levels found in their prey.

Although most panthers live in central Florida, an estimated population of five live in Everglades National Park, isolated by the waters of Shark River Slough. The numbers in the park are small because the wet nature of the area means fewer of their natural prey – deer and wild pigs – are found. However, the Everglades group is healthier than panthers in other parts of Florida, since they bred with partners escaped or released from captivity that were imported from Central or South America, thus adding outside genes to the shrinking local gene pool.

SAVE THE PANTHER

There are two approaches to saving the Florida panther. Controversial captive breeding programs (said to interfere with nature and rob the noble animals of the dignity of their species' natural death and decline) are attempting to increase the population. The other approach involves securing large land packages to be set aside as preserved panther habitat. Since the range of a panther can be as much as 25 square miles, a huge amount of land needs to be bought. Several organizations are involved in what is probably the only approach that might offer long-term possibilities for maintaining a viable population of wild panthers. Development interests and the enormous influx of people into Florida make the process difficult. Of course, hunting deer and wild pigs could be restricted, thus increasing the panthers' access to prey, but the powerful hunting lobby has fierce resistence.

Every year, cars hit cats as they attempt to cross highways in their long-range rambling. Wildlife tunnels under I-75 (Alligator

Alley), built at a cost of over $1 million each, may help solve this problem. Some panthers are simply shot for sport or greed. Even though they rarely attack cattle, humans or pets, many people fear them and would shoot them on sight.

Panthers are extremely shy and reclusive. Even studying biologists rarely see them, so the chances of visitors to the park seeing one are close to zero. But just knowing they are there, lurking in the palmetto thickets, gives a special thrill to the Everglades experience.

"Panther Crossing" sign.

■ Deer

Some deer are left in the Everglades, but casual visitors do not usually see them. However, it is not at all unusual to spot the exotic and tiny **Key deer** when driving through the Lower Keys, especially around Big Pine Key. The first time I saw a Key deer off in the distance I thought it was a Doberman, given its size, its pointy ears and its lean, long-legs. If you want to look for them, you may have luck simply cruising just before sunset through the back streets of Big Pine Key, where some undeveloped lots offer privacy. I've had the best luck just past the end of the bridge to No Name Key. I suggest you park by the side of the road in a place where you can see well down the road in either direction. Turn off the motor and wait inside the car for a half-hour or so.

■ Insects

Any entomologist will tell you there are hundreds more insect species in the Everglades and the Keys than all the other types of living creatures combined. You will rarely be aware of more than a few – **mosquitoes**, **no-see-ums**, **green flies**, **horse flies** and **common houseflies** are about all you will notice. Fortunately, window screens, air-conditioning and bug repellent with a high amount of DEET make living with such an interesting population of insects bearable.

> **WILDLIFE WATCH:** *Forty different species of mosquitoes inhabit the Everglades. Most have no interest in humans.*

Although rare, the **Schaus swallowtail butterfly** can be found in the Upper Keys.

MOSQUITO REPELLENT

The most effective mosquito and no-see-um repellents contain DEET (diethylmetaoluamide) as the main active ingredient. Check the label before you buy to make sure you get one with plenty of oomph. The strongest brands contain as much as 90% DEET. That's the kind you want; stay aware from mixes with very low percentages of DEET.

I'm unsure of the health consequences of spraying DEET on your body for weeks at a time, but I can assure you it does keep the bugs away. There have been times when I would have happily drenched myself from head to toe in diesel fuel just to keep mosquitoes at bay. Skin-So-Soft lotion is rumored to ward off ankle-biters.

Take more repellent than you think you will need. If anyone knows of a pleasant repellent that works under heavy-duty mangrove swamp-conditions, I would like to hear about it. Be sure to give your dog a spritz of bug repellent as well.

■ Raccoons

The cute little raccoons found in the Keys and Everglades have raided more picnic baskets and garbage cans than Yogi Bear ever thought about. There are lots of them, and they tend not to be terribly shy. I've had raccoons approach within just a foot or two of me looking to snatch food scraps off my picnic table. This is too close. Raccoons can carry unpleasant diseases and may bite or scratch. Wild ones are not cuddly. Look for the cartoon bandit mask and ring-encircled tail.

■ Reptiles

Reptile and amphibian-fanciers will be well satisfied with the plethora of dangerous and unusual snakes, lizards and frogs. There are approximately 38 species of snakes in the area, only five of which are poisonous. Some of the more menacing snakes are best imagined, rather than encountered. The notorious **Eastern coral snake** is so pretty it begs to be examined closely. Please don't approach. **Timber, diamondback** and **pygmy rattlesnakes** are not uncommon.

Crocodiles are seen mostly in the Everglades areas near the coast and in a few quieter parts of Key Largo. Even though they are not common, the Eco Pond near the Flamingo campground is usually stuffed full of crocs. American crocodiles grow to 15 feet and tend to be a bit shyer than alligators. You can easily tell a crocodile from an alligator by the croc's more pointed snout. Crocodiles like salty or brackish water. They attack people, so give them plenty of room.

Caimans are smaller than crocs or alligators, and are comparatively rare in Florida, but thrive on nearby Caribbean islands. All caimans in Florida are thought to be the offspring of animals imported for pets or zoos that have escaped or been released into the wild. Caimans have a narrow snout with a curved, bony ridge on it.

Although **alligators** were considered endangered for many years, they are making a strong comeback and you will see plenty of them with little effort. You can make a back-seat game of counting the alligators as you whiz along the Tamiami Trail. Alligators make a very loud croaking or roaring sound unlike anything else. If you walk the short Anhinga Trail (see page 279) you will certainly see and hear enough alligators to suit even the most jaded fan. Alligators have a distinctive snout shaped like a shovel – broad with a rounded tip. They grow to well over 15 feet long and have been known to attack dogs, cats and, occasionally, humans.

Alligators are making a comeback after years of population decline.

Life in the Sea

The rich sea life in and around the Keys and Everglades is one of the prime attractions of the region. Since the area is still relatively undeveloped and hard to access, much of the marine environment is in good shape, meaning there is a lot to see. Coral reefs are well known to be teeming with colorful creatures. The flats of Florida Bay and mangrove islands of the Everglades are breeding and nursery grounds for hundreds of marine species, from shrimp to blue marlin. Getting out on the water by whatever means – glass-bottomed boat, canoe, wading – is obligatory.

A sand crab hides.

■ Dolphins

South Florida waters, both shallow and deep, abound with dolphins. The most common kind is the **bottlenose**, but other types (such as the **spotted dolphin**) are also often seen. The athletic **spinner dolphin** is sometimes seen.

■ Fish

There are more than 600 species of fish in the Florida Keys and Everglades. More than 100 of them are game fish species. The coral reefs teem with seemingly thousands of tiny fish all trying to out-do the others in style, makeup and weird behavior. Even if you don't get into the water to see any of these fish up close, you can at least eat some of them. In fact it's hard not to eat seafood in the Keys; **snapper**, **grouper**, **yellowtail** and **mahi** (dolphin) are the most common fish on the menu. If you want to see them but don't want to get wet, go on a glass-bottom boat tour or look down from a bridge.

RED SNAPPER – ARE THEY REALLY RED?

Of course they are – that's why they call them "red" snapper. But snappers come in many colors, including gray, yellow and brown. When you see them underwater the color is not apparent, but that's because some colors, especially red, become less distinct the deeper you go. Regardless, once in the pan, the color is only a memory. If you see whole red snapper on the menu, order it! It may even have some red skin left on it after broiling. Red snapper has a characteristic flaky texture and is one of the sweetest fish on the menu. Yellowtail is a close relative and is also one of the best fish to order.

Some of the old Overseas Highway bridges have been converted into fishing or walking piers and offer a good chance to see shallow-water species such as **sharks**, **leopard rays**, **barracuda** and the occasional **tarpon**. Snorkeling or scuba diving gets you close up to zillions of colorful reef fish, as well as some deep-water species like **Goliath groupers** (jewfish), **jacks**, **blue runners** and many types of **snappers** and **grunts**. For close encounters with top-tier game fish (**bonefish, sailfish, kingfish, permit, tarpon, wahoo** and even **marlin**), you need to charter or rent a boat and head a couple of miles offshore.

RECIPE – Grilled Whole Red Snapper

❐ 2-5 lbs fresh whole red snapper
❐ 3 onions
❐ 2 sweet peppers, 1 red and 1 yellow
❐ 1 head of garlic, peeled
❐ 2 limes
❐ Salt
❐ Fresh ground black pepper
❐ Olive oil
❐ Balsamic vinegar
❐ 1 mango, peeled and pip removed
❐ A few sprigs of cilantro
❐ 1 hot pepper (jalapeño), seeded and stemmed

❒ 1 teaspoon Dijon mustard (optional)
❒ 2 teaspoons sesame oil (optional)
❒ 1 teaspoon honey (optional)

If the onions are big, put them in the oven at 350°F for a half-hour before you start broiling the fish. (If you put raw onions and the fish under the broiler at the same time, the fish will be done before the onions.)

Prepare the marinade. In a blender, place the mango, half the garlic, peeled, ½ teaspoon salt, 1 teaspoon fresh ground black pepper, the juice of a lime, 1 cup olive oil, 2 tablespoons balsamic vinegar and the hot pepper. Pulse the blender until you have a slushy texture.

Make sure the snapper has been gutted, scaled and cleaned properly. Leave the head on. Wash in cold water. Make three or four diagonal slits about a half-inch long across the body on both sides of the fish. Place in a large plastic bag and add most of the marinade. Seal and shake to ensure marinade covers the fish. Put it in the refrigerator for one hour or even overnight, turning occasionally.

Take the fish out of the bag and place it on a broiler pan or onto the charcoal grill. Surround it with the partially cooked onions, remaining garlic cloves (you don't have to skin them) and sliced sweet peppers. Broil for five-10 minutes on each side. Cooking time varies with fish size and oven/grill temperature; stick a fork in a thick part of the fish to see if it's done. The peppers should be partially black and the skin of the fish crispy.

Place fish on a serving platter with the best looking side up; make sure the eyeball is still in place – it may look gross, but a socket without an eyeball looks worse. Arrange the peppers and garlic around the fish. Just before serving, squeeze the last lime and drizzle the reserved marinade over the entire dish. Garnish with a few sprigs of cilantro.

■ Manatees

Manatees, or sea cows, are very like cows: in size, in eating habits and in their docile nature. Most people would call them ugly. They float about serenely consuming literally tons of vegetation every day. Manatees inhabit shallow coastal areas and, although endangered, they are not all that hard to spot. I've seen them near the marina in Flamingo and in the bay in back of Key Largo.

> **WILDLIFE WATCH:** *The leading cause of death for manatees is collisions with powerboats. Go slow when boating in manatee habitats.*

■ Turtles

Five of the world's eight sea turtle species are found in the Everglades and Keys. **Loggerheads**, **green turtles** and **leatherbacks** are the most common. **Ridley's** and **hawksbills** are seen occasionally. It is estimated that turtles make as many as 50,000 nests every year on the few sandy beaches in the area. Turtles nest only in sandy areas and almost always do so at night. They are shy of coming ashore if there are lights or activity of any sort. Sandy beaches are rare in the Everglades and Keys and almost all are active nesting areas. Nesting is usually done between May 1 and the end of October. If you happen to see sea turtles on the beach, keep your distance. The best place to find sea turtles is in and around the Keys named for them: the Dry Tortugas. At the right time of year, it is possible to see hundreds of these marine animals as you travel by boat or plane from Key West to Fort Jefferson.

> **WILDLIFE ALERT:** *You could cause sea turtles to abandon their egg-laying activities if you get too close to their nesting area.*

Introduction

■ Whales

Although the stranding and death of numerous pilot whales near Big Pine Key recently made the international news, whales are rarely spotted in the Keys. The waters around Everglades National Park are too shallow for them, but the Gulf Stream is a logical route for migrating cetaceans. Killer, humpback, gray and pilot whales are the most commonly spotted types.

The Florida Keys & the Everglades Today

Few places in North America have changed as much as South Florida has in the last 100 years. Few places in South Florida have changed as little as have the Keys and the parts of the Everglades that are now Everglades National Park. Fortunately, preservation efforts have saved the Everglades from the worst development pressures and the Keys wears well the modest amount of development that has occurred.

■ The Arts

The Keys have long been a refuge for the independent-minded and have attracted creative types since they was first settled. Key West is famous as the home of many noted writers and artists.

Galleries

The elegant gallery at the **Kona Kai** resort on Key Largo is open to the public and features such artists as Ruth Bloch, Vincent Magni, Clyde Butcher and Dirk Verdoorn. See page 122. Key West is almost overflowing with art and noted galleries, including **Cuba! Cuba!**, the **Lucky Street Gallery** and the **Pura Vida Gallery**.

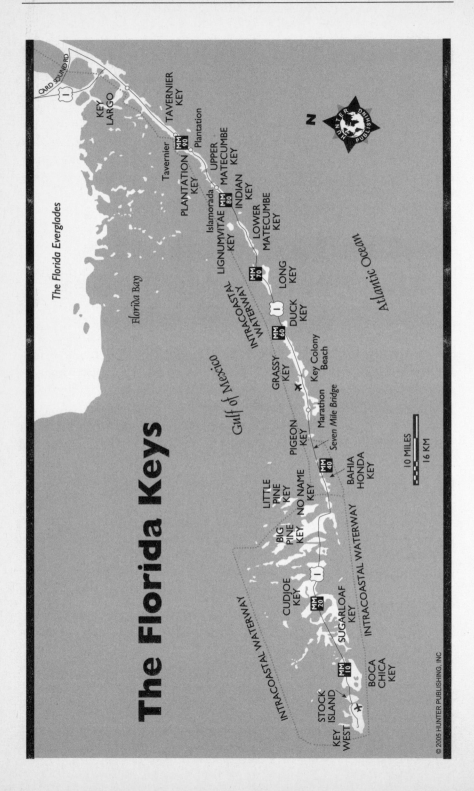

LOCAL ARTISTS OF NOTE

Noted artist **Sarah Stites** and her photographer husband **Bill Stites** own the Seascape Ocean Resort in Marathon. Her art adds ambiance to all the rooms. **Sandford Birdsey**'s watercolors capture the "Old Key West" spirit. Renowned artists like **Suzie De Poo, Judy Waterman, George Carey** all have their works in Key West galleries.

■ Museums

Even though there are no grand publicly supported museums in the traditional sense, there are a couple of real stand-outs among the tourist-oriented offerings. **Mel Fisher Maritime Heritage Society and Museum**, *200 Greene Street, Key West,* ☎ 305-294-2633, is famous for its impressive displays of gold, jewelry and artifacts retrieved from the *Atocha* and other wrecked Spanish treasure ships. The **Little White House Museum**, *111 Front Street,* ☎ *305-294-9911, Key West,* is one of the most interesting of the historical attractions in the Keys. The amazingly twee and boring **Key West Shipwreck Historeum**, ☎ *305-292-8990, www.shipwreckhistoreum.com,* caters to the cruise ship crowd milling about Mallory Square.

■ Fairs & Festivals

Whether your idea of culture is sipping tea while listening to lectures on fine art or guzzling margaritas served from a hose while enjoying a wet T-shirt contest, the Keys have something to suit all tastes. Events like Fantasy Fest, various arts and crafts and exotic food festivals, as well as weird underwater concerts fill the calendar. See *Holidays & Cultural Events* for details on the region's fantastic celebrations.

■ Food

Even a picky eater like me has a hard time complaining about the great seafood found in Keys' restaurants.

Fresh fish, shrimp, local lobster (called "lobster," but actually the Florida crawfish or spiny lobster) and crab are everywhere. It's hard to go wrong eating local seafood, but steer clear of restaurants where the "fresh local seafood" actually comes to their back door pre-breaded and frozen. It's packed in cardboard boxes with the layers of breaded "units" separated by thick wax paper. That's why the shrimp are unnaturally flat. The breading is usually a bigger part of the serving. I am also dismayed by what even some upscale restaurants serve as "steamed vegetables." These come, you guessed it, frozen and already steamed in large plastic bags. They all look the same and the cooks just shake them out of the bag and put them in a hot table until needed. When I'm paying $20 and more for my meal, I expect fresh food.

With the help of this book, you can find real, fresh seafood for reasonable prices. The "Author Picks" listed in this book are places I have eaten at over and over again and know to be good. Still, places change. If you find any of my recommendations to be incorrect, please let me know so I can revisit and update my review for future readers. Send your feedback to comments@hunter-publishing.com.

My general advice is to stick with local specialties, which are usually very good. Ask the locals where they eat. If you order snow crab or halibut (neither one found alive anywhere near the Keys) you are getting a frozen dinner. If you order yellowtail, it is very likely you'll be enjoying a fish that was caught in the last day or so within a few miles of where you're sitting.

Cost

With the variety of restaurants in the Keys, you can expect to eat a great meal for under $10 if you select carefully. You can also spend well over $50 for a great meal. The listings in this book concentrate on restaurants I rate from good to great. No matter the price range. The same as anywhere, some of the most visible and talked-about restaurants actually serve mediocre or even poor food, relying on atmosphere or location to keep the cash registers ringing. I like a good atmosphere, but I go out to eat primarily to feast on good chow. Any restaurant listed as an "Author's Pick" is a place I go back to with my family and friends.

The price symbols for each listing consider the average cost of main courses listed on the menu.

RESTAURANT PRICE CHART

$	Under $8
$$	$8-12
$$$	$12-20
$$$$	Over $20

Local Specialties

It's no surprise that the local food is what makes the best eating. Some dishes unique to the Keys simply must be tried at least once during your visit.

Conch fritters and chowder are popular. Conchs have a large, spiral-shaped shell. In the old days, these shellfish were a staple in the regional diet and locals became known as "conchs." Conch chowders are usually milk-based.

> **LOCAL LINGO:** Be sure to pronounce it "CONK" and not the way it is spelled.

Mahi (or sometimes mahi-mahi) is the fish formerly known as "dolphin" or *dorado* in Spanish. When the TV character Flipper educated the public that what had been called a "porpoise" was more properly referred to as a "dolphin," restaurant owners found the eating public confused. Often, they refused to eat the fish, and so the name was changed to mahi. The fish is almost always served filleted and has a flaky texture and slightly sweet taste.

Grouper appears in sandwiches with cheese, lettuce, tomato and tartar sauce and is usually served filleted. The fillets are chunky and the flakes of flesh prominent. The best grouper sandwiches are messy affairs, their quality being judged by the level of messiness. If you find juice dripping off your elbow while eating a grouper sandwich, you are probably eating one of the best.

You don't find **yellowtail** served many places besides the Keys and South Florida. A member of the snapper family, yellowtails don't get very big and are therefore often served whole. This is one of the best eating fish in the Keys.

Steamed **shrimp** served peel-and-eat style, either hot or cold, are a staple in every restaurant in the Keys. **Key West Pinks** are probably the plumpest, most flavorful kind. Expect to pay anywhere from $10 on up to $20 for a half-pound of these puppies. If you find an all-you-can-eat deal or a pound for around $14, gorge yourself. Shrimp cocktails here are like those found anywhere else – four jumbo-size shrimp with cocktail sauce that somehow leaves you feeling that you came up short on the deal.

Stone crabs are unlike any other type of crab. They are caught locally in traps and only one of the huge claws is taken off before the crab is dropped back into the water. The crabs grow a replacement claw and, with one claw for protection while they rejuvenate, they can be harvested again year after year. Once in a while you can find an all-you-can-eat stone crab deal. Ballyhoo's (see page 130) has such a deal in season for a mere $24.95. The same meal will cost you well over $50 in Miami.

Key lime pie is known the world over for its tangy lime flavor. Key limes are very small with a yellow skin and, although they did not originate in the Keys, can now be found all over Florida and even in the Kroger's near my house in Tennessee. Almost every restaurant claims their pie has been voted "the best Key lime pie in the Keys." There are a few styles and aficionados are ferocious about supporting one or other of the preparation techniques. The pies come with or without meringue, with or without either whipped cream or "dairy topping" and either frozen (ice-box style) or simply cool. They can be made with egg yolks, flour or corn starch and almost always involve a secret ingredient. My preference is for the icebox style with no toppings, a form that is getting harder to find.

> **AUTHOR TIDBIT:** If the pie is green, it has been dyed. Real Key limes are yellowish and the juice is clear-to-yellow in color.

Cuban Influence

As in most of South Florida, Cuban-American restaurants and Cuban-influenced cooking can be found everywhere in the Keys. Although food in Cuba itself is sadly lacking in interest and often bland, Cuban-American food, as I call it, is brilliant, tasty and usually cheap. I mention a few good Cuban eateries in this book and you should not pass them up. Don't miss the wonderful Cuban coffee served strong and black, something like espresso, or *con leche*, with hot milk. Every time I drive through Key Largo I have to stop at Denny's Latin Café (see page 130) for a cup of this Cuban nectar.

THE BLACKENED TRUTH

Blackened fish (or chicken) was originally a Cajun specialty prepared by heavily coating the fish with spices and then "blackening" it by tossing it for a few moments onto a red-hot skillet. The fish cooks very quickly and the spices burn a bit, creating a black coating. Red-hot skillets are difficult to work with, so nowadays real blackened food is almost unheard of. Restaurant kitchen preparation of blackened food now consists of simply pouring a big pile of black pepper and Cajun spices over the fish before cooking it in traditional ways. You can buy Cuban spice powder of varying quality in almost any supermarket. For reasons I have never been able to figure out other than perhaps greed, some restaurants charge $1 extra for this treatment.

Many people fear Cuban food will be too spicy for their palate, but Cuban food is relatively bland, served with a bottle of Louisiana hot sauce on the side. In Cuba these days, hot peppers are almost unknown, and even a pepper shaker is a rarity. Spices don't go much further than lime juice and a little salt. Cuban food in the US may include a little saffron to make the rice yellow.

Fine Dining

Although most of the tourist restaurants claim to offer fine dining and charge accordingly, a few places exist where talented chefs push the boundaries and offer truly wonderful fusions of local ingredients and continental or Asian traditions. Linen napkins and candles do not tell the whole story. You'll find my recommendations of the best places listed in the *Where to Eat* sections of each regional chapter.

■ Music

One of the nice things about a visit to the Keys is the opportunity to hear live music. Strolling around the entertainment areas of Key West you can listen to a wide variety of musical styles. While the Jimmy Buffet-influenced Caribbean sound is a little too common for my taste, blues, rock, folk and occasional jazz can be found. The unfortunate effects of karaoke and DJs are felt perhaps a little less here than in other parts of the country. Live music is provided in many clubs, bars and restaurants up and down the Keys. The **Hurricane** in Marathon (page 172) and the **Geiger Key Smokehouse** (page 199), next to Big Coppitt Key, are oases of live music. Noted entertainers include **Big Dick and the Extenders** (quite good in spite of their unfortunate name), **Alfonso** (known as "Fonz"), the **Charlie Morris Blues Band** (led by my brother), and **Barry Cuda** (also with an unfortunate name, but very good).

Although good live music can be found in the Keys, economic reality is that few groups are paid more than $100 per man per night, and it is a rare hotel in Key West that charges much less than $100 per night. Entertainers interested in actually making a living tend to avoid the area, so many bars hire fairly inexperienced or desperate acts. One notable exception in Key West is **Sloppy Joe's** (page 263). Sloppy's does a bustling business and can afford to hire good musicians. **Pete & Wayne**, although not noted for musical excellence, are regulars there and they are, without a doubt, the premier act in the Keys. Also check out the **Green Parrot** (page 262), where local musicians go after work for reliably good sounds.

■ People

The Keys and the Everglades have been attracting adventurers and nonconformists since the area was first settled. It continues to be a haven for the counterculture and those whose chosen lifestyles may not be completely suitable for conservative middle America. As a visitor, be prepared to be surprised, shocked and even titillated by how the locals and other visitors comport themselves. Many people come here to live a quiet life in the warm climate enjoying the proximity of the sea. Others come to party, flaunt themselves in front of like-minded crowds dancing to a Caribbean beat or simply watch as others stretch the "anything goes" atmosphere to the limits. If public nudity and public drinking offend you, avoid Key West during its notorious partying events like Fantasy Fest.

Gay Life

Few places in the US are as tolerant of gay lifestyles as Key West. The town attracts permanent residents and visitors who appreciate non-traditional lifestyles. Gays and straights get along famously in the Keys. Many hotels, bars, restaurants and entertainment establishments welcome all, whatever their sexual proclivities. Others try to limit their patrons to one particular lifestyle; gay-only and lesbian-only venues exist, and many bars and entertainment spots are aimed at particular sexual orientations. Enjoy the show. You might learn something.

Gay or lesbian visitors may want to contact the **Gay & Lesbian Community Center**, *513 Truman Avenue*, ☎ *305-292-3223, www.glcckeywest.org.*

Indigenous Cultures

There are no remnants of pre-Columbian people left in Florida. Near Everglades National Park, Seminole Indians, a tribe that moved to the area well after Columbus passed nearby, has settlements.

Retirees

As is true throughout the state, the Keys have attracted retirees from all over the US and other countries. They come for the warm weather, fabulous outdoor life, modern shopping centers and the proximity of advanced medical care. Due to high demand for limited real estate, the Keys are rated Florida's most expensive place to live. Small, rundown mobile homes on tiny lots away from the water sell for upwards of $150,000. However, neighborhoods near Everglades National Park, such as Homestead, offer much more economical housing choices, along with the proximity of the Keys, the park and the delights of nearby Miami.

Conchs

Florida Keys natives are known as "Conchs" after the mollusk that was their culinary staple during early settler times. Conchs are proud of their culture and defend it. They tend to be friendly and welcoming to the tourists who are providing a living for many year-round residents. They have a unique Southern accent that reminds me of the thick drawl of North Carolina. But Conchs are a definite minority and sometimes feel put upon by the hoards of tourists who flood the area. Some feel the influx of big money investors have displaced them from their rightful place in business and commerce.

> **AUTHOR NOTE:** Due to the influx of tourists and retirees and the limited amount of land, residential real estate is out of reach for many of the middle class who serve the tourist hordes, such as cab drivers, restaurant and hotel workers, policemen, shop owners and small business people. Many who work in the Keys commute from Homestead or South Miami.

Tourists

Tourism is by far the largest industry in the area and provides jobs for or influences the prosperity of almost all area residents. The population of Key West doubles or triples during special events, and when a couple of cruise ships are in town, Key West bursts at the seams with camera-wielding, fanny pack-wearing, water bottle-clutching tourists. Hey, it's a tourist town, but a great one.

Many of the area's natural attractions are offshore or way back in the mangroves and are relatively unaffected by the tourist traffic. But some areas are shopworn due to the heavy tramp of tourist feet. The Keys and Everglades remain delicate and the excesses of tourism could still spoil them.

Adventures

■ On Land

Hikes & Walks

Everglades National Park is well planned so that people can enjoy some of the US's most pristine wild areas on foot. More than 20 trails are maintained through saw grass, swamps, mangrove and cypress hammocks, small wilderness ponds and sloughs. Many are raised wooden walkways and can be easily enjoyed by most able-bodied visitors.

The Keys have a number of parks and beaches where you can stretch your legs and watch for birds and other wildlife. Walks over the flats and channels of Florida Bay along the bridges from the old Overseas Highway are a wonderful way to observe sea birds and marine life from on high. Turtles, sharks, stingrays and horseshoe crabs are easily seen from the old bridges that have been converted into fishing piers.

Beachcombing

Although there's not much in the way of nice sandy beaches in the Keys or Everglades, there are plenty of wonderful waterfronts that run alongside mangroves. Where there is sand, you can walk for a mile or so poking through washed-up turtle grass and other seaweed looking for flotsam and jetsam treasures. If you are the hardy type, you can push your way through the mangroves just up from the beach where the real beachcombing treasures can be found. Beachcombers know that early morning beach walkers scoop up anything of real interest or value. But hurricanes and other storms wash floating junk waaay back into the mangroves and, if you can stand the mud, mosquitoes and heat, you might find old bottles or relics from one of the many wrecks that ended up on the reefs.

Cycling

A well-maintained bike path runs from MM 106 (Key Largo) to the Seven Mile Bridge (Marathon); after that point, it becomes inconsistent. Although road traffic is heavy in this stretch, most of the bike path is well off to the side. Concentrate when you need to cross the road as the cars travel at high speeds. Most of the bridges are wide enough for bicyclers, but you do need to be careful. The bike path peters out entirely as you get close to Key West.

> **WARNING:** The main road south from Homestead has no bike path and the traffic is legendary for being dangerous to bikers.

Bike rentals are available up and down the Keys and in Key West.

By Moped

Zipping around on a moped is a fun way to enjoy yourself in Key West. Rental agencies appear on almost every street corner. Many of the people renting out mopeds work on commission and some will bargain. You can definitely negotiate prices, so call around.

■ In the Water

Water is what makes the Everglades live and is what makes the Keys so attractive. Visiting without getting out on the bay or in the ocean is like eating an ice cream sundae with no ice cream, cherry or chocolate. Although the views of the bay and ocean are wonderful from land, you'll miss most of the fun if you stay there. Zillions of places rent all manner of watersports equipment and another zillion places offer tours of Florida Bay, snorkeling or scuba trips to the reefs and fishing charters. Open your wallet a bit and take advantage of the exciting and beautiful opportunities. You'll need a proper boat to get out to the reefs. Although the water is usually fairly calm, the reefs are mostly a few miles offshore and are certainly not a good place for kayaks or canoes. Small motorboats suitable for visits to the reefs or for enjoying Florida Bay can be rented from around $100 per day and up.

SAFETY FIRST

Equipment needed for even short paddling trips should include at least one life preserver for each person (required by state law), paddles (of course), bailing can, one gallon of water for each person, mosquito repellent, hats, charts, long pants, long-sleeved shirts, sunglasses and sunscreen.

Everglades National Park has its own opportunities for enjoying the water. Fishing is permitted in most of the park and the area is justly famous for backcountry fishing for snook, redfish, snapper and spotted sea trout. A small canoe or kayak is perfect for getting into the heart of the park.

Beaches

There are beaches (very interesting beaches in the Keys), but they are not wide expanses of sand like those you see in Miami Beach, Sanibel or Daytona. Marathon, Bahía Honda and Key West have sandy beaches; most other shore areas are shell, gravel or coral rock. Almost impenetrable mangroves line much of the coast. But these conditions are what make these beaches unique and interesting. Birds hang out in the mangroves and all sorts of interesting animals live in the turtle grass just beyond the sand.

Boating

The Keys are one of the finest boating areas in the world, offering relatively calm waters and plenty of water-based activities. The water is quite shallow in large areas, so shallow-draft boats are essential. (The draft of a boat is the distance between the waterline and the bottom of the boat). Sailboats drawing over four feet should stick to the Intercoastal Waterway and Hawk Channel.

Marinas come in all sizes and styles, from seedy shacks with one crumbling concrete launch ramp to high-roller haunts with fancy bars and expensive shops. Public boat ramps are few but adequate.

There are hundreds of places to rent a boat for the day or the week. Marinas are the usual place to look, but some hotels also have rental boats. Prices for a small boat with an outboard motor start at $100 for the day and go up from there. Most vessels come with no more than basic safety equipment. Due to the very shallow water in the Keys, propellor damage can be a real problem. Outfitters have safeguarded themselves against paying for such damage by hitting your credit card up for any damage you cause, and it's clearly stated in the rental agreement. Be sure to ask if there are any restrictions on where you can take the boat – some operators don't want you going into Florida Bay since the water is shallow in many places. One operator I checked into supplies only a very short anchor rope to prevent you from going out to the reefs. This same operator also did not want customers going into Florida Bay. They are no longer in business.

> **WARNING:** Currents in the Keys, especially near bridges, can be swift and can change direction in a matter of only a few minutes. It is vital that you take this into account when planning your paddling excursions. Throughout the text of this book, I mention conditions, such as currents, relevant to planning your itinerary.

Canoeing & Kayaking

The shallow and calm waters of Florida Bay and the sand and turtle grass flats and shallow reefs on the ocean side offer wonderful paddling opportunities. Thousands of large and small mangrove islands a-flutter with birds and scuttling crabs are a delight (bring mosquito repellent). Whitewater Bay and Shark River in Everglades National Park are world-famous paddling destinations. Commercial outfitters offer guided tours and basic equipment rentals at both locations. You can go out for an afternoon on the flats or a week-long adventure through the 'glades. If you bring your own watercraft, it's little trouble to find a place to pull off the road and plop into the water. As kayaking explodes in popularity, more and more hotels and resorts offer basic kayaks to their guests.

> **WILDLIFE WATCH:** *Kayaking is an easy way to get close up to fascinating sea life and birds – don't miss at least a half day exploring the flats and mangroves.*

Dolphin Interaction

I can't help feeling that interacting with dolphins in an organized manner is a bit cheesy. I am told that the dolphins enjoy the opportunity to play with tourists. Almost all operators cover themselves with a veneer of science or therapy as an excuse for trousering tourist dollars. Some also offer opportunities to do similar things with sea lions, although what sea lions have to do with the Keys escapes me.

At one of the dolphin centers I visited the "marine biologists" consisted of five or six attractive young blond girls in matching, skimpy bathing suits. They seemed to know how to handle the dolphins and put on a good show, but this really seemed a bit like exploitation for the purpose of making a profit.

I've been lucky enough to encounter dolphins at sea and have been in the water with wild ones. They went slightly out of their way to give me a passing glance, which was still a thrill for me.

Fishing

Few places in the US offer the spectacular fishing opportunities found here. Light tackle backcountry fishing, shore and bridge fishing, as well as offshore charter boat fishing are all available, offering the chance to catch small but tasty snapper or have a back-breaking battle with sailfish, tarpon and marlin.

FISHING ETIQUETTE

■ Be sure to respect the rights of other fishermen.

■ Don't anchor or set up close to someone who is already fishing.

■ Don't take your boat close to other fishing boats or to bridge and shore fishermen. While bridge fishing, I've "caught" several boats that didn't think this point of etiquette applied to them. I lost lures and line, but had the last laugh as the boaters struggled to untangle my fishing line from their props.

■ Do unto others....

Some charter captains who peg you for a tourist will simply take you out for a boat ride while slowly trolling plugs dropped into the water just outside the harbor. This conserves their fuel. Other captains bite their nails in anxiety and zoom all over the Gulf Stream trying to find you the fish. I've sorted through them all and list only the latter.

BACKCOUNTRY & LIGHT TACKLE FISHING NEAR SHORE: Anglers with smaller boats enjoy the pleasures of fishing on turtle grass flats and nearby channels, as well as around bridge pilings and trolling the near-shore patch reefs. Catches include bonefish, kingfish, redfish, permit, snapper, grouper, tarpon and spotted weakfish (known as "sea trout"). Most of these can be caught year-round. Tarpon season usually begins around late April or early May, but the silver kings can be caught almost any time of year.

CATCH & RELEASE WITH CIRCLE HOOKS

It's a mystery to me how circle hooks work at all, but it's no mystery that they tend to hook in the lip or jaw and not in the guts of a fish, making it easier to release the fish unharmed. Tournament fishermen swear by circle hooks and I've been slowly switching over myself, with positive results. Some tournaments even require that participants use circle hooks, citing studies that show higher survival rates for released fish.

SHORE & BRIDGE FISHING: You don't need a boat of your own or an expensive charter to enjoy good fishing in the Keys. The many bridge pilings you see make great artificial reefs – they're well known to be very fishy territory. Don't look down your nose at people you see fishing around the Keys' many bridges – they're on to something. Best of all, the Keys have lots of good bridges for fishing. You can fish either around the pilings or on remnants of the old Overseas Highway now set aside specifically for fishing. Families devote entire weekends – days and nights – to bridge fishing. They bring chairs, coolers, radios, umbrellas and food and drink for the whole family. Just ask "Doin' any good?" and perhaps they'll share with you where the big 'uns are.

To learn where the hot spots are, pick up a copy of the local fishing paper, such as *The Weekly Fisherman*, available free at fine bait and tackle shops and grocery stores.

I like to visit several bridges and try tossing a plug or spoon around for an hour or so at each one. I'll hit four or five spots in an afternoon. The best bridge and shore fishing is in the Middle Keys. The Upper Keys don't have very many bridges and most of the shoreline is privately owned. The Lower Keys have several excellent fishing bridges, but those closer to Key West tend to be over water too shallow for good fishing.

> **AUTHOR TIDBIT:** As you walk down behind a row of bridge fishermen it is okay to discretely peer into people's buckets to see what they have caught.

If you are fishing with a guide, ask where he's taking you. Many backcountry or inshore guides take their clients to "special" spots right next to bridges occupied by the bridge fishing brigades... who are fishing the same spot for free.

BAIT FOR BRIDGE FISHING

Pinfish, mullet and live and dead shrimp are the usual baits for fishing from the shore or bridges. I like to have one pole set up for fishing with shrimp and a heavier pole set up with a large egg sinker to put a mullet or pinfish on and leave on the bottom for the big boys to gobble. I usually set the poles (securely fastened to a tree or bridge railing) and then walk around nearby casting various plugs and lures to likely looking spots. Most of the time I don't catch anything more than small snapper and grunts, but every now and then I come home with a real adventure story. At the very least, bridge fishing is a good excuse to get out of the house or hotel and soak up some sun while fiddling around with fishing tackle and talking about fish with the other anglers.

PARTY BOAT FISHING: Let's face it, the big fish aren't going to grab your plug from the dock in front of the hotel. They're somewhere else and you need a boat and an expert to help you find them. But if you don't want to spend a lot of money on the project – you just want to catch some fish – a party boat is a good idea. Party boats usually take from 20 to 30 people out to the reefs for a half- or full day of bottom fishing. Some offer night fishing trips as well. The boats provide all the tackle and bait; you bring lunch and drinks, hat and sunscreen. Call ahead to reserve a spot and find out when to be at the dock. You can expect to come back with yellowtail, various types of snapper and maybe a grouper, kingfish or dolphin. Prices vary from $35 to $50 per angler. A variety of party boats are located up and down the Keys.

OFFSHORE FISHING: The Florida Keys might just be the world capital for sportfishing. Marlin, known as "the man in the blue suit," and sailfish, known as "the man in the pin-striped suit," are what the big boys want. The catch is almost always released. Dolphin (actually *dorado* or mahi-mahi), amberjack and kingfish are pursued for the table and are much more likely catches. Experts will tell you that, even at the height of the season, you can expect to actually catch only one marlin for every three to four days spent fishing for them and only one sailfish for every two days. This makes for some expensive and boring boat rides. But that's why it's called "fishing" and not "catching."

Sailfish can be caught from almost any point in the Keys. Marlin are most commonly caught on the "wall," an underwater canyon southeast of Key West. The best time for sailfish is usually January through March, while marlin are caught in small sizes (150-300 lbs) in the summer and large sizes (400-1,000+ lbs) in the winter months. *Dorado* season usually begins in late April or early May.

Licenses, Laws & Limits

Out-of-state anglers must obtain a fishing license. Charter captains and guides almost always provide a day license in the cost of their trip. If you plan to fish from the shore, a bridge or from your own boat, you can purchase a fishing license at any bait shop or even at Kmart. You can buy one by phone at ☎ 888-FISH-FLORIDA (347-4356), or online at www.eangler. com. There are separate licenses for fresh water and salt water and you can buy a combination if you plan on doing both. Non-resident licenses are offered for seven days or one year. If you are under 16 you can fish for free. Check www.floridafisheries. com/license.html for the latest details on prices and for more information.

Fishing Charters

All charters are not the same, and it is not unusual for visitors to talk to several charter captains before making a decision. Finding a charter is vastly easier than finding the fish. It's a rare hotel or resort that doesn't have a couple of favorite skippers to which they refer their guests. In the text, I have selected a few backcountry and offshore captains who have a good reputation for providing a high-quality fishing experience. I also list a few charter boat associations that can provide a list of guides. Local Chambers of Commerce can also point you in the right direction. Call one of my recommendations, let your hotel help you or simply go by one of the many marinas in the late afternoon to see the boats come in and talk to the skippers yourself.

A day with a backcountry guide using the guide's boat and equipment runs anywhere from $350 to $550. The maximum number of guests for the flats boats is almost always two. Offshore trips start around $550 for a day and can usually handle four people; some larger boats carry six. Half-day charters can be arranged for $400 or so. Some guides have a no-fish, no-pay policy. Party boats charge about $35 for each angler and most go out twice a day for half-day trips. Of course, bridge and shore fishing cost no more than whatever you spend on bait, refreshments and busted tackle. I sometimes lose a couple of expensive lures on my bridge fishing expeditions, the cost of which easily tops my bait and refreshment outlays of around $10 for an afternoon out.

Scuba Diving

Without a doubt the best place to dive and snorkel in the US, the Keys are blessed with a carefully managed park system that protects large areas of reefs. **John Pennekamp Coral Reef State Park**, just off Key Largo, is easily accessible. This undersea park is one of the main reasons many people visit the Upper Keys.

There are dozens of dive shops lining the highway as you drive through the Keys. Most run their own dive trips or will refer you to a charter. In addition, many hotels have their own dive shops and offer reef trips as well. Some boats carry as many as 20 or 30 divers and insist they are not "cattle boats." Discerning divers will pay a couple of dollars more and look for a "six pack," a boat taking no more than six divers at a time. With fewer divers in the water at the same spot, the undersea denizens seem friendlier.

Training at all levels is widely available. Most operators rent all equipment you need for scuba or snorkeling, but some are more knowledgeable, professional and friendlier than others.

In Everglades National Park, little scuba diving is done except by a few avid lobster hunters way out in Florida Bay. For the most part, the park is simply not deep enough for scuba. Snorkeling could be done over the flats and in the channels, but it is not an activity that is promoted.

WRECK DIVING: Divers love wrecks and there are plenty of them in the Keys. The *Thunderbolt*, off Marathon, is probably the most interesting, as it can be easily penetrated and is fairly intact, allowing visitors to completely indulge their *Sea Hunt* fantasies. Large pelagics, tarpon, Goliath grouper (jewfish) and other monsters lurk here. Wrecks tend to be deep and lack the myriad of small colorful reef fish found on shallow reefs. Also, due to the deep location of most wrecks, bottom time is limited. Still, divers love 'em. Trips to the *LSD Spiegel Grove, Benwood* and the *City of Washington* are mandatory for hardcore wreck hounds.

THE BEST DIVES

Spectacular reefs follow the curving line of the Keys from above Miami to way past the Dry Tortugas. You can head out from almost any point in the Keys and find wonderful dives. Some of the most spectacular dive spots are:

- **Looe Key**, with its tongue-and-groove reef pattern.

- **Sombrero Key**, with locomotive-sized chunks of coral.

- **John Pennekamp Coral Reef State Park**, which has thousands of tiny fish.

- Probably the most popular dive is a visit to **"The Statue,"** a replica of Christ of the Abyss. The statue itself is interesting for about three minutes and the area around it is heavily visited, which can drive off some of the large and more skittish fishy inhabitants.

- The reefs around **Dry Tortugas National Park** are the best in the Keys due to their relative inaccessibility (read fewer visitors stirring things up) and slightly more tropical location.

- In general, the reefs north of **Key Largo**, off Elliot and Old Rhodes Keys, and off the **Lower Keys** are harder to reach and see less dive traffic. As a result, they are more pristine.

Snorkeling

Unfortunately, it is hard to get to the really good snorkeling spots from the Keys. While you can find interesting things right in front of your hotel or campground on the bay and the ocean side, the lush coral reefs that are so famous lie a couple of miles offshore. You'll need a boat. You can bring your own, rent or go on a snorkeling charter. If you are a beginner and need rental equipment, a charter is the way to go. Of the hundreds of operators here, some cater specifically to snorkelers. If you opt for a mixed scuba/snorkeling trip, you may find the water at some sites too deep for comfortable snorkeling. I suggest a snorkeling-only trip.

I find snorkeling over the turtle grass and sand flats to be interesting, but you have to look for tiny marine creatures lurking in the seaweed – most of the fancy, highly colorful reef fish you see in *National Geographic* magazine are offshore. Still, snorkeling in the shallow water near your hotel can be rewarding, and it's certainly worth doing if you are a beginner or just want a little practice.

COSTS & EQUIPMENT CONCERNS

Most snorkeling or scuba diving trips cost $50 for a two-tank, half-day dive; some operators charge a bit more, some a bit less. Most rates include use of tanks and weights, but any other equipment you might need is additional. Boats for only six divers, called "six packs," sometimes charge the same price as boats that take as many as 30 people at a time.

Almost all snorkel and scuba charters supply cold drinking water and some offer complimentary soft drinks and snacks. Since most trips are for a half-day, you usually don't have to worry about bringing lunch. Many people show up for a dive with nothing but swim trunks and rent everything they need. Simple. I like to bring my own regulator and buoyancy compensator, as well as my own fins and prescription lens mask. This way I know I'll have a good fit. I rent only tanks and weights. Sunscreen is essential.

AUTHOR TIDBIT: If you are prone to seasickness, take your Dramamine pills at least two hours before you leave the dock to give the medicine a chance to take effect.

Better-equipped shops rent underwater photography equipment, still and video. Some of the larger boats send down a video or still photographer/diver who will record the splendors of your underwater adventure to sell you as a keepsake. Check the cost of this service before you plunge.

Some operators like to extract a mandatory charge for a companion diver if you have not been diving in the last six months. If you a true novice, this is a service you might need, but if you are a solid diver who has simply not been in the water for a year or so, this is a rip off.

■ In the Air

Flightseeing Tours

Few sights top flying over the shallow reefs and flats around the Keys and Everglades. Photo opportunities from the air are unique and make for special pictures to show off back home. Low-altitude flights are perfect for eco-sightseeing. Tours leave from the airport at Marathon or Key West; services are listed in the relevant chapter. Ultra light rentals and instruction are offered at several locations.

A seaplane trip to the Dry Tortugas is a unique opportunity for sightseeing and adventure. The planes fly at 500 feet so you really get a good look at the extensive system of flats and channels west of Key West, around the Marquesas and toward Fort Jefferson. If you're lucky, you'll see schools of sharks, pods of dolphin and brigades of turtles from the plane window. Keep an eye out for Mel Fisher's treasure salvage boat stirring up the sand for emeralds just west of the Marquesas.

Author's Top Things to Do

1. BIRDING AT FLAMINGO. The single best place to see the unusual birds of the area and add significantly to your life list is Flamingo on Florida Bay.

2. HISTORIC WALK THROUGH KEY WEST. Hemingway, cigar factories, forts, turtles, Spanish galleons and Henry Flagler – what a strange lot to encounter on an afternoon walk.

3. FORT JEFFERSON. Take the seaplane to the Dry Tortugas for the day or just a couple of hours. Snorkeling from the shore is some of the best in the Keys, and the birding is intense.

4. DOLPHIN INTERACTION HAWK'S CAY RESORT. The resort's lagoon sits right in front of the main lodge. Even if you are not the one actually interacting with the dolphins, you can enjoy the show while sipping a cocktail.

5. WALKING THE ANHINGA TRAIL. This half-mile trail in the Everglades is an easy and intense wildlife experience with a soundtrack provided by dozens of bellowing alligators and thousands of birds. You can get some great pictures from the boardwalk above the gator holes.

6. BACKCOUNTRY & LIGHT TACKLE FISHING. Bonefish, pompano, snapper, trout and redfish abound in the backcountry. Fly-fishing from a flats skiff is one of the great fishing adventures to be had.

7. GUNK HOLING IN FLORIDA BAY & TEN THOUSAND ISLANDS. Floating quietly among thousands of small mangrove keys and drifting over turtle grass flats is relaxing and the best way to enjoy the wildlife and encounter fascinating sea creatures.

8. HANGING OUT & GOING TO SEED AT GEIGER KEY MARINA. Among the seemingly thousands of thatched Tiki bars, the outdoor bar at this marina stands out as being a waaay laid back place to sip draft beer or rum drinks out of plastic cups and watch the world go by as your beard grows longer. Blues plays over the stereo. The breeze blows gently and Bowser, the dog, jumps into the drink from time to time in an attempt to catch mullet. This is a good place to be sure *you* don't fall in the drink.

9. OFFSHORE FISHING IN THE GULF STREAM. Trolling for billfish or deep jigging for amberjack over The Hump has to be the premier deep-sea fishing experience in the Keys.

10. SNORKELING/SCUBA DIVING AT LOOE KEY. Looe Key or the coral heads just off the beach in the Dry Tortugas offer the best snorkeling and scuba diving in the Keys.

11. CANOEING IN EVERGLADES NATIONAL PARK. Until very recently venturing into the Everglades was a daunting and uncomfortable proposition. Explorers and adventuresome tourists became disoriented in the sameness of the saw grass and cypress hammocks and never returned. The National Park Service now maintains well-marked canoe and boat trails that run through the wilderness and swamps. Simple campsites dot the route. This is the best way to see the heart of the Everglades.

12. PUB CRAWLING IN KEY WEST. Start at the **Pier House** for a noisy sunset cocktail, followed by catching Pete &

Wayne's act at **Sloppy Joe's**. Honk down a slab of ribs at the **Meteor Smokehouse** and check to see if there are any good bands playing at the **Green Parrot**. Follow your ears as you walk around town and wander in and out of the dozens of bars and clubs offering live entertainment. If you must, choke down a powdered mix margarita at the **Hard Rock**, **Hog's Breath**, **Dirty Harry's**, **Margaritaville**, and on and on. Even if you confine yourself just to Duval Street, your choice of bars is vast.

13. EATING SEAFOOD AT BALLYHOO'S. Head to Ballyhoo's in Key Largo for the seasonal all-you-can-eat stone crab claws, which can't be beat. **Seven Fish** in Key West serves creative fish plates.

14. BEST WILD NIGHT OUT. Pete & Wayne at Sloppy Joe's is the way to get in the mood for Key West wildness. I suggest forgetting about your usual proclivities and let yourself be entertained by the more outrageous lifestyles that are on display in the bars and clubs around Duval Street. End up at the Green Parrot with the locals in the wee hours. Enjoy the sunrise from Smathers Beach.

15. MEL FISHER MARITIME HERITAGE SOCIETY AND MUSEUM, *200 Greene Street,* ☎ *305-294-2633,* in Key West is the best museum in the area. A visit here rekindles the small boy's dream of pirates and doubloons that still lurks inside most of us.

16. LIVING THE GOOD LIFE AT PALM ISLAND. Come here to experience elegant and luxurious living.

17. PEOPLE-WATCHING IN KEY WEST. Sprinkled among the tourists, there are more strange people walking down Duval Street than almost anywhere else in the US. Find yourself a table with a view of the sidewalk at one of the fine beverage emporiums on Duval Street and prepare your mind to be boggled by the exotic lifestyles flaunted by residents and visitors alike.

18. BAHÍA HONDA STATE PARK. This has, by far, the best beach in the Keys.

19. KEY LIME PIE AT THE BLOND GIRAFFE. It must be the icebox type, of course. The Blond Giraffe in Marathon does it best.

Bahía Honda Bridge.

20. VISIT THE BAHÍA HONDA BRIDGE. This old bridge is the most mysterious, awe-inspiring and architecturally interesting bridge in the old Overseas Highway system. The structure owes its humpbacked appearance to the unique engineering feat of elevating a road for car traffic directly over the old railroad tracks. The bridge looms huge from the flats and Bahía Honda (deep bay) channel. Unfortunately, you can't walk on it.

Travel Information

The Region At a Glance

■ The Keys

 With 43 bridges, 46 inhabited keys and thousands of square miles of shallow water to explore, the Florida Keys have attracted outdoor enthusiasts for decades. Their quiet resorts, wonderful seafood restaurants, laid-back lifestyle and throbbing nightlife seem to have something

for all tastes. The comfortable lodging found in the Keys is almost always smack dab at the edge of an underwater wilderness teeming with life. Coral reefs, miles of turtle grass-covered flats and the nearby Gulf Stream attract anglers, divers and boaters tasting something natural and untouched.

Key West

A party town with charm, Key West's attractions include unique architecture, historical interests, a joyous, festering gay colony, wonderful seafood, twee tourist attractions, sportfishing, diving, birding, margarita- drinking, music, people-watching and more. The water-based and other outdoor adventures are rivaled by the pleasures of a sophisticated tourist town.

■ Everglades National Park

Everglades National Park is all about wildlife and unique natural beauty in one of the few relatively unspoiled places left in Florida. Even if you are not a birder, it is hard not to be impressed and fascinated by the abundant and varied bird life in the park. Deer, crocodiles, alligators, turtles, raccoons and snakes compete for your attention. Life in the shallow waters in and around the Everglades is remarkable and prolific. But perhaps the best thing is that you don't need to spend weeks crouched in a camouflaged blind hoping for a glimpse of anything wild. Well-maintained and easily accessible footpaths and paddling trails lead through hammocks groaning with birds and through swamps chock-a-block with gators. Shaded, cushioned seats on stable tour boats take visitors in comfort on outings through what, until recently, has been one of the most inaccessible regions in North America. After a day spent outdoors enjoying the wildlife and natural beauty, air-conditioned comfort and restaurant meals await the tired tourist. For the more adventurous and those with stamina, miles of lakes and creeks lead to campsites in the heart of this exceptional park.

When to Visit

Of course, most visitors come to the area when it is cold up north, after hurricane season, between November and April. This time of year offers the most pleasant weather, the biggest crowds, least mosquitoes and, according to some tastes, the most fun. But several organized events, like Bike Week, Key West Summer Food and Wine Festival, and the Underwater Music Festival, fill up the area during quieter times. My advice is to come when you can. Even in the heat of summer the weather is nice, with reliable trade winds and cooling afternoon rain squalls. Fishing, diving and enjoying the outdoors are good all year.

■ Holidays & Cultural Events

 Most traditional holidays (and some manufactured especially with tourism in mind) are celebrated in the Keys with gusto. Quilt shows may not draw the same kind of crowd as Spring Break, so select your punishment carefully ahead of time. Fishing tournaments, powerboat races, food fests, drinking fests and art shows vie for your attention.

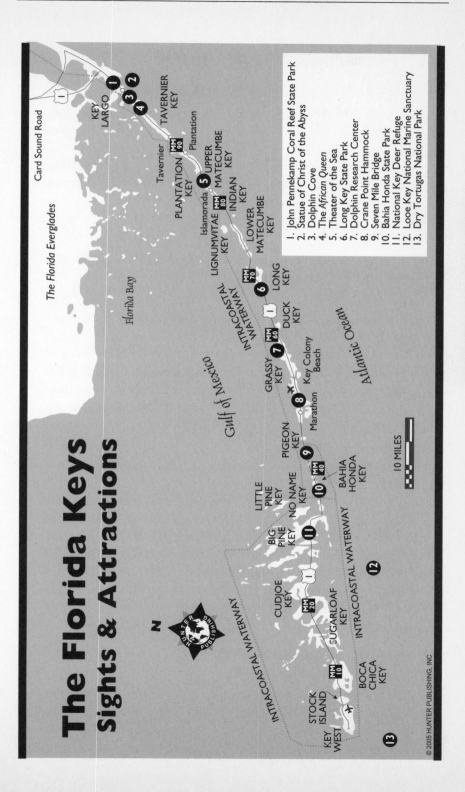

The Florida Keys
Sights & Attractions

Card Sound Road

The Florida Everglades

Florida Bay

Gulf of Mexico

INTRACOASTAL WATERWAY

Atlantic Ocean

KEY LARGO

TAVERNIER KEY

Tavernier

Plantation

PLANTATION KEY

Islamorada

UPPER MATECUMBE KEY

LIGNUMVITAE KEY

INDIAN KEY

LOWER MATECUMBE KEY

LONG KEY

DUCK KEY

GRASSY KEY

Key Colony Beach

PIGEON KEY

Marathon

LITTLE PINE KEY

NO NAME KEY

BAHIA HONDA KEY

BIG PINE KEY

CUDJOE KEY

SUGARLOAF KEY

INTRACOASTAL WATERWAY

BOCA CHICA KEY

STOCK ISLAND

KEY WEST

MM 90
MM 80
MM 70
MM 60
MM 40
MM 20
MM 10

N

10 MILES

1. John Pennekamp Coral Reef State Park
2. Statue of Christ of the Abyss
3. Dolphin Cove
4. The African Queen
5. Theater of the Sea
6. Long Key State Park
7. Dolphin Research Center
8. Crane Point Hammock
9. Seven Mile Bridge
10. Bahia Honda State Park
11. National Key Deer Refuge
12. Looe Key National Marine Sanctuary
13. Dry Tortugas National Park

Travel Information

© 2005 HUNTER PUBLISHING, INC

Many of the dates vary from year to year. Call the contact number to verify this year's event dates.

■ ARTS, CRAFTS & CULTURAL EVENTS

Arts & Crafts Festival. *Thanksgiving weekend, Islamorada;* ☎ *305-664-2321, 800-327-7070; www. holidayisle.com*
This three-day festival features booths of Keys artists and craftspeople. Expect to find everything from carved coconuts to conch shell jewelry.

Florida Keys Art Guild Outdoor Art Festival. *February/March; Islamorada;* ☎ *305-743-6148*
The show concentrates on one-of-a-kind original artwork and discourages flea market-type crafts.

Key West House & Garden Tour. *Held on various weekends throughout January, February and March;* ☎ *305-294-9501.*
One of the most enjoyable things to do in Key West is walking or biking around the back streets of Old Town admiring the beautiful old homes and their riotous gardens. As part of Old Island Days, volunteers lead groups through the more significant Key West architectural gems

Underwater Music Festival. *June/July; Big Pine Key;* ☎ *305-872-2411*
In a unique musical event, classical and popular music is broadcast underwater at Looe Key Marine Sanctuary. People come from around the world, and numerous scuba and snorkeling charters from Ramrod Key to Big Pine Key transport music fans to the reef for the six-hour performances. You can also attend by private boat. Formal attire is not required – bathing suits or wetsuits only.

■ FISHING TOURNAMENTS

Fishing tournaments easily number in the hundreds. Visitors can charter a boat to get in on the action. Non-participants can usually watch the weigh-in without charge. Below are a few of the larger or more interesting tournaments.

Key Largo Sailfish Challenge. *January; Islamorada; Jan Moore,* ☎ *305-664-4735*

Pursuit Sailfish Open. *End of January; Islamorada (tournament takes place out of Duck Key); Charlotte Ambroggio,* ☎ *305-664-2444*

Islamorada Women's Sailfish Tournament. *February; Islamorada; Tammie Gurgiolo,* ☎ *305-852-9337*

Sunset Tarpon Tournament. *Mid-March; Marathon; Gary Ellis,* ☎ *305-664-2002*

Mercury Celebrity Sunset Tarpon Tourney. *Mid-March; Islamorada; Gary Ellis,* ☎ *305-664-2002*

Islamorada All-Tackle Spring Bonefish Tournament. *Mid-March; Tavernier; Jim Bokor,* ☎ *305-852-1694*

World Sailfish Championship. *April; Key West; Mike Weinhofer,* ☎ *305-294-3399*

Key West Classic. *End of April; Key West;* ☎ *305-294-4042; www.texacokeywestclassic.com.*

Ladies Tarpon Tournament. *Early May; Marathon; Dave Navarro,* ☎ *305-743-6139*

Rolex/IGFA Inshore Championship Tournament. *May; Islamorada; Mike Myatt,* ☎ *954-927-2628*

McDonalds Invitational Tarpon Tournament. *May; Marathon; Dave Navarro,* ☎ *305-743-6139*

Marathon International Tarpon Tournament. *May; Marathon; Dave Navarro,* ☎ *305-743-6139*

Scientific Anglers Women's World Invitational Tarpon Series. *June; Islamorada; Suzan Baker,* ☎ *305-531-1233*

Drambuie Key West Marlin Tournament. *Mid-July; Key West; Scott Greene,* ☎ *305-292-2710*

Mercury S.L.A.M. Celebrity Tournament. *September; Key West; Gary Ellis,* ☎ *305-664-2002*

Mercury Outboards Bonefishing World Championship. *Mid-October; Islamorada; Fred Troxel,* ☎ *305-872-2366*

■ FOOD FESTIVALS

Keys food is seafood, seafood, seafood and Key lime pie.

Key West Summer Food & Wine Festival. *First two weeks of August; Key West;* ☎ *305-296-6909; www.kwrba.com/festival.htm*
This big festival digs deep into wine-tasting and international food enjoyment, but also diverts into rum drinks and local food delights. Participants can enjoy such special events as champagne brunches, dessert-only tastings and a red & white party.

Lobster Fest. *August 8-10; Holiday Isle;* ☎ *305-664-2321*
Boiled, broiled, baked, smoked and roasted lobster tails are on the menu.

■ GOLF TOURNAMENTS

Golf Classic. *November 3; Islamorada;* ☎ *305-664-2321, 800-327-7070; www.holidayisle.com*

Hole-In-One Golf Tournament. *April 19; Marathon;* ☎ *305-743-8291*
Held at the Sombrero Country Club. All proceeds go toward the Rotary Club of Marathon Scholarship Fund.

NASCAR Golf Tournament. *November 12; Islamorada;* ☎ *305-664-2321, 800-327-7070; www.holidayisle.com*

■ OTHER FUN EVENTS

Bike Week/Poker Run. *September; Key West;* ☎ *305-294-3032*
Even though the city has recently passed a noise ordinance that prohibits motorcycles from loudly revving up their engines, Key West welcomes bikers with open arms and blender drinks topped by paper umbrellas. Leather clothing, chrome accessories and tattoos are what to wear. Over 10,000 motorcyclists ride down from

Miami to Key West during the Poker Run, culminating in the notorious and wonderful Bike Week. As participants head south, they stop at specified points to pick up cards in an attempt to configure the best poker hand and win valuable prizes at the trip's end. The best part of the show is the informal fancy bike parade down Duval Street that lasts for the entire week – 24 hours a day. This is one of the bigger events of the year and hotels fill up well in advance.

Conch Republic Days. *Mid-April; Key West; www. conchrepublic.com*

At one point in the drug wars, the US Border Patrol set up roadblocks on the Overseas Highway and searched cars looking for drugs and illegal immigrants. This caused traffic jams many miles long and also hurt the tourist business in Key West. In response, Key West Mayor Dennis Wardlow (now Prime Minister Dennis Wardlow) declared the area South of Skeeter's Last Chance Saloon to be The Conch Republic, seceded from the Union and declared war on the US. One minute later he surrendered and demanded $1 billion in foreign aid and war relief. Believe it or not, the Monroe County Commission passed a resolution legitimizing all this. The Republic offers passports, diplomatic passports, T-shirts and various indulgences.

> **AUTHOR TIDBIT:** 13 Caribbean nations, as well as Germany, Sweden, Cuba, Mexico, France, Spain, Ireland and Russia accept Conch Republic passports.

The Republic's founding is celebrated every year on Independence Day: April 23. The celebrations include a bed race down Duval Street conducted by the most notorious of the island's drag queens and other baffling and hilarious events. "We seceded where others failed."

Fantasy Fest. *October 22-31; Key West; www.warptime. com*

Not for the conservative, Fantasy Fest is a raucous party inspired by Carnival. If you are offended by public nudity and drunkenness, avoid Key West during this world-famous party. Elaborate body painting is all that covers many of the participants. The scene is on the streets. People come to see and be seen. One participant said "where else can a third-grade teacher from Ohio walk down the street butt-naked drinking a beer right out of the bottle?" The crescendo is the Saturday night parade sponsored by Coors Light.

Hemingway Days. *Mid-July; Key West*
Although shunned by the "real" Hemingway family as being too commercial, Hemingway = big party in Key West. Probably most famous for its Hemingway look-a-like contest, Hemingway Days is a good excuse, if you need one, to do all the usual Key West party things late into the night.

Lighted Boat Parade. *December; Key West.*
See hundreds of boats festooned with fairy lights parading up and down the harbor to the delight of merrymakers.

Spring Break

Spring breaker lemmings descend on the Keys, and especially Key West, by the hundreds. The main period of spring break occurs in mid-March, but things remain crowded and wild for a week or so afterwards. The crowds are intense on Duval Street and all of the bars sponsor highbrow celebrations like wet T-shirt contests and best buns and bartending competitions. These are not for the faint of heart. Even the swankiest resorts fill up well in advance, and a good time is generally had by all. Underage drinkers picked up by the tolerant local cops usually spend the night in the can and the next day wear an orange jumpsuit as they pick up trash around town.

Lobster Season

August 1 is the first day of lobster season and bug hunters from all over converge in a gold-rush mood to root out a limit of these scrumptious crustaceans for themselves. Hotels and campgrounds fill up well in advance, so if you plan to be in the area the couple of days before and after this date be sure you arrange everything well in advance. March 31 marks the end of the lobster season.

■ How Much Time to Allow

Quit your job and come to stay. Seriously, though, a week is sufficient time to fly into Miami, rent a car, spend a day or two in Everglades National Park, enjoy fishing and diving in the Lower Keys and still allow plenty of time to wallow in the earthly pleasures of Key West. If you fly to Key West or Marathon with your tourist objectives planned in advance you can enjoy the best of fishing, diving, eco-touring or Key West nightlife in just a day or two – but you'll wish your trip had not been so short.

DAY-TRIPS FROM MIAMI

It's about 150 miles from Miami to Key West, which would be short enough for a day-trip to many destinations, but keep in mind that much of the route is on a two-lane road, which makes for slow going at times. Weekends can see bumper-to-bumper traffic from Homestead seemingly all the way to Key West on Fridays and the reverse on Sundays. If you want to do anything other than drive, you should restrict a day-trip to the Upper Keys or Everglades.

What to Wear

At any time of the year the sun is a big deal, a big reason many come, so bring a wide-brimmed hat and sunscreen. The idea of any sort of dress code at all is foreign; this is one of the few destinations where you can wear almost any old thing that pleases you. At times, you can even get away with wearing nothing more than body paint. It's a rare establishment that would refuse admittance to someone based on what they are wearing. "No shirt, no shoes, no problem" is a sign frequently seen in the Keys. Shorts, T-shirts and flip-flops are appropriate almost anywhere.

Travel Information

I've even seen real estate agents wearing this outfit, and am unaware of anyplace where a tie is needed. The only reasons to wear more would be to avoid sunburn or to keep warm during a cold snap. When I go to a fine restaurant for dinner I might put on a shirt with a collar, but keep my shorts and flip-flops.

■ Winter, the High Season

 They don't call it the high season for nothing. Prices and crowds are higher between November and April, but the weather is at its best. Temperatures can dip into the 60s during the day and can get as low as 50 at night. A light jacket or sweater and a pair of jeans or khakis are about all you'll need for warmth.

■ Summer, the Low Season

The height of summer can get very hot, but almost never does the temperature rise above the mid-90s. Cooling trade winds and afternoon rain showers keep things bearable. If a little warm weather doesn't bother you, this is the time to come. The crowds are smaller and prices in hotels, restaurants and shops can be as much as 20% lower than in high season. Bring your thinnest T-shirts and roomiest Hawaiian shirts. A bathing suit, even a wet one, will be comfortable at any time of day or night. You may need to cover up to avoid sunburn, but for almost no other reason. A light shirt (unbuttoned) over a bathing suit or wrap for the ladies is all the concession to modesty needed.

Costs

Everything costs more in the Keys. Since everything but sunburn needs to be shipped in from the mainland, prices reflect that. Don't be surprised by high prices for gas, meals and hotel rooms. You can count on **gasoline** costing at least 25¢ more than on the mainland.

▪ Food

Meal prices are generally even higher than normal during the high season, when a modest lunch for two with beer for under $30 is hard to find (I wouldn't attempt to eat with less than $50 in my pocket). Dinner costs more. That said, travelers on a budget can find some real bargains and eat well for substantially less. The laws of capitalism state you can charge whatever the market will bear and the market in the Keys will apparently bear quite a bit. If you go into the main tourist venues, you will pay tourist prices and enjoy tourist food and drink. Even modest restaurants somehow feel they are in the same league as high cuisine, big-city linen napkin joints and charge accordingly. Seafood is expensive everywhere; at least in the Keys it is almost always fresh and wonderful. I try to eat it twice a day while I'm here and examine myself in the mirror each night to see if I am starting to grow gills. A mixed drink costs well over $5 in most places. See page 33 for price chart.

▪ Adventures

Charter-boat fishing is a high-dollar sport, but credit cards are accepted. A half-day offshore trying for sailfish or dolphin starts at $450 and goes up to somewhere north of $650 for a whole day on the nicer boats. You can fish the reefs on party boats for a mere $35 or so (see my recommendations in each chapter) and are much more likely to come home with something to eat. Any day spent fishing is better than a day at the office (unless you are a travel writer, when there is an overlap), so take a couple of pals along and have a good time. Hooking up with a sailfish, tarpon or other game fish may take several trips and, if you really have your heart set on a catch, you'll need to absorb the cost of a few boat rides in pursuit of your goal. You have a good chance of catching some dolphin in season (May through September), but realize that most trips after sailfish come up empty. Backcountry flats guides charges start at $250 per half-day, and usually offer you a good chance of battling barracuda, if not bonefish. Bonefish are elusive and rarely caught by the average tourist. Some people think bonefish are a figment of the imagination invented by guides as an excuse for coming back empty-handed day after day. But rest assured, they do live. I caught one in 20 feet of water while bottom fishing for snapper. Boat rentals start at $100 per day, with wave runners and Jet Skis going for $25 and up per hour.

■ Hotels

 Few hotel rooms go for less than $60 per night, and most run well over $100 for even a modest room in the high season. A good number of rooms draw over $300 nightly.

SENIOR DISCOUNTS

Come armed with your AARP card and you'll find plenty of opportunities to save 10% or more. Many hotels offer discounts for AARP, AAA, military or other group memberships. Be sure to ask when you make your hotel reservation, rather than upon arrival or on check out.

AUTHOR TIDBIT: Beware of places that advertize T-shirts at three for $10. They do have some at that price, but they usually fit only newborns and are made from the cheapest materials. Upon inquiring, you will be shown to these with a sneer.

The bottom line is that you're on vacation, so try not to focus on how much you could buy something for back in Frostbite, South Dakota and have a good time. You probably didn't come to Key West for the quality and low price of the margaritas anyway – you came to check out the scene, have a few drinks and look at the sights.

Transportation

▪ Getting Here

Regional Airports

Miami International Airport, ☎ *305-876-7000, www. miami-airport.com,* serves all major carriers and hundreds of smaller ones. It is one of the major airline hubs in the world and is the key airline hub for Latin America. It is located off I-95 and is handy to the Florida Turnpike, I-95 and I-75. Rental car services are available, though most of their lots are away from the terminal and are served by brightly marked shuttle buses. The airport is about 60 miles from Key Largo, 80 miles from Islamorada, 115 from Marathon and 160 from Key West.

> **WARNING:** The airport is located in a bad neighborhood and tourists have been robbed shortly after leaving the rental car lots. If you are not familiar with the area, it is always a good idea to review your route so you can get on your way quickly.

Currently, the **Florida Keys Marathon Airport**, *MM 52 BS, Marathon,* ☎ *305-743-2155*, has no scheduled, major airline service. **Florida Coast Airlines**, ☎ *888-435-9322, www.flyfca.com,* offers flights from Ft. Lauderdale. The extensively improved and expanded modern terminal houses rental car agencies for Budget, Enterprise and Avis, as well as the Greyhound Bus terminal.

Key West International Airport, *Roosevelt Boulevard,* ☎ *305-296-5439*, is served by **American Eagle**, ☎ *800-433-7300*, **Cape Air**, ☎ *305-293-0603*, **Delta**, ☎ *800-221-1212*, **Continental Connection**, ☎ *305-294-1421*, and **USAir Express**, ☎ *800-428-4322*. Most flights feed from Miami, Tampa, Orlando and Fort Lauderdale.

Best Access Routes

Highway 1 (Overseas Highway). Known as Dixie Highway as it crawls through South Miami, US 1 becomes the Overseas Highway once it reaches Key Largo. It is the only road that can be called a "highway" in the Keys. In most of the Keys, it serves as the only road.

> **AUTHOR TIDBIT:** Keep your pets close if you stop along the roadside in the Everglades as hungry gators have been known to gobble up small dogs and cats.

The scenic **Tamiami Trail** blasts straight and long from Miami west toward the Gulf coast. For most of its length it borders either Everglades National Park to the south or Big Cypress National Preserve to the north. If you can bring yourself to drive slowly along this route, you'll be rewarded with views of wildlife from your car. The canal that parallels the road is home to gigantic gators, which are a common sighting.

■ Directions from Miami International Airport

The area around the airport is not salubrious; it's best to get onto the Florida Turnpike as directly as possible by following the signs from the airport for 836 West. It's possible to go all the way from the airport in Miami to the bottom of Homestead without getting off modern, controlled-access interstates. To do that, you must stay on the **Florida Turnpike** until the end.

If you don't want to pay tolls you can go down the **Palmetto Freeway** and then follow **Route 1** through a few hundred stop lights to Homestead and then the Overseas Highway. This is a long slog through suburban sprawl, but there are no tolls. The best way to get to Homestead without paying tolls is to go down **Krome Avenue** (Highway 997). Krome runs arrow-straight from well north of Miami to Homestead, where it gently merges into US 1 leading to Key Largo and the Overseas Highway. The route goes past seemingly thousands of commercial nurseries and huge trucks can slow things down on the two-lane road, but it sees much less traffic than US 1. This bit of local knowledge alone is worth the price of this book.

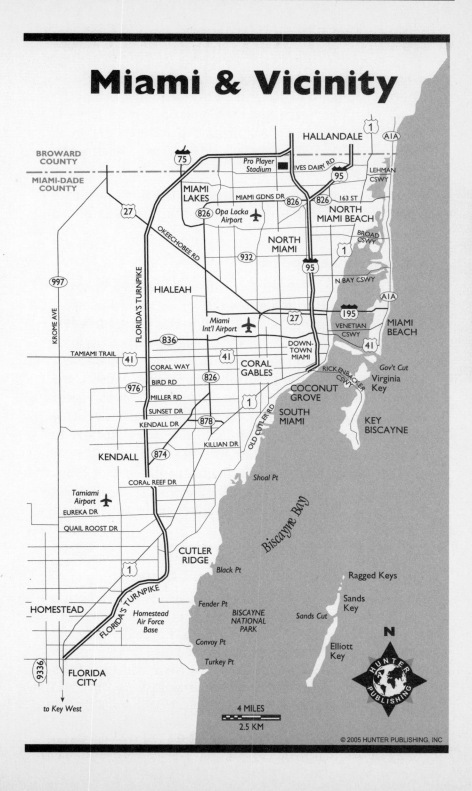

Miami & Vicinity

GOOD STOPS ON THE DRIVE DOWN

■ Last-Minute Shopping

There is a huge **Wal-Mart** in Homestead just before the road splits off to Everglades National Park or the Keys. If you are traveling on the Florida Turnpike, which ends south of the Wal-Mart, you would need to go back north just a bit on US 1.

Gas is cheaper in Homestead than in the Keys, so top up here. The gas station at the Wal-Mart is usually the cheapest around.

■ Great Places to Eat

Over the years I have discovered a few really great places to either grab a quick bite or settle in for a fine meal before making the long haul to the Keys. **Shivers**, *28001 Dixie Hwy, Homestead*, is a no nonsense BBQ joint on the left as you head south. Great seafood and sandwiches can be had at **Alabama Jack's**, *58000 Card Sound Road, Key Largo,* ☎ *305-248-8741*, on the Card Sound route to North Key Largo. Near the Ernest Coe entrance to Everglades National Park is the **Robert Is Here Fruit Stand**, *19200 SW 344th Street, Florida City*, a funky place selling fruit smoothies and other yummies. It's right in front of you at the "T" as you head to the park. You have to make a left there so you can't miss it.

■ Directions from Florida's West Coast

The scenic **Tamiami Trail** (Highway 41) runs through the Everglades from the Naples area alongside Everglades National Park to Miami. It's really the only way to cross the state, unless you head farther north and use I-75, **Alligator Alley**. **Highway 29** runs from Alligator Alley straight down to join the Tamiami Trail right at the turn for Everglades City. It's a fast four-lane highway and a good shortcut. If you want to skip the mess of Miami completely, turn right off the Tamiami

Trail just after the huge Indian casino onto **Krome Avenue** (Highway 997). This two-lane route can have heavy truck traffic, but it offers a direct route to Homestead, where it meets up with US 1 heading south to the Keys and the Overseas Highway.

Transportation Companies

Shuttles & Limos

Even without a car, you can get to and from Miami or regional airports by shuttle with very little difficulty – in style and comfort.

Emerald Transportation, ☎ *305-852-1468, 800-524-7894, www. emerald- transportation.net*, operates 24-hour vans, executive cars and limos with door-to-door service from Key West to Palm Beach. Prices start around $100.

Keys Shuttle, *Marathon,* ☎ *305-289-9997, 888-765-9997, www. floridakeysshuttle.com*, offers door-to-door shuttle service between the Florida Keys and Miami and Ft. Lauderdale airports. Shuttles leave five times a day, seven days a week. From Miami International to Key West runs $70.

To'n'fro, ☎ *305-852-4514, www.tonfro.com*. When you get off the plane at any South Florida airport, these guys can be there to meet you. They even hold a little sign with your name on it. Prices (one to four people in a car) are a bargain, at $100 for the whole car from Miami to Islamorada.

Buses & Coaches

Greyhound Bus Lines, *Key West International Airport,* ☎ *305-296-9072, 800-231-2222, www.greyhound.com*. Four times every day buses leave from Key West for Miami International Airport. The numerous stops on this 4½-hour journey are marked by small "Greyhound" signs. The fare is $32 one-way for the entire trip.

Rental Car Companies

Be sure you have car rental agents inspect the car carefully for dents, scratches, and missing spare tires or jacks before you set off. Any issues should be detailed in writing on the rental contract. Be aware that your homeowners or auto insurance may of-

Travel Information

fer sufficient coverage for cars you rent on vacation, so you may not need a supplemental policy. Some rental companies quote very low prices but charges for supplemental insurance can more than double the rate you have been quoted.

The Keys have sun aplenty so this trip would be a good time to splurge a bit and plunk down for an upgrade to a convertible.

There's an **Alamo** office at Key West International Airport, ☎ *305-294-6675, 800-327-9633, www.alamo.com.*

Avis, *www.avis.com*, ☎ *800-831-2847*, is at Marathon (MM 52 BS, ☎ *305-743-5428*) and at Key West International Airport (☎ *305-296-8744*).

Budget, *www.budget.com*, ☎ *800-527-0700*, is also in Marathon (*MM 52 BS*, ☎ *305-743-3998*) and at Key West International Airport (☎ *305-294-8868*).

Dollar is at Key West International Airport, ☎ *305-296-9921, 800-800-4000, www.dollar.com.*

Enterprise, *www.enterprise.com*, ☎ *800-325-8007*, has offices in Key Largo (*MM 100.2 OS*, ☎ *305-292-0220*), Marathon (*MM 52 BS*, ☎ *305-289-7630*) and at Key West International Airport (☎ *305-292-0220*).

Hertz is at Key West International Airport, ☎ *305-294-1039, 800-654-3131, www.hertz.com.*

One local company I can recommend is **Just Jeeps of the Keys**, *MM 98.1 in the median, Key Largo*, ☎ *866-587-8533.*

Arriving by Cruise Ship

The cruise dock at Mallory Square is right at the edge of the action and the island is so small that cruise passengers are able to get a good feel for it even on a short stop. Most cruise ships are required by local ordinance to get out of town before sunset, which means passengers miss the legendary Key West nightlife.

Several cruise lines stop in Key West. I suggest visiting their websites to see what each ship offers. Many cruise lines don't encourage potential passengers to contact them directly, steering web visitors instead to travel agencies.

Carnival, ☎ *888-CARNIVAL, www.carnival.com.* Their less-than-useful website (without phone numbers!) offers very little practical help. This is the bottom of the barrel, economy cruise line. Their cruises can be fun, but don't expect luxury or peace and quiet. The food is a little better than school cafeteria food.

Royal Caribbean, ☎ *800-256-6649*, *www.royalcaribbean.com*. Their site has a good description of each ship, destination, stateroom options and prices.

Celebrity Cruise Line, ☎ *800-722-5941*, *www.celebrity.com*. Their excellent website has detailed descriptions of each stateroom category on every ship. Their schedules and contact information is easy to find. This is one of the premier cruise lines operating in the region.

Disney Cruise Line, ☎ *800-951-3532*, *www.disneycruise.com*. Disney's site offers cool 360° views of staterooms and gives contact information on the main page. Mickey and Goofy seem to be everywhere on this kids-oriented line.

Norwegian Cruise Line, ☎ *800-327-7030*, *www.ncl.com*, is considered a little more upscale than some of the other lines. Its ships offer all the fun and amenities you could want. Their website has good descriptions and 360° views of staterooms.

Radisson Seven Seas Cruises, ☎ *877-505-5370*, *www.rssc. com*. The Rolls Royce of luxury cruise lines, Radisson smothers guests in comfort and sumptuousness. Cruises just don't get any better.

■ Getting Around

There is only one highway in the Keys and routes in and out of Everglades National Park are limited. Both destinations are difficult to explore without a car. Cyclists enjoy the bike trails in the Keys, but Everglades National Park is best enjoyed by car, foot and kayak or canoe.

By Air

There are commercial airports at Marathon, Key West and Homestead. Daily commuter flights between them cost from $100 to $300. At press time, no major airlines served Marathon. Private planes can use the airports at Marathon and Key West.

By Car

It may not look like a long drive from Key Largo to Key West, and it is *only* about 100 miles, but be forewarned that the trip can take several hours. Traffic on the long, mostly two-lane Overseas Highway is often packed bumper-to-bumper for much of the way. There is a large weekend movement from Miami down through the Keys to Key West that usually begins late Friday afternoon; it reverses towards Miami late Sunday afternoon. The last few miles into Key West on a weekend evening are often a slow, stop-and-go slog.

MILE MARKERS

A convenient system of navigation called Mile Markers (MM) is used in the Keys and directions are often given by MM. Look for the small green signs on the roadside to figure out how far you are from the middle of Key West (MM 0). Most of the hotels, restaurants and attractions listed in this book list their MM. Not every mile has a mile marker and you may have to keep your eyes peeled to spot them when you need them. Many of the mailing addresses along the Overseas Highway are close to the actual mile measurement, so 89240 Overseas Highway will probably be close to MM 89. You can often look at mailboxes along the road to get an idea of where you are. Unfortunately, everybody in the Keys uses this system except for the US Post Office, which refuses to acknowledge it and will return mail that uses only mile markers for an address.

If you aren't in a hurry and plan in advance, getting from place to place through the Keys can be the most enjoyable part of your trip. The views over Florida Bay and out to the Gulf Stream change with the weather and continue to hypnotized me whenever I drive through the Keys. I make it a point not to rush.

Key Largo (MM 110) is approximately 60 miles from Miami airport. The roads are all freeway, so you can usually make it in a bit more than an hour. Islamorada (MM 86) is about 24 miles farther, Marathon (MM 65) is another 21 miles, Big Pine Key (MM

39) is 26 miles more and MM 0 in Key West is about 160 miles from Miami International Airport. Speed limits drop to 35 mph in some places and much of the Overseas Highway is only two lanes.

By Bicycle

Busy highways with no bike lanes deter casual bikers from making the long run down from Miami. Once in the Keys, a wonderful bike trail runs most of the way from Key Largo to Key West, although biking it can still be dangerous. The path peters out in the Lower Keys and picks up again near Key West. Bridges in the Keys are relatively wide and have enough room for moderately comfortable biking.

In spite of the traffic, many bikers do make the trip from Miami. A few are killed each year. My suggestion is to find another way of getting yourself and your bike to Key Largo before starting off on your two-wheeled adventure. Buses will carry bicycles with some packing restrictions. Greyhound, for example, will carry bicycles packed in a "substantial" container no larger than 8" x 32" x 60". For $10, Greyhound sells boxes suitable for packing a bicycle.

By Boat

The absolute best way to get to and enjoy the Keys is by boat. The routes down along the Intracoastal Waterway or on the ocean side through Hawk Channel are two of the best boat rides in the country, with calm, clear water and relatively undisturbed wildlife. Getting from key to key is a pleasure. Although the entire area is very shallow and requires your attention, the channels and flats are well marked.

For the purposes of this book, the **Intracoastal Waterway** runs south from Miami through Biscayne Bay (to the north, it continues a long way up the country's East Coast). It hits Key Largo at Jewfish Creek and continues through Florida Bay alongside Everglades National Park, past Big Pine Key to Key West. Boaters frequently cross from the bay side to the ocean side of the Keys at either Elliot Key, just north of Key Largo, or at Tavernier Creek, just south of Key Largo. The well-traveled **Hawk Channel** runs on the ocean side about two miles off from the chain of the Keys all the way to Key West and is a delightful sail.

Travel Information

NAUTICAL CHARTS

NOAA charts are a must. I suggest selecting the detailed charts for the areas you will be passing through or spending time in. NOAA's website is difficult to navigate. Instead, visit **www.nauticalcharts.com**, which has an easy-to-use interface and allows you to order charts online. Most NOAA charts sell for $17.75. You can also buy them in the keys at major marine supply stores, such as **World Class Angler** in Marathon or **West Marine** on Caroline Street in Key West.

Communications

■ Telephone

 The area code for Everglades National Park and the Keys is 305 throughout, but starting sometime in 2005, area code (786) will be used for new listings. Long-distance charges may apply when calling out of the immediate area. A call from the Keys to Miami is charged at long-distance rates, for sure.

Cell phones work fine in most areas of the Keys. There are occasional dead spots, and I find poor coverage, if any, in Flamingo. Hotels typically charge 75¢ for local calls. Ask about charges if you plan on making lots of long-distance calls.

■ Internet Access

Most of the major providers have service in the Keys and offer local dial-up numbers. When dialing from your hotel room, use a local number (call your provider before you leave home and ask for their access Keys number). A number with a 305 area code may not be a local call. Check with the front desk if you are unsure. A few of the upscale hotels have high-speed connections in the rooms, but it is not common.

Special Concerns

■ Accessibility

Handicapped access is becoming more and more common and you will find the Keys to be on par with other parts of the US. Some of the trails in Everglades National Park are designed for wheelchair use. The Old Town Trolley in Key West can accommodate wheelchairs and is a great way to see the town.

■ Gay & Lesbian Travel

The Keys, and Key West in particular, are famous for their tolerant lifestyle. Whatever your sexual preferences, you will probably feel quite comfortable here. To help you get what you want from your trip, I mention guesthouses, bars and other establishments that cater specifically to gay or lesbian travelers. The **Gay & Lesbian Community Center**, *513 Truman Avenue*, ☎ *305-292-3223, www.glcckeywest.org*, can provide more information.

■ Hospitals

Fisherman's Hospital, *MM 48.7, Marathon*, ☎ *305-743-5533*

Lower Keys Medical Center, *5900 College Road, Stock Island*, ☎ *305-294-5531*

Mariner's Hospital, *MM 91.5, Plantation Key*, ☎ *305-852-4418*

■ Public Nudity

Topless or nude bathing is against the law on all Florida Keys beaches. It is tolerated on a few resort beaches, but don't expect to toss off your clothes wherever you feel like it. While body painting replaces actual clothing during some party events in Key West and nudity is more or less tolerated at those times, it is still against the law and people go to jail for it. You should avoid Key West's notorious Fantasy Fest if public nudity offends you. Some guesthouses encourage nudity around their pool areas, but ask before you strip.

■ Traveling with Pets

 Many hotels remain hostile to our fuzzy animal companions, but others have more enlightened attitudes. Traveling with a dog may seem crazy to some but, for many people, traveling without their pet seems like traveling without their spouse or kids. Florida is a popular destination for empty nesters and many drive down with pets on board. Wise hoteliers welcome neat pets and their money-spending owners. Most pet-friendly hotels will ask for a cleaning deposit and some charge a bit extra (up to $25/night) if you bring a pet. Some otherwise pet-friendly hotels refuse large dogs. Many hotels refuse animals of any type. Fines or ejection can occur if you are caught sneaking around the no-pet rule. Be sure to check before booking. Everglades National Park allows pets if kept on a leash and away from public trails.

> **AUTHOR NOTE:** Gators gobble up small dogs and cats from time to time, so keep your pets close to you and away from the edge of ponds and swampy areas.

Information Sources

■ Weather

National Weather Service, ☎ *305-295-1324, www. nws.noaa.gov,* features national and local weather maps and warnings.

www.keysnews.com, is a local site offering news and weather.

www.fla-keys.com/weather.htm, has regional weather reports and forecasts.

▪ Reading Resources

 Swamp Screamer, At Large with the Florida Panther, Charles Fergus, North Point Press, 1996, ISBN 0865474915. A well-written description of various conservation efforts for the Florida panther.

Bone by Bone, Peter Mathiessen, Random House, 1999, ISBN 0375501029. A fictional account of rough life in Ten Thousand Islands at the turn of the 19th century.

Last Train to Paradise, Les Standiford, Three Rivers Press, ISBN 1400049474. Good history of the old Flagler railroad and how it was built. However, the author seems not to have actually been to the Keys, getting directions wrong and, very incorrectly, stating that visitors cannot see evidence of the old railroad. Still a good read, though.

Storm of the Century, Willie Drye, National Geographic Society, 2002, ISBN 0792280105. A well-researched and highly readable account of the 1935 Labor Day hurricane, one of the most powerful hurricanes to hit the US in modern times.

To Have and to Have Not, Ernest Hemingway, Simon & Shuster, ISBN 0684818981. A classic that gives a good feel for life in "old" Key West.

The Key West Reader, Various, Tortugas, ISBN 0962418412, is a compilation of works by respected writers.

Don't Stop the Carnival, Herman Wouk, Little, Brown and Company, 1965, ISBN 0316955124. A fictional but very Keys-like account of adventures on a tropical isle. This should get you in the mood. If you're a Parrot Head, you'll love it.

BOOKSTORES

☆ **AUTHOR'S PICK** - **Key West Island Books**, 513 Flemming Street, Key West, ☎ 305-294-2904

Walden's Books, 2212 North Roosevelt Boulevard, Key West, ☎ 305-294-5419

Valladares L and Son, 1200 Duval Street, Key West, ☎ 305-296-5032

Hooked On Books, MM 82.6 OS, Islamorada, ☎ 305-517-2602

■ Newspapers

 Islamorada Free Press. Weekly newspaper with up-to-date Middle Keys information on their website, www.keysnews.com.

The Reporter. Weekly newspaper for the Upper Keys region. Their website is www.UpperKeysReporter.com.

The Weekly Fisherman. Free weekly paper with all the latest fishing news and ads from marinas, boat captains and bait shops. Their website is www.weeklyfisherman.com.

Key Largo, Islamorada Times. Free weekly paper with local news and reviews. www.keysnews.com.

■ Chambers of Commerce

 Islamorada, *MM 82.5 BS, Islamorada,* ☎ *305-664-9767, 800-322-5397.* Look for the little red caboose and stop in for advice on where to go and how to get there. They have racks and racks of tourist brochures for browsing. You can call for lists of fishing and diving guides, resorts and restaurants.

Key Largo, *MM 106 BS, Key Largo,* ☎ *305-451-1414, 800-822-1088*

Key West, *Mallory Square, Key West,* ☎ *305-294-2587, 800-648-6269*

Lower Keys, *MM 31 OS, Big Pine Key,* ☎ *305-872-2411, 800-872-3722*

Marathon, *MM 53.5 BS,* ☎ *305-743-5417, 800-262-7284*

■ Websites

WWW Most of the newspapers run websites that offer the latest news on life in their area of coverage. See above. Other useful sites include The Keynoter, **www.keynoter.com** and Key West Citizen, **www.keysnews.com**.

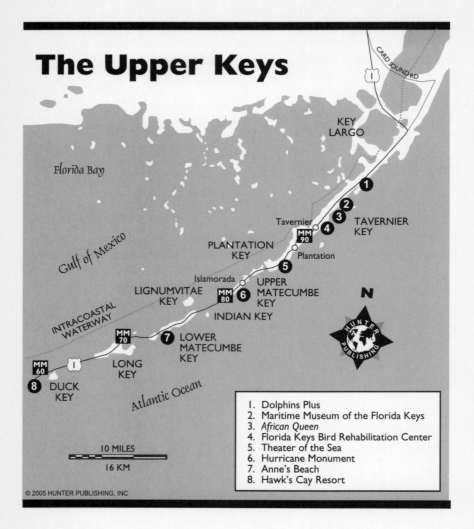

The Upper Keys

KEY LARGO

Florida Bay

Gulf of Mexico

Tavernier

MM 90

Plantation

PLANTATION KEY

TAVERNIER KEY

1
2
3
4
5
6
7
8

Islamorada

UPPER MATECUMBE KEY

LIGNUMVITAE KEY

MM 80

INDIAN KEY

INTRACOASTAL WATERWAY

MM 70

LOWER MATECUMBE KEY

MM 60

LONG KEY

DUCK KEY

Atlantic Ocean

CARD SOUND RD

N

HUNTER PUBLISHING

10 MILES

16 KM

© 2005 HUNTER PUBLISHING, INC

1. Dolphins Plus
2. Maritime Museum of the Florida Keys
3. *African Queen*
4. Florida Keys Bird Rehabilitation Center
5. Theater of the Sea
6. Hurricane Monument
7. Anne's Beach
8. Hawk's Cay Resort

Upper Keys

At a Glance

LARGEST TOWN: Key Largo, population 11,886

ELEVATION: Six feet

AREA: 12.2 square miles

COUNTY: Monroe

MAJOR ROUTES: Overseas Highway (US 1)

NEAREST AIRPORTS: Marathon (51 miles); Miami International (48 miles)

ZIP CODE: 33037

AVERAGE TEMPERATURE: January 68°; August 83°

PRECIPITATION: January 2.4 inches; August six inches

Getting Here & Getting Around

Unless you arrive by boat, the only options are to drive down from Miami or fly to Key West and drive back to the Upper Keys area.

The **Overseas Highway** (US 1) is the only major road through the Keys. It is four lanes in some places, but narrows to two lanes for most of its length. Speed limits are 55 mph for the most part, but drop down to 45 in some areas and 30 for school zones. Even 45 seems a bit fast at times as businesses line the road on both sides and local as well as through traffic clogs things up on weekends. Since most visitors drive down from Miami or arrive by air at Key West, car rental companies in the Upper Keys are non-existent. See *Middle Keys Car Rental Agencies*, page 142, for information about renting cars in Marathon, or check out those companies with desks at Miami International Airport, page XX.

There is no **airport** in the Upper Keys area and the Marathon airport has been abandoned by major airlines due to high operating fees imposed by the county.

Area History & Highlights

Other than Key West, the Upper Keys are of slightly more historical interest than other parts of the Keys. Fishermen, pineapple growers, wreckers and a few leftovers from the railroad work crews inhabited parts of Key Largo and Islamorada in the early 1900s.

The 1935 **Labor Day Hurricane** piled storm surge water up to 18 feet deep over the higher parts of Plantation Key and Windley Key. As you drive down the Overseas Highway, imagine the water being that deep. Few people survived the storm and thousands drowned, including many Depression-era "Bonus Marchers" sent to the Keys to work on the new road from the mainland to Key West. The hurricane uprooted miles of railroad track and basically ended the railroad for good. Cut off, Key West went into an economic decline that lasted for years. The building that is now the **Green Turtle Inn** (see page 134) used to be the general store and filling station for the area and is one of the few buildings that survived the hurricane. The **Hurricane Monument** at MM 82 OS serves as a reminder of those who lost their lives. There is still a small disaster victims' cemetery on the grounds of the **Cheeca Lodge** (see *Where to Stay*, page 119).

MILE MARKERS

Addresses on the Atlantic (ocean) side of the Over-seas Highway are abbreviated to OS and those on the Florida Bay side are abbreviated to BS. So, if you're in Key Largo heading towards Key West, MM 102.5 OS would be on your left and MM100.2 BS would be a little further down the road on your right.

Lauren Bacall, Humphrey Bogart and Edward G. Robinson probably brought more fame to Key Largo than Jimmy Buffet ever brought to Key West. Most of the 1948 film *African Queen* was shot on a Hollywood sound stage, but some of the exterior images were reportedly filmed at the **Caribbean Club**, MM 104 BS, Key Largo. In spite of this fame, it's a bit of a local late-night hangout and worth a visit just to hear the long-running house band.

Foul-mouthed baseball player Ted Williams was a big fan of fishing for tarpon and bonefish in the Islamorada area and a huge fan of Cuban restaurant **Manny & Isa's**, MM 81.6 OS, profiled on page 136.

Information Sources

Islamorada Chamber of Commerce, *MM 82.5 BS, Islamo-rada,* ☎ *305-664-9767, 800-322-5397.* Look for the little red caboose and stop in for advice on where to go and how to get there. They have racks and racks of tourist brochures for browsing. You can call for lists of fishing and diving guides, resorts and restaurants.

Key Largo Chamber of Commerce, *MM 106 BS, Key Largo,* ☎ *305-451-1414, 800-822-1088.*

Upper Key

Sightseeing

There is plenty to do and see in the Upper Keys – much of it involving the water. There's the backcountry to scout out, reefs to dive, turtle grass flats for snorkeling and canoeing and mangrove islands to explore. Most activities require hat, sunscreen and plenty of liquids.

■ Suggested Itineraries

If You Have One Day

1 DAY You can drive down from Miami for only a day and still have a great time. Reserve in advance for any activities you are interested in so you don't waste your limited time. Even though most fishing, diving and snorkeling trips take place twice a day, don't try to do two (you would be returning from one about the same time you should be aboard for the other). Simplify. Take a leisurely sightseeing drive in the morning and leave the half-day trips for the afternoon.

Leave Miami early and, where the Overseas Highway splits just past Homestead, take Card Sound Road. Stop at **Alabama Jack's**, ☎ *305-248-8741*, for refreshments. Continue on Card Sound Road until it joins back up with the Overseas Highway on Key Largo. Java lovers should stop at **Denny's Latin Café**, *MM 100*, for a cup of Cuban coffee before heading down the Overseas Highway as far to **Anne's Beach**, ☎ *305-852-7161, MM 73.5 OS, Lower Matecumbe Key*, for a stroll along the boardwalk that leads through mangroves. Back in the car again, continue southwest to MM 78.5 OS, Lower Matecumbe Key, for a walk along the old **Overseas Highway bridge** to check out the sea life on the flats and look for tarpon. If you must frolic with the dolphins, drive farther southwest to **Hawk's Cay Resort**, ☎ *305-742-7000 or 888-443-6393, MM 61 OS, on Duck Key*. The **dolphin encounter** here takes an hour or so and requires advance booking. About this time you should be ready for a great lunch at **Ballyhoo's**, MM 97.8 in the median.

After you've eaten, go **fishing** with **Captain Ron Green**, ☎ *305-852-9577 or 305-766-7078*, for mahi, grouper, kingfish and barracuda. You'll need to make a reservation at least two months in advance for Captain Ron. If you have a productive day, the mate will prepare your catch so you can take it to the **Fish House**, ☎ *305-451-HOOK, 888-451-4665, MM 102.4 OS, Key Largo,* where they will prepare your catch deep-fried, broiled or sautéed.

If you have any energy left, stop in for some live music at **Coconuts Lounge**, MM 100 OS, Key Largo in the Marina del Mar Resort, ☎ 305-453-9794. Tuesday is Blues Night. Don't miss it if the Charlie Morris Band is playing.

Drive back to Miami tired and sunburned but well satisfied with your day in the Keys.

If You Have Three Days

3 DAYS Three days gives you time to sample the outdoor adventures and a couple of seafood dining experiences. This is a pretty short trip so be sure you make hotel, diving and fishing reservations in advance. Figuring you will spend time on Days One and Three traveling, you should plan the activity that is most important to you for Day Two so you won't be pressed for time. A half-day diving or fishing on the first or last day is certainly practical (most dive spots are not far offshore). If you want the full fishing experience, book a guide for Day Two and head offshore to wrestle a few sailfish.

> **AUTHOR TIP:** If you do a dive on your last day, you may have to check out of your hotel in the morning. Even if you dive boat has a freshwater shower, you will still be a little sticky for the trip back in the afternoon without a proper shower with shampoo, etc.

On Day One drive down from Miami with stops at **Alabama Jack's**, ☎ *305-248-8741*, Card Sound Road, for refreshments or **Denny's Latin Café**, *MM 100*, for a cup of Cuban coffee. Check into your hotel and have a seafood lunch at **Ballyhoo's**, *MM 97.8 in the median*. Set the afternoon aside for a two-tank dive in **John Pennekamp Coral Reef State Park**, *MM 102.5 OS, Key*

Largo, ☎ 305-451-1202, with **Dual Porpoise Charters Inc.**, *MM 100, Holiday Inn Docks, Key Largo,* ☎ *305-394-0417.* After the dive, head back to the hotel for a shower and a change of clothes. Have a great dinner at **Bentley's Restaurant & Raw Bar**, *MM 82.8 OS, Islamorada,* ☎ *305-664-9094.*

Start Day Two with an early breakfast at **Harriette's**, *MM 95.7 BS, Key Largo,* ☎ *305-852-8689,* then head for the *Day Tripper* for a day hunting down sailfish with **Captain Ron Green**, ☎ *305-852-9577, 305-766-7078* (get Harriette's to pack you a lunch). If you are lucky enough to catch your dinner, head to the **Fish House**, *MM 102.4 OS, Key Largo,* ☎ *305-451-HOOK, 888-451-4665,* where they cook it for you.

Everglades National Park is only a mile or so out into the bay from the Upper Keys. You can find guides who will take you back country fishing, birding and eco-touring near mangrove islands and over the fascinating turtle grass and sand flats. I would make this a half-day trip in the morning on Day Three. Reserve several weeks in advance with **Florida Bay Outfitters**, *MM 104, Key Largo,* ☎ *305-451-3018,* for a morning guided kayak tour in Florida Bay through Everglades National Park. If you didn't eat at the Fish House last night, stop by for lunch today. Anglers can spend the afternoon **bridge fishing** on the old Overseas Highway bridge at MM 78.5 OS, Lower Matecumbe Key, or just go for a walk along the bridge looking at the sea life on the flats. You're bound to see some stingrays or small sharks.

Head back to Miami stopping in Homestead at **Shivers**, *28001 Dixie Hwy*, a no-nonsense BBQ joint on the right as you go north.

If You Have a Week

7 DAYS Now you're talking! A week will give you plenty of time to indulge deeply in all the best activities of the Upper Keys and even allow you to buzz down to Key West for an afternoon or evening of wildlife observation (or participation). Snorkeling or scuba diving trips to John Pennekamp Coral Reef State Park take only a half-day. If you are a Diver Dan-type, you can spend every day doing reefs, wrecks or even a night dive. Guides will combine backcountry fishing with eco-touring through the nearby Everglades. However, if it's very hot, a full day may be a little draining.

Drive down from Miami on Day One stopping for a BBQ lunch at **Shivers** and a Cuban coffee at **Denny's Latin Café** (both mentioned above). Spend the afternoon on a guided **kayak tour** in Florida Bay through Everglades National Park. As suggested on the Three-Day Itinerary, reserve several weeks in advance with **Florida Bay Outfitters**. Zip back to the hotel to freshen up before the first of many wonderful seafood dinners. Try **Marker 88**, *MM 88 BS, Islamorada,* ☎ *305-852-9315*, for yellowtail.

On Day Two, go for an early morning breakfast at **Harriette's** in Key Largo (see above), then spend the morning driving along the Overseas Highway sightseeing and walking along some of the old bridges starting at MM 78.5 OS in Lower Matecumbe Key.

Nearby **Hawk's Cay Resort**, *MM 61 OS, Duck Key,* ☎ *305-742-7000 or 888-443-6393,* offers a frolic with the dolphins. It only takes about an hour, so fit this in whenever it seems best. Hawk's Cay insists on advance reservations, although you could make arrangements when you first arrive for later in the week.

If that cup of Cuban coffee got your taste buds going on Day One, have a *muy autentico* Cuban lunch back at **Denny's Latin Café**, MM 100. This is close to **John Pennekamp Coral Reef State Park**, *MM 102.5 OS, Key Largo,* ☎ *305-451-1202,* so you'll be well positioned for an afternoon, two-tank dive with **Dual Porpoise Charters Inc.**, *MM 100, Holiday Inn Docks, Key Largo,* ☎ *305-394-0417.* Clean up back at the hotel then go out for a fabulous dinner at **Pierre's at Morada Bay**, *MM 81.6 BS, Islamorada,* ☎ *305-664-3225.*

Day Three should be reserved for a full day offshore on the *Day Tripper* fishing with **Captain Ron Green** (see above). Don't forget to have Harriette's pack a lunch. The **Fish House**, *MM 102.4 OS,* ☎ *305-451-HOOK, 888-451-4665,* will prepare your catch deep-fried, broiled or sautéed for dinner.

In the evening, catch the blues show at the **Hurricane Lounge**, *MM 49.5 BS, Marathon,* ☎ *305-743-2220.* Call ahead to see if the Charlie Morris Band will be playing anytime during the week you will be in the area.

Get another packed lunch on Day Four for a half-day fishing on the ***Gulfstream* party boat**, *MM 99.5 Key Largo, Ocean Bay Marina,* ☎ *305-451-9788.* Trips are fairly long, running from

Upper Keys

8:30 am to 3:30 pm. Clean up and have a cocktail at the hotel, then enjoy some great pizza at **Tower of Pizza**, *MM 100 BS, Key Largo* and *MM 81.5 BS, Islamorada,* ☎ *305-664-0634, 305-664-8246.*

Start Day Five by once again getting a lunch to go at Harriette's. You can spend the day exploring the backcountry of Florida Bay into Everglades National Park flats **fishing** and **sightseeing**. Reserve several months in advance with **Captain Jimmy Johnson**, *Coconut Cove Resort, MM 85, Key Largo,* ☎ *305-852-6322, 305-393-2500.* You'll come home tired after a long day in the sun, so take a cool shower and relax before heading out for a fine seafood dinner at **Snappers**, *MM 94.5 OS, Key Largo,* ☎ *305-852-5956.*

Blow all of Day Six in **Key West**. If you head out early in the morning, stop at **Baby's Coffee Bar** close to Key West at *MM 15 OS,* ☎ *800-523-2326,* for a brew. In town, park in the Old Town Parking Garage on the corner of Caroline and Grinnell streets and take the shuttle to Duval Street. Slowly walk the whole length of Duval, admiring the freedom of expression allowed in this quaint outpost of artistic sensibilities. Stop and shop, but avoid most of the cheesy restaurants on this street for anything other than a drink. Instead, save room for an unforgettable lunch of conch fritters at **Johnson's Café**, *306 Petronia Street / 801 Thomas Street,* ☎ *305-292-2286.* Waste the afternoon walking along the back streets of Old Town admiring the Caribbean architecture, shopping or simply people watching while sipping a cooling beverage in a bar with a good view of Duval Street – **Mangoes**, *700 Duval Street,* ☎ *305-292-4606*, is a good choice.

Just before sunset it is obligatory to stroll along the waterfront by Mallory Square checking out the street theater, musicians and small-time hustlers. As soon as the sun goes down, head quickly to **Sloppy Joe's**, *201 Duval Street,* ☎ *305-294-5717, www.sloppyjoes.com,* where Pete and Wayne's childish adult comedy should still be in full swing (they usually start at 5 and do two sets). Unless you're brave, stick to beer at Sloppy Joe's but go easy; save some spending money to splurge on an elegant dinner at **Café Marquesa**, 600 Fleming Street, ☎ 305-292-1244. After dinner, force yourself to the **Green Parrot**, *601 Whitehead Street,* ☎ *305-294-6133, www.greenparrot.com,* for blues, blues, and more blues. Check their website to see who is playing. When you have had enough blues and beer, with your designated driver driving, trudge back up the Overseas Highway to your hotel.

Day Seven is a good day to sleep late after your debauch the previous night in Key West. Treat yourself to a hangover-curing breakfast of bacon, eggs and biscuits at – where else? – **Harriette's**. If you have energy this morning, take a tour of **Indian Key** from **Robbie's Marina**, *MM 77.5 BS,* ☎ *305-664-4815*. They also rent kayaks and conducting your own tour is an easy alternative to the tours Robbie's offers.

Head northeast up the Overseas Highway towards home in the early afternoon with a stop for a huge fish sandwich dinner at **Alabama Jack's**, ☎ *305-248-8741, on Card Sound Road.*

> **AUTHOR NOTE:** Make sure you keep going straight ahead as the Overseas Highway splits off to the right in Key Largo heading towards Jewfish Creek. Take the alternate route straight to Card Sound Road and take the toll bridge back to Homestead.

■ Attractions

 Maritime Museum of the Florida Keys, *MM 102.5 BS,* ☎ *305-451-6444, $5, Monday-Saturday, 10 am-4 pm.* The theme is shipping, shipwrecks and treasure hunting. There's a great collection of old bottles. If Spanish treasure and old wrecks interest you, this is a good stop for an hour or so.

African Queen. Yes, this is really the one in which Humphrey Bogart and Katherine Hepburn aggravated each other. It sits next to the Holiday Inn at Key Largo Harbor Marina, *MM 99.7 OS,* ☎ *305-451-4655*. You can also see the *Thayer IV* from *On Golden Pond*. Call in advance to make arrangements for a boat ride in one or the other. This could be that special romantic sunset cruise. But you have to have seen the movie to get in the mood.

Florida Keys Wild Bird Rehabilitation Center, *MM 93.6 OS, Tavernier,* ☎ *305-852-4486, donations accepted, sunrise to sunset*. This is a good place to get close to birds you may see wing-ing by in the distance. The aim here is to rehabilitate wild birds and set them free, but some are too damaged to ever survive on their own. Take plenty of film – you can brag to people back home about what a skilled wildlife photographer you are, all without using one of those three-foot telephoto lenses.

Theater of the Sea, *MM 84.5 OS, Islamorada, ☎ 305-664-2431, www.theaterofthesea.com, $18.50 general admission, 9:30 am-4 pm.* Theater of the Sea has been a popular Keys attraction since time began (1946). The continuous dolphin shows here are the second-oldest in the world (the first one was Marineland of the Pacific). Snorkeling and glass-bottom boat trips are also offered. For $125 you get a brief swim with the dolphins and for $85 you can swim with loveable, frisky sea lions. Although some therapy sessions have been donated to Jackson Memorial Hospital, the dolphin swim is, refreshingly, not promoted as anything other than an educational tourist attraction. You'll need to reserve by phone for the dolphin, sea lion or other special activities.

Hurricane Monument, *MM 81.6 OS*, marks the grave of 423 people who died in the Labor Day Hurricane of 1935. Many of them were workers on the Overseas Highway. The train sent to rescue them was overturned by the storm surge. Unless you need to get out and stretch your legs, you can see enough without getting out of the car.

■ Beaches

Anne's Beach, *MM 73.5 OS, Lower Matecumbe Key, ☎ 305-852-7161,* has a boardwalk that leads through a hammock to picnic areas and a modest but enjoyable beach. Snorkeling is good. There are restrooms and covered picnic tables, as well as a freshwater shower for a quick rinse after swimming. There is no charge to enter the area. The beach is dedicated to the memory of Anne Eaton, longtime Lower Matecumbe Key resident and noted environmental preservation activist.

Open to the public, **Harry Harris County Park**, ☎ 305-852-7161 (see below) has the only other bit of sand in the area that might merit the name "beach." An enclosed area offers good swimming for small children and the flats in front of the park offer reasonable snorkeling for beginners. There's a boat ramp, bathrooms, picnic tables and a playground. To get here, follow the signs as you turn to the ocean side at MM 93 OS.

At MM 86 OS, the **Holiday Isle Resort**, ☎ *305-664-2321, 800-327-7070, www.holidayisle.com*, complex has a sandy beach that is open to the public. You may have to pay for parking during high season or on the weekends. Every imaginable watersport is catered to with equipment rentals, charter fishing boats, a scuba shop and dive charters. Most watersports equipment can be rented by the hour, half-day or longer. The complex has several restaurants, four hotels (see *Where to Stay*) and includes the happening nightspot Rum Runners (see *Nightlife*). The ever-popular "sandbar" is a party spot on an actual sandbar about a half-mile offshore. Reachable by boat, sailboard, swimming or kite ski, the sandbar teems with young life on weekends. There is no bar in the commercial sense; it's BYOB affair.

■ Parks

Crocodile Lake National Wildlife Refuge, ☎ *305-451-4223, http://southeast.fws.gov/CrocodileLake/*, is almost completely undeveloped and is one of the few places where you can see wild crocodiles in the US. There are no facilities whatsoever and little more than a small sign to greet visitors. If you can find a place to park (not easy, since most of the surrounding property is privately owned) there is excellent canoeing and kayaking. The park is on the bay side of the northern part of Key Largo, before you get to the Ocean Reef Club.

Dagny Johnson Key Largo Hammocks State Botanical Site, ☎ *305-451-1202, free, www.floridastateparks.org/key-largohammock/, 8 am-5 pm*, a relatively undeveloped park, has picnic tables and restrooms but not much more in the way of facilities. The park's 2,400 acres protects crocodiles, Key Largo wood rats and other species. Self-guided tours by foot or bike on the paved road are the main activity. A Ranger leads tours on Thursday and Sunday at 10 am. Pets on leash are allowed. There is no charge for the guided walks, but there is a $2 entry fee paid on the honor system at the park entrance.

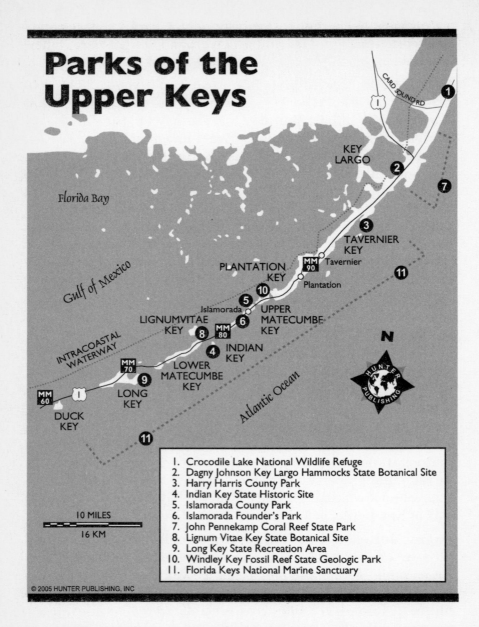

Parks of the Upper Keys

KEY LARGO

Florida Bay

TAVERNIER KEY

PLANTATION KEY

MM 90 Tavernier

Plantation

Gulf of Mexico

Islamorada

UPPER MATECUMBE KEY

LIGNUMVITAE KEY

MM 80

INDIAN KEY

INTRACOASTAL WATERWAY

LOWER MATECUMBE KEY

MM 70

Atlantic Ocean

N

MM 60

LONG KEY

HUNTER PUBLISHING

DUCK KEY

10 MILES

16 KM

1. Crocodile Lake National Wildlife Refuge
2. Dagny Johnson Key Largo Hammocks State Botanical Site
3. Harry Harris County Park
4. Indian Key State Historic Site
5. Islamorada County Park
6. Islamorada Founder's Park
7. John Pennekamp Coral Reef State Park
8. Lignum Vitae Key State Botanical Site
9. Long Key State Recreation Area
10. Windley Key Fossil Reef State Geologic Park
11. Florida Keys National Marine Sanctuary

© 2005 HUNTER PUBLISHING, INC

Harry Harris County Park, ☎ *305-852-7161,* has swimming, a playground, a boat ramp, softball diamonds, picnic tables and bathrooms. Entrance is free during the week, and there is a small charge on the weekends for out-of-towners. To get here, turn off the highway at MM 93 OS in Key Largo and follow the signs.

Indian Key State Historic Site, MM 78.5 OS, off Lower Matecumbe Key, is the location of a famous massacre of settlers by Indians. Guided trips to both Indian Key and Lignum Vitae Key are $25 or $15 to just one of the Keys and they leave every day from **Robbie's**, *MM 77.5 BS, ☎ 305-664-4815*. Robbie's also has kayak rentals and other services. Contact for the historic site is via Long Key State Recreation Area, ☎ 305-664-4815.

There is a good swimming beach and the island has several hundred yards of trails with ruins of a wrecker's home. It is dripping with Old Florida history. You can access the island only by boat, so bring your own, rent one, or sign up for a tour at Robbie's. Unless you've read up on the island, Robbie's is a good way to learn about what happened among all the mangroves. You should stop at the marina even if you don't need any of the services. The docks teem with tarpon and are in a frenzy whenever tourists feed them.

Islamorada County Park, MM 81.5 BS, behind the library, has picnic tables, a playground, restrooms and a small but nice beach. This is a good casual snorkeling spot, but watch the current when the tide is changing.

Islamorada Founder's Park, MM 86 BS, is a public park free to residents and those staying in a local hotel (use of the huge pool costs $3). It has extensive facilities, including dog and skate parks, a beach, a marina, sports equipment rentals and bathroom/shower facilities.

John Pennekamp Coral Reef State Park, ☎ *305-451-1202, MM 102.5 OS, Key Largo, $2.50 per vehicle/50¢ per person, 8 am to sunset, www.johnpennekamp.com*, was the first undersea park in the US and, with the adjacent Florida Keys National Marine Sanctuary, it covers approximately 178 square nautical miles of reefs, mangroves and a small bit of Key Largo where park headquarters is located. The park is named for the late *Miami Herald* editor John Pennekamp, who was instrumental in creating both this park and Everglades National Park.

Upper Keys

The area preserves not only the famed offshore coral reefs, but a small portion of mangrove swamps and a huge area of turtle grass and sand flats, both of which are nurseries for shrimp, lobsters, crabs and a wide variety of sport and commercial food fish. The reefs here are the best preserved in the US and are spectacularly diverse, with beautiful gardens of living coral, sponges, sea fans and thousands of insanely colorful reef fish.

Park facilities are designed to make enjoying the offshore reefs easy, even for people who cannot swim or have never even snorkeled or scuba dived. Glass-bottom boats make quick trips to the nearest shallow reefs so visitors can view the underwater splendor in air-conditioned comfort.

For serious scuba divers and snorkelers, the park concessionaire and numerous nearby charter boats offer trips to shallow and deep reefs, wrecks and the famous underwater statue of Christ. All necessary equipment is available for rent, from mask and fins to tanks and regulators. PADI diving instruction is available, from beginner through Divemaster level. Diving and snorkeling trips with the park's concessionaire tend to go to nearby reefs suitable for intermediate divers at best. Most of the sites are visited over and over again every day and, although well preserved, you may find the more remote, less-visited sites to be of more interest.

The signs you will see on the Overseas Highway pointing to the park are for the land-based headquarters, which has everything you need to get into the heart of the offshore reefs or just have a nice picnic by the water with the kids. Kayaks, canoes, and snorkeling and diving equipment are all available. There's a dive shop, marina, campsites, two small beaches, kayak, canoe and boat rentals, showers, changing rooms and a snack bar. The area around the land-based portion of the park is an excellent kayaking spot, with hundreds of small trails leading through mangroves and many miles of flats to explore.

Pets are not allowed on the beach, concession or camping areas, which doesn't leave much besides the parking lots. They must be on a leash at all times and should not be left unaccompanied.

Lignum Vitae Key State Botanical Site, *MM78.5 BS off Lower Matecumbe Key,* is named for the extremely hard Lignum Vitae tree that grows on the island. There is a dense subtropical forest with Ranger-led hikes through the trails. Access is by boat only. Trips are arranged from **Robbie's**, a small marina at *MM 77.5 BS,* ☎ *305-664-4815*. Information about tours and access is available from the Islamorada Chamber of Commerce, ☎ *305-664-4503*.

Long Key State Recreation Area, ☎ *305-664-4815, MM 67.5 OS, 8 am to sunset, $3.75 for first person; 50¢ for each additional person*. Canoe rentals are available by the hour or day. The area's Golden Orb Trail is a boardwalk that runs through a mangrove swamp with a plethora of water birds. Facilities include a campground, picnic area, restrooms, showers and canoe trail. There is good snorkeling on the flats. Layton Nature Trail, across the street at MM 67.7 BS, goes through a tropical hardwood grove.

Windley Key Fossil Reef State Geologic Park, *MM 85.5 BS,* ☎ *305-664-2540*, features a petrified reef and an abandoned rock quarry that worked until the early 20th century. The vertical quarry cuts slice through the remains of old coral reefs, giving an educational view of reef fossils. The Alison Fahrer Environmental Education Center here is open weekdays, 8 am-5 pm). There's a $1.50 entrance fee to access the trails running through the quarries.

Adventures

■ On Foot

There simply aren't many beaches for strolling, so you have to be creative about what you can do on foot in the Upper Keys.

Beachcombing

It's hard to find a long stretch of undeveloped beach, but once you do, you can spend hours looking for treasures washed up in the mangroves and on the sand. **North Key Largo** has a very long, relatively undeveloped section of beach made up of coral rock, mangroves and a few areas of narrow sand. There are few access points and no decent places to park, but if you can get dropped off by boat or simply beach your own boat, the area is usually deserted. Prime beachcombing can be found on **Elliot Key** and **Old Rhodes Key**, north of Key Largo and reachable only by boat.

Birding

The "beach" on the ocean side of **North Key Largo** is hard to access due to lack of parking and large tracts of private property. However, if you have stout shoes and bug spray, the long shoreline is a good place to admire sea birds.

On the other side of the highway is **Crocodile Lake National Wildlife Refuge**, a completely undeveloped protected area that's home to a healthy crocodile population. There are no public facilities whatsoever and, without a kayak or canoe, the refuge is almost impossible to access. There is a parking area and boat ramp on the other side of the highway suitable for parking and launching a canoe or kayak.

■ OUTFITTERS

Several outfitters offer birding trips in the mangroves and shallow flats.

Bay & Reef Company, *MM 79.7, Islamorada,* ☎ *305-393-0994, www.bayandreef.com*. Specializing in small, custom environmental tours, Bay & Reef leads snorkeling, fishing, birding and Everglades tours from Islamorada. The Everglades trips go to Cape Sable and Flamingo. They don't take casual drop-ins, so call in advance to book your spot. Their service is really for people who want a personalized experience. Prices start at $300 per day.

Caribbean Water Sports, *MM 82 OS, Islamorada at the Cheeca Lodge & Spa,* ☎ *305-664-9547*, offers daily mangrove tours, snorkeling trips and tours of historic Indian Key and Lignum Vitae Key. Call ahead for reservations and prices. Two-hour Zodiac enviro-tours cost $45 and snorkel tours start at $40.

Caribbean Watersports, *MM 97 BS, Key Largo at the Sheraton Resort,* ☎ *305-852-4707, www.caribbean-watersports.com*, runs mangrove tours in a Zodiac inflatable as well as a Hobie Cat sailboat tour that goes to small, remote keys in Florida Bay. Both vessels have very shallow draft, so you have a good chance to see bird and aquatic life in areas not accessed by other craft. Birders or anyone fascinated by life on the flats should not miss this tour. The same company offers trips from Islamorada to Indian and Lignum Vitae Keys. Trips start around $40. Be sure to make reservations in advance.

Everglades Safari Tours, *MM 102 BS, Key Largo at the Quay Restaurant,* ☎ *305-451-0943*, has two-hour sunset cruises through the mangroves. These trips are a very good birding opportunity.

Bridge Walks

The old bridges of the Overseas Highway offer a unique opportunity to get out to sea on your own two feet. In particular, the bridges by **Indian Key**, **Lignum Vitae Key** and **Long Key** have wonderful views of the flats and channels. Rarely without a fisherman or two, the bridges offer the chance to see sea birds, stingrays, sharks and maybe even a turtle or two.

Golf

There is a nine-hole, nicely maintained course at **Cheeca Lodge**, *MM 82 OS, Islamorada,* ☎ *305-664-4651, www.Cheeca. com*. Cheeca Lodge is a full-service luxury hotel with, in addition to golf, tennis, watersports and a top-quality restaurant. The $39 per-room resort fee covers the resort's most popular activities, including golf and tennis.

■ On Wheels

 A **bike path** runs alongside the Overseas Highway all through the Upper Keys. There's not as much room on the bridges as bikers would like, but it's still a wonderful route. Keep in mind that, other than a few side streets in Key Largo, there really are no alternate places to cycle.

Upper Keys

■ **OUTFITTER**

Tavernier Bicycle & Hobbies, *MM 91.9 BS*, ☎ *305-852-2859*, has children's and adult bikes from $8 per day.

■ On Water

Water is what the Keys are all about (although some would say rum) and the Upper Keys have all the very best of the Keys watersports to enjoy. **Harry Harris County Park**, ☎ *305-852-7161*, has a small boat ramp and parking for vehicles with trailers. The turnoff for the park is to the ocean side at MM 93 OS.

> **AUTHOR NOTE:** Personal watercraft are prohibited in all areas of Everglades National Park, which covers most of Florida Bay.

Boat Tours

African Queen, *MM 100 OS, Key Largo at the Holiday Inn*, ☎ *305-451-4655*. The *African Queen* putters around the harbor and weaves through some meager mangroves. But if you're a Bogart or Hepburn fan you'll love it – this is the actual boat on which Humphrey Bogart reluctantly hosted Katherine Hepburn in the movie *African Queen*. The vessel is coal-powered and did service early in the last century on Lake Albert in East Africa. You need to call ahead to check on departure times and prices for the half-hour trips. The same owner also keeps the vintage mahogany launch used in the movie *On Golden Pond*.

Spirit of Pennekamp, *MM 102.5 OS, Key Largo*, ☎ *305-451-1621, $20 adults, $12 children*. Going all the way out to some of the best reefs in the park, this catamaran is a stable platform perfect for viewing the undersea world through its glass bottom. Tours last about 2½ hours and leave from park headquarters on Key Largo every day at 9:15, 12:15 and 3 pm.

Key Largo Princess, *MM 100 OS, Key Largo*, ☎ *305-451-4655, $18.50 adults, $8.50 children*, has a basic glass-bottom viewing area. It runs two-hour trips over coral reefs. You won't be disappointed – the reefs are beautiful and you cannot have a better view without getting your feet wet.

Sailing

Treasure Harbor Marina, *200 Treasure Harbor Drive, Islamorada,* ☎ *305-852-2458, fax 305-852-5743, www. treasureharbor.com.* Treasure Harbor offers daily and weekly sailboat charter, either bareboat (without crew) or with captain and crew. Rates run from $100 per day to $1,700 for a week-long bareboat charter.

Offshore Sailing School, *MM 61 OS, Hawk's Cay Resort,* ☎ *800-221-4326*, offers sailing lessons from beginner to advanced levels. It was founded in 1964 by Olympic sailor Steve Colgate and is flexible enough to arrange everything from three-hour introductory sessions for a family or a week-long offshore courses aboard a 46-foot yacht. Accommodations can either be on board or at Hawk's Cay Resort. Pricing varies depending on the number of people involved and length of instruction desired.

Canoeing & Kayaking

The area around largely undeveloped **North Key Largo** and **Card Sound** is one of the best for paddling in the entire Keys and can be reached from a variety of roadside launch points. **Crocodile Lake National Wildlife Refuge** is closed to the public and hard to access from the Key Largo side, but you can put in along Card Sound and poke around the mangroves at the edges of the refuge.

Farther south, it's simply a matter of finding a good place to leave your car while exploring the tiny keys and mangroves. Paddling across the flats is a good opportunity to get very close to stingrays, sharks and, sometimes, turtles.

Indian Key State Historic Site, *MM 78.5 OS, off Lower Matecumbe Key.* Small Indian Key is a history buffs dream that's accessible from the shore. It is only about a half-mile offshore, over very shallow grass and sand flats. Wading around these flats is great fun. It gets a little too deep to actually wade out to the island, but there are always things to see in the shallow water here. Watch for currents to the east.

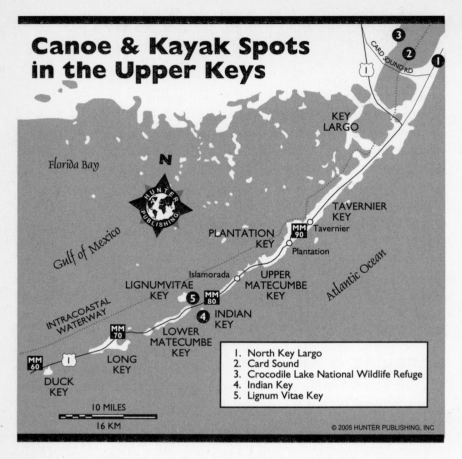

Canoe & Kayak Spots in the Upper Keys

1. North Key Largo
2. Card Sound
3. Crocodile Lake National Wildlife Refuge
4. Indian Key
5. Lignum Vitae Key

© 2005 HUNTER PUBLISHING, INC

Lignum Vitae Key State Botanical Site, *MM 78.5 BS, about a mile north of Lower Matecumbe Key,* has a mostly shallow route with a few deeper channels to cross. This is quite a good paddle if you like to see birds and, of course, the sea life on the flats. Currents can be strong.

> **AUTHOR TIDBIT:** Plan your trip to go out on an incoming tide and return after the tide change.

■ OUTFITTERS

Caribbean Watersports, *MM 97 BS, Key Largo, at the Sheraton Beach Resort,* ☎ *305-852-4707, www.caribbeanwatersports.com,* covers just about every tropical watersport you can think of, including kayaks. A boat trip with dolphin-sighting guarantee is coupled with a visit to Dolphins Plus, billed as marine mammal research and education center (see below).

Coral Reef Park Co., *MM 102.5 OS, John Pennekamp Coral Reef State Park,* ☎ *305-451-1621*, rents canoes, sailboats, windsurfing equipment.

Florida Bay Outfitters, *MM 104, Key Largo,* ☎ *305-451-3018, www.KayakFloridaKeys.com*, runs three-hour kayak tours and rentals get you to the backside of the park from Key Largo. They can also arrange for guided multi-day trips in some of the less-traveled parts of the park. These guys have a reputation as being real pros, taking care to know each customer's needs and skill levels.

Robbie's (see *Equipment Rentals*, page 115) rents kayaks and personal watercraft

Dolphin Encounters

If you can't resist messing around with dolphins, two of the best-known dolphin places are in the Upper Keys.

Dolphin Encounters are offered at Hawk's Cay Resort.

Upper Keys

Dolphins Plus, *31 Corrine Place, Key Largo*, ☎ *305-451-1993, www.dolphinsplus.com.* Billing themselves as a "marine mammal research & education center," Dolphins Plus claims to have developed a "totally new procedure in acclimating dolphins to humans...," but that sounds like a marketing blurb to me. An attempt to make the operation more legitimate requires advance reservations, although when I showed up unannounced they seemed ready to go. The price for a half-hour swim starts at $125 per swimmer. Children under 12 must be accompanied by an adult and also pay the full price. I'd rather go fishing.

Hawk's Cay Resort, *MM 61 OS, Duck Key*, ☎ *305-742-7000, www. hawks- cay.com,* offers both in-the-water Dolphin Discovery and what they call Dockside Dolphins. Guests pay $100 for a 45-minute Dolphin Discovery session (includes 25 minutes actually in the water with the loveable dolphins) and non-guests pay $110. They have an enclosed lagoon directly in front of the main pool and convention center, making it easy for bystanders or family to enjoy the show as well. The dolphins and staff seem to love what they do. Professional-quality digital photos of the sessions are available at an extra cost. Both programs spend time discussing how dolphins live in the aquatic ecosystem, and the behavior and training techniques used to care for and husband these marine mammals. To get in the water with the frolicsome critters you must be at least 54 inches tall, not pregnant and in good health. Dockside Dolphins allows smaller people to participate, but children under five years old must be accompanied by a paying adult. The programs allow only a very small number of people to participate (make reservations in advance) and run every day. The "marine biologists" who work with visitors and dolphins all seem to be young, blond, good-looking females in matching blue swimsuits. I didn't hear any complaints from human participants or dolphins.

Fishing

The Upper Keys – Islamorada in particular – calls itself the sportfishing capital of the world. Hundreds of charter boats and guides offer their services to the tourist trade. Bridges left over from the old Overseas Highway and railroad have been converted for fishing and offer structures that lure fish. When I come here, the first thing I do is head to the nearest tackle shop, grab a copy of the free *Weekly Fisherman* and chat up the staff and other customers to find out who's catching what, where, and, if possible, how.

You can arrange for guides and charter boats by asking at your hotel or simply by going down to one of the charter docks. Try **Bud & Mary's**, **Holiday Isle**, **Whale Harbor** or **Tavernier Creek Marina** (all listed below). You could also call one of the fishing guide associations, such as **Key Largo Guides Association**, ☎ *305-451-9493*, or **Islamorada Charter Boat Association**, ☎ *305-852-7430*. Below, I suggest a few established operators that offer good value (and I've been out with a few bozos).

■ BACKCOUNTRY & LIGHT TACKLE GUIDES

☆ **AUTHOR'S PICK** - **Lyin' Hawaiian**, *MM 104 at the Marriott*, ☎ *305-451-1097, 305-522-4724, www. lyinhawaiian.com*. Captain Tony DelosSantos has been fishing and guiding in the Keys for over 15 years and is one of the most recognized backcountry guides in the Keys.

☆ **AUTHOR'S PICK** - **Captain Jimmy Johnson**, Coconut Cove Resort MM 85, Key Largo, ☎ *305-852-6322, 305-393-2500, jjfishy@bellsouth.net*, usually booked months ahead, but if you manage to get a day with him you'll be pleased. He's been fishing in the area for decades and knows all the best places and techniques. Half-day trips start at $325 and full-day trips start at $425.

Dockside Charters, *MM 84.5 OS at the Pelican Cove Resort, Islamorada*, ☎ *305-451-5903, www.docksidecharters.com*. IGFA-certified Captain Jeff Pfister specializes in light tackle and fly-fishing and offers no-fish-no-pay tarpon hunts.

■ OFFSHORE CHARTERS

☆ **AUTHOR'S PICK** - **Day Tripper Charters/Captain Ron Green**, *128 Plantation Drive, Tavernier*, ☎ *305-852-9577, 305-766-7078, 800-336-9093, www. daytrippercharters.com*. One of the best-known charter captains in the Keys, Captain Ron Green, boasts numerous tournament wins and has been the subject of articles in major fishing magazines. More than once he has helped me and my family haul in huge wahoo, amberjack, kingfish, dolphin and sailfish. He tends to be a live bait fanatic, which is essential if you expect to catch big pelagics. Rates run from $350 for a half-day to $450 for a full day.

☆ **AUTHOR'S PICK** - *Dream Maker*, Holiday Inn Docks, *Slip #2, MM 100, Key Largo,* ☎ *305-451-2418, 800-451-2418, www.fishkeylargo.com. Dream Maker* is a 34' Hatteras skippered by Captain Jim Arnold. He'll take you out for dolphin, wahoo, sailfish, marlin, tuna and reef fish.

■ PARTY BOATS

Several fine party boats go out for half-day, full day or even night trips. Costs run from $35 up to $50. You take food, drinks, a hat and sunscreen. You bring back fish. It's a pretty good deal. I like party boats.

Gulf Lady, *MM 79.8 OS at Bud and Mary's Marina,* ☎ *305-664-2628, 305-664-2461.* Call ahead to book day or night trips.

Gulfstream, *MM 99.5 at Ocean Bay Marina, Key Largo,* ☎ *305-451-9788.* Trips are fairly long, running from 8:30 am to 3:30 pm and 7 pm to midnight. Costs are $50 for adults/$35 for children on day trips and $35 for adults/$20 for children on night trips. Most excursions involve bottom fishing for snapper, grouper or yellowtail on inshore reefs. Ask about senior discounts.

Miss Tradewinds, *MM 83.5 at Whale Harbor Marina, Islamorada,* ☎ *305-664-8341, 800-883-5336, www. misstradewinds.com*, charges $35 with all gear and bait included. Half-day trips leave at 9:30 am, 1:45 pm and 7:30 pm.

Robbie's, *MM 84.2.5 BS, 77520 Overseas Hwy., Islamorada, FL 33036,* ☎ *305-664-9814, 877-664-8498, fax 305-664-9857, www.robbies.com, robbies@gate.net.* Robbie's Captain Michael party boat leaves at 9:30 am,

1:45 pm and 7:30 pm on two four-hour day-trips and a five-hour night trip.

Sailor's Choice, *MM 100 OS at the Holiday Inn Marina, Key Largo, ☎ 305-451-1802, www.sailorschoicefishingboat.com*, charges $33 for a four-hour trip, gear included. *Sailor's Choice* is a new party boat with daily trips and night fishing on Friday and Saturday. It leaves from the dock at the Holiday Inn at 9 am and 1 pm.

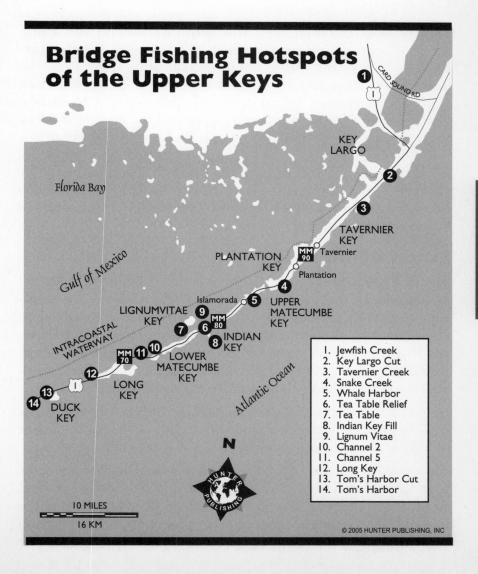

Bridge Fishing Hotspots of the Upper Keys

Florida Bay

Gulf of Mexico

INTRACOASTAL WATERWAY

KEY LARGO

TAVERNIER KEY

Tavernier

PLANTATION KEY

Plantation

Islamorada

LIGNUMVITAE KEY

UPPER MATECUMBE KEY

INDIAN KEY

LOWER MATECUMBE KEY

LONG KEY

DUCK KEY

Atlantic Ocean

1. Jewfish Creek
2. Key Largo Cut
3. Tavernier Creek
4. Snake Creek
5. Whale Harbor
6. Tea Table Relief
7. Tea Table
8. Indian Key Fill
9. Lignum Vitae
10. Channel 2
11. Channel 5
12. Long Key
13. Tom's Harbor Cut
14. Tom's Harbor

N

HUNTER PUBLISHING

10 MILES

16 KM

© 2005 HUNTER PUBLISHING, INC

Upper Keys

Bridge & Shore Fishing

Key Largo is one long island with only a small canal crossing it from Florida Bay to the ocean side. Most of the shoreline is inaccessible, allowing few opportunities for fishing without a boat. The **Marvin D. Adams Waterway** at MM 103 is fairly swift depending on the tide and, although I'm sure a few interesting things swim by from time to time, it's just not that fishy looking. A couple of better spots are the bridges over **Tavernier Creek** and **Snake Creek**. The current is swift when flowing and there are lots of interesting structures.

Farther west, the bridges by **Tea Table Relief** and **Tea Table** are good spots with decent parking. The bridge by **Whale Harbor** has a lot of boat traffic and no good parking spots. I like the bridges and shore spots opposite Indian Key and Lignum Vitae Key, and sometimes fish under the bridge opposite **Robbie's**, hoping some of the tarpon that hang around the marina will find their way over to my bait. So far: no luck. **Long Key Bridge** is a well-known tarpon hot spot and there can be literally hundreds of boats anchored just off from the bridge waiting patiently for the "silver king." Bridges do get busy with the boatless, who hope to catch tarpon. However, actually landing one from a bridge would be pretty hard.

Scuba Diving

The Key Largo area is justifiably considered the premier diving destination in the US. The lushness of the coral reefs just offshore has been perhaps slightly lessened over the years due to development, pollution and overuse, but the huge protected areas in Everglades National Park and John Pennekamp Coral Reef State Park have ensured that the biggest part of this valuable resource is, and will remain, in excellent shape.

Large state and national parks have kept the reefs in the Upper Keys in great condition, but that will change if over-development proceeds, as seems possible.

The main dive areas are on the ocean side and are, for the most part, focused on dozens of sites within **John Pennekamp Coral Reef State Park** (see page 95). Shallow (three-15 feet) patch reefs lie about a mile offshore in many places. Dive sites on these reefs include **Mosquito Bank**, **Hen & Chickens** and **Cannon**

Above: Fort Jefferson in the Dry Tortugas.

Below: Sunset sailing off the coast of Key West.

Above: A fine example of Old Key West architecture.
Opposite: The Dolphin Encounter at Hawk's Cay Resort.
Below: Bahía Honda State Park.

Above: Pelicans.
Opposite: Tarpons fill the water at Robbie's Marina.
Below: Boats transport visitors through Everglades National Park.

Above: A family of herons search for food.
Opposite: Widow walks in Key West were once used as lookout posts for returning sailors.
Below: Cruising the waters in a small boat.

Above: The flats are home to all kinds of sea life.

Below: Canoeing is a peaceful way to look for wildlife.

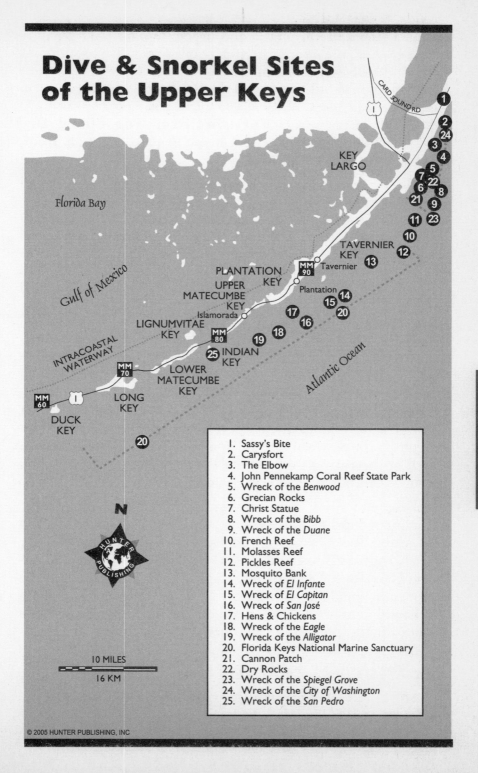

Dive & Snorkel Sites of the Upper Keys

CARD SOUND RD

KEY LARGO

Florida Bay

Gulf of Mexico

TAVERNIER KEY

Tavernier

PLANTATION KEY

MM 90

UPPER MATECUMBE KEY

Plantation

Islamorada

LIGNUMVITAE KEY

MM 80

INTRACOASTAL WATERWAY

INDIAN KEY

MM 70

LOWER MATECUMBE KEY

Atlantic Ocean

MM 60

LONG KEY

DUCK KEY

N

HUNTER PUBLISHING

1. Sassy's Bite
2. Carysfort
3. The Elbow
4. John Pennekamp Coral Reef State Park
5. Wreck of the *Benwood*
6. Grecian Rocks
7. Christ Statue
8. Wreck of the *Bibb*
9. Wreck of the *Duane*
10. French Reef
11. Molasses Reef
12. Pickles Reef
13. Mosquito Bank
14. Wreck of *El Infante*
15. Wreck of *El Capitan*
16. Wreck of *San José*
17. Hens & Chickens
18. Wreck of the *Eagle*
19. Wreck of the *Alligator*
20. Florida Keys National Marine Sanctuary
21. Cannon Patch
22. Dry Rocks
23. Wreck of the *Spiegel Grove*
24. Wreck of the *City of Washington*
25. Wreck of the *San Pedro*

10 MILES

16 KM

Upper Keys

Patch. Often more dramatic and deeper (from awash to 120+ feet) reefs are found bordering the Gulf Stream five to six miles offshore. These are the barrier reefs that crop up from just south of Miami and run all the way to the Dry Tortugas. The dives on these reefs can begin quite shallow and run down to over 100 feet. Major sites include **Carysfort Reef**, **The Elbow**, **Dry Rocks**, **Grecian Rocks**, **the Christ Statue**, **French Reef**, **Molasses Reef** and **Pickles Reef**.

Outside the park off the north part of Key Largo, Elliot Key and Old Rhodes Key are less-frequented sites. Because there are not so many facilities in this area and access is difficult, the reefs suffer less from pollution. About six miles off Elliot Key, past Bache Shoal, are two huge piles of coral (starting in about 30 feet of water) facing each other over a sandy passage or "bite." These are the ends of large reef systems that meet at a channel called **Sassy's Bite**, one of the best dive sites in the Upper Keys. Few dive operators know where it is and, if they do, will not take you there (it takes some time and gasoline). It is enough off the beaten path to entice only the "in-the-know" locals and hard-core lobster grabbers. A steep drop-off down into the blue of the Gulf Stream borders the site on the east side. The bite leads through the reefs to the Hawk Channel side of the reef system with vast areas of sand and turtle grass. Sharks and jewfish (Goliath grouper) pass between the piles of coral through the bite in search of the careless or weak. I've seen tuna, amberjack and marlin at this big fish feeding ground.

Wreck diving off Key Largo is awesome. There are several large accidental wrecks, as well as some purposely sunk for diving. You could spend weeks just diving wrecks. The **Spiegel Grove, City of Washington, Benwood, USCG Bibb, USCG Duane, El Infante, San José, El Capitan, Eagle, USS Alligator** and the **San Pedro** should keep you busy for some time. Some of these wrecks are merely piles of corroded metal and ballast and some are hauntingly preserved. The lure of wreck diving can be indulged so thoroughly in only a few other places in the world.

■ DIVE SHOPS & CHARTERS

American Diving Headquarters, *MM 105.5 BS, Key Largo,* ☎ *305-451-0037, www.americandiving.com*. Reef dives with tanks and weights start at $70.

Amy Slate's Amoray Dive Center & Resort, *MM 104.2 BS, Key Largo,* ☎ *305-451-3595, www.amoray. com, NAUI, PADI, YMCA, BSAC*

BlueWater Divers of Key Largo, *MM 100 OS, Key Largo,* ☎ *305-453-9600, www.BlueWaterDiver.net,* runs two-tank dives twice a day for a bargain $55, including tanks and weights. They'll take you on wreck dives, drift dives, twilight dives and all the John Pennekamp Coral Reef State Park sites you can handle. All levels of PADI instruction are offered, including Nitrox. Their boat has a nice platform that makes getting back aboard easy and is roomy enough when they keep the trip limited to six people.

☆ **AUTHOR'S PICK** - **Dive In**, *MM 97.5 OS, Key Largo,* ☎ *305-852-1919, www.diveinflkeys.com.* Located in Mandalay Marina, Dive In offers six-person dives to all the Upper Keys, including wrecks such as the *Speigel* and *Eagle.* They rent underwater digital still and video cameras so you can go home with a DVD of your dive. A two-day trip with night dive as well as private charters can be arranged. Prices start at $50 with no tank. This is an owner-operated business and offers custom trips.

☆ **AUTHOR'S PICK** - **Dual Porpoise Charters Inc.**, *MM 100, Holiday Inn docks, Key Largo,* ☎ *305-394-0417, www.dualporpoise.net.* Cutely named Dual Porpoise takes only six passengers at a time on its two scheduled trips a day. John Pennekamp park and the *Speigel Grove* and *Bibb* wrecks are regular stops. All equipment is available for rent. Scuba instruction and guided tours are offered in English and German. Two-tank dives run $55.

Florida Keys Dive Center, *MM 90.5, Tavernier,* ☎ *305-852-4599, 800-433-8946, www.floridakeysdivectr. com.* This PADI Five-Star IDC facility has been serving the Upper Keys since 1983. They offer two half-day tours daily and have classes from beginner to advanced Nitrox diving. A concession operates out of John Pennekamp State Park.

Upper Keys

Holiday Isle Dive Shop, *MM 84 OS, Islamorada,* ☎ *305-664-DIVE, 800-327-7070, www.diveholidayisle. com*, is a full-service PADI Gold Palm Resort located at the Holiday Isle Resort. Their 35-foot boat takes 22 snorkelers and scuba divers every day at 9 am and 1 pm for a half-day reef trip. This can be a fairly large crowd, but is fine if you are a beginner. Trips start at $45 with no equipment (rentals are available). You may have to pay for parking on weekends. The shop itself is large and comprehensive.

Ocean Divers, *MM 105.8, Key Largo,* ☎ *305-451-1113, 800-451-1113, www.oceandivers.com*. Set right in the Marina del Mar complex, Ocean Divers operates a larger boat than most, taking 20+ divers for $65 apiece, including tanks and weights. They have a wide-ranging schedule of dives covering all levels of experience up to wreck dives that go down 130 feet. Day-trips leave at 8 am and 1 pm. Night dive departure times vary. Ocean Divers offers all levels of PADI training courses.

☆ **AUTHOR'S PICK** - **Quiescence**, *MM 103.5 BS, Key Largo,* ☎ *305-451-2440, www.quiescence.com*, is one of the more professional operations in the area. Many of the other shops send you here for equipment repairs. They have a small stock but are helpful and knowledgeable. And with six boats devoted exclusively to small groups, you are likely to be paired up with other divers of similar experience and interests. Their two-location trip with tanks starts at $60.

☆ **AUTHOR'S PICK** - **Rainbow Reef Dive Center**, *MM 84.9 BS at Tropical Reef Resort,* ☎ *305-664-4600, 800-457-4354, www.rainbowreef.us*, is a full-service PADI Five-Star Gold Palm Resort facility, offering lessons, referrals, guided dives, full gear rental and sales, Nitrox certification and lodging, as well as bike, canoe and Sunfish rentals. Their dive trips are in small boats with no more than six divers. They offer drift, wall and night dives as well as two-tank trips twice a day. A two-tank dive with tanks and weights is $56. Rainbow Reef has a reputation as one of the better dive operators in the area.

Tilden's Scuba Center, *MM 51 OS, Hawk's Cay,* ☎ *305-289-4931, www.tildensscubacenter.com*. Tilden's has a shop in Marathon and another one where their boats dock at Hawk's Cay Resort Marina. They are a full-service operation with complete PADI training courses, including Nitrox certification. Their fleet includes both six-pack and larger boats holding as many as 16 divers. I found them to be professional and knowledgeable. The training I observed was very well run – these people try hard to do things right. Each trip has both a captain and Divemaster. Destinations range from the patch reefs directly offshore from Duck Key to deeper dives on the outer reefs and the *Thunderbolt* wreck. Their boats are well set up and roomy. A basic trip (a good choice for beginners and the less experienced) with two tanks and weights is $59; snorkelers can go along for $30. If you want a more advanced dive, ask to be included in a more experienced group.

Snorkeling

As in most of the Keys, the best snorkeling is on the reefs a few miles offshore. Still, there are plenty of interesting things to see in the shallow waters around **Key Largo** and the nearby **Upper Keys**. Most snorkel trip operators take customers to both the nearby and more offshore reefs. Make sure you go on a trip that caters specifically to snorkelers, since dive trips usually go much deeper than you need.

■ OUTFITTERS

Keys Diver Snorkel Tours, *MM 100 BS (next to Wendy's), Key Largo,* ☎ *305-451-1177, 888-289-2402, www.keysdiver.com*, offers three daily snorkel-only tours to John Pennekamp Coral Reef State Park and Key Largo National Marine Sanctuary. They visit the Christ statue and other popular spots. All equipment is provided, including dry snorkels, masks, fins, safety vests and instruction.

Sundiver Snorkel Tours, *MM 103, Key Largo,* ☎ *305-451-2220, 800-654-7369, www.snorkelingisfun. com*, goes to all the hot spots: John Pennekamp Coral

Reef State Park, the Christ statue and some of the more interesting inner reefs. They run three trips a day and provide everything you need. Call for departure times.

Caribbean Watersports, *MM 97 BS, Key Largo, at the Sheraton Beach Resort,* ☎ *305-852-4707, www.caribbeanwatersports.com*, has a snorkeling-only trip good for beginners and more advanced snorkelers. You are guaranteed to spend the whole time in shallow water suitable for snorkeling, rather than diving.

SHORE-ACCESSIBLE SNORKELING SPOTS

Unless you're staying in a hotel with water frontage, it's hard to find an interesting snorkeling spot without a boat. **Harry Harris County Park**, *MM 93 OS,* ☎ *305-852-7161*, has a small beach suitable for beginning snorkelers. The water is shallow. Park amenities include restrooms and showers.

Sunset Cruises

Horizon Catamaran Sail Cruise, *MM60 OS, Duck Key,* ☎ *305-743-7000, ext. 3555, $30 per person*. The nightly trips on a 40-foot catamaran include refreshments and champagne. If you don't have your own boat, this is a good way to see the area from a little ways offshore at the very best time of the day.

Captain Sterling's Champagne Sunset Cruises, *Dolphin Cove MM 102, Key Largo,* ☎ *888-224-6044*, offers nightly cruises and wedding specials aboard a 30-passenger boat.

Nautilimo, *MM 80.5 BS, Islamorada,* ☎ *305-942-3793, www.nautilimo.com*. Captain Joe Fox has taken a stretch limo and made it seaworthy. The combination boat/car, which can be driven on the road and floated over the flats, is an amusing way to arrive at waterside events. It's a real hoot. Two-hour sunset cruises aboard the unique *Nautilimo* start at $75.

Watersports

The popularity of windsurfing seems to be declining in favor of kite boarding. And the trade winds and flat water in the Keys make good conditions for both.

■ EQUIPMENT RENTALS

Robbie's, *MM 77.5 BS, Islamorada,* ☎ *305-664-9814, 877-664- 8498, www.robbies.com, robbies@gate.net.* Robbie's has been around for more than 20 years and is a good place to find a simple, cheap boat rental. They also rent kayaks and personal watercraft for trips out to Indian Key and Lignum Vitae Key. Over the years, tarpon have learned they can get a handout from Robbie's dock and literally hundreds of the silver sides weighing up to 100 lbs mill about the dock waiting for tourists to feed them. There is a $1 charge just to walk out on the dock and witness this; $2 gets you a small pail of fish scraps to feed them.

Tarpoms create a frenzy in the water at Robbie's.

Bump & Jump, *MM 81.5 OS Islamorada,* ☎ *305-664-9404, www.floridakeyswindsurfing.com.* Bump & Jump has rental equipment for catamaran sailing, windsurfing and the more popular kite boarding. They offer complete instruction, and even deliver to your hotel. Check

Upper Keys

their web site for specials but don't look there to find out where they actually are.

Pelican Cove Resort, *MM 84.5, OS, Islamorada,* ☎ *305-664-4435, 800-445-4690, www.pcove.com*, rents every conceivable type of watersports gear and they are just onshore from the famous "sand bar" where young folks from all over the world congregate in bathing attire to flirt and socialize.

■ In the Air

 If you have the guts, flying an ultra-light is probably the very best way to enjoy a leisurely view of the reefs and flats.

■ OUTFITTER

Flying Fish Flight School, *Windley Key in the Coconut Cove Marina,* ☎ *305-664-4055, seagliders@yahoo. com*, offers ultra-light flying lessons in Quicksilver craft with floats for water landings. For $55, you can get a short introductory flight. If you want to go the full course and become a licensed ultra-light pilot, you will need 10 hours of lessons, which runs about $1,000.

Where to Stay

■ Ratings & Prices

 All the room prices in this book are for two people staying in a double room during high season. Taxes and meals are not included unless so mentioned. Hotels and lodges marked "Author's Choice" are my personal favorites, offering top quality lodging and services but, more importantly, something of particular interest or charm.

ACCOMMODATIONS PRICE CHART

$ . . . . Under $100
$$ $100-200
$$$ $200-300
$$$$ . . . . Over $300

■ Hotels & Resorts

HOTEL **Amy Slate's Amoray Dive Center & Resort**, *MM 104.2 BS, Key Largo,* ☎ *305-451-3595, 800-426-6729, fax 305-453-9516, www.amoray.com, amoraydive@aol.com,* $$$. If you're looking for an underwater wedding or honeymoon, Amy Slate can arrange it all for you. The unusual name came from the *Miami Herald*. It cleverly headlined "That's Amoray" to describe one of the resort's undersea weddings that was crashed by a huge moray eel. The hotel has a variety of pleasant rooms from simple singles to luxurious "villas," some with great views of Florida Bay. Many rooms have a dock at the back door so you can step directly from your room onto a dive boat. Amy Slate's is an all-inclusive dive center.

Anchorage Resort & Yacht Club, *MM 107.5 BS, Key Largo,* ☎ *305-451-0500, fax 305-451-2565, $$$.* The Anchorage is located at the northernmost end of Key Largo and appeals primarily to anglers. It is well situated to take advantage of great flats and reef fishing. The quiet location is about nine miles from the bustle of "downtown" Key Largo. The one-bedroom suites are timeshare rentals, fully furnished and usually rent by the week. Amenities include pool, tennis courts and a marina. You must book quite early since few of the condos are available for rental.

Bay Breeze Resort Motel, *MM 92.5 BS, Tavernier,* ☎ *305-852-5248, 800-937-5650, fax 305-852-5758, www.baybreeze-motel.com, $-$$$.* The Bay Breeze is on a beautiful piece of property tucked well away from the highway with good views of Florida Bay. Snorkeling directly from the small sandy beach in front of the motel is shallow but nice for beginners. A local secret "deep hole" is nearby and the story goes that it holds some enormous goliath grouper. Check out one of the kayaks and find out for yourself. Some of the rooms are motel-style that have been nicely modernized. There are some detached cottages as well –

quite elegant. Guests can keep their boats at the dock for no extra charge. There is a small boat ramp. The heated pool is partially shaded by an interesting selection of sub-tropical palms and bougainvillea. The office closes at 6 pm so be sure you arrive before then or call ahead. All units have efficiency or full kitchens. Check out their website for pictures of the rooms.

Bay Cove Motel, *MM 99.4 BS, Key Largo, 99446 Overseas Highway,* ☎ *305-451-1686, $$*. Clean and neat with 11 motel-style rooms, the Bay Cove is a good budget choice. They have a dock for guest use. Pets are not allowed.

Bay View Inn and Marina, *MM 63 BS, Conch Key,* ☎ *305-289-1525, 800-289-2055, www.bayviewinn.com, $*. This good budget choice is usually busy with a diving crowd. The regular rooms have two queen-size beds and refrigerator and the "waterfront efficiencies" sport full kitchens.

Breezy Palms Resort, *MM 80 OS, Islamorada,* ☎ *305-664-2361, fax 305-664-2572, www.breezypalms.com, $$*. A bit of a beach sets Breezy Palms apart from other oceanside lodging. All the accommodations (except the older motel-style rooms) have full kitchens. One- and two-bedroom apartments front either the beach or the pool. The Breezy Palms is in a laid back location with a good dock for night fishing and great access to the reefs around Alligator Light and the flats in Florida Bay.

Bud & Mary's Fishing Marina, *MM 79.8 OS, Islamorada,* ☎ *305-664-2461, 800-742-7945, $$*. Bud & Mary's is the premier charter boat marina in the Keys and has a few motel-style rooms for the budget-conscious. If you're going to be out fishing all day, this is a convenient place to base yourself. No pets allowed.

Caloosa Cove Resort, *MM 73.8 OS, Islamorada,* ☎ *305-664-8856, 888-297-3208, fax 305-664-8856, www.caloosacove.com, $$$*. Caloosa Cove has efficiencies with private balconies and one-bedroom suites. The resort sits by the ocean and has a restaurant, lounge, boat rentals, tennis courts, pool, grocery store and full-service marina.

☆ **AUTHOR'S PICK** - **Casa Morada**, *MM 82 BS, Islamorada, 136 Madeira Road (turn at the Lor-E-Lei),* ☎ *305-664-0044, fax 305-664-0674, www.casamorada.com, $$$-$$$$*. Completely renovated in 2003, Casa Morada is a comfortable, quietly elegant boutique hotel with pool, dock and bocce. The rooms are light, large and very nicely appointed with DVD players, a small library featuring books on local history and piles of large, fluffy pillows. They offer meals and drinks by the pool or in your room. If you're the active type they have bicycles ready for use and can arrange for kayaks, fishing, diving, snorkeling and eco-trips to the nearby Everglades. A continental breakfast with cereal, good coffee, fresh-squeezed orange juice, delicate croissants and the daily papers is served on an upper-level veranda overlooking Florida Bay. The landscaping is tasteful, with orchids and winding sandy trails that lead over a small bridge to "the island," where there is a pool and open-air bar. Each bathtub comes complete with the usual small bars of interesting soaps, shampoo, body oils and rubber ducky. Pets are allowed.

Cheeca Lodge, *MM 82 OS, Islamorada,* ☎ *305-664-4651, fax 305-664-2893, www.cheeca.com, $$$-$$$$.* With a small nine-hole golf course, six tennis courts, eco-tours and elaborate pool, Cheeca Lodge is a large, luxury resort with everything for the Keys adventurer. Home to several major fishing tournaments, this is the place for serious anglers with some money to spend on nice lodgings. They have a good website, but it lacks direct e-mail capability – fill out the reservation form or call if you have questions. The Cheeca Lodge is one of the luxury hotels owned by Rock Resorts, which tends towards exotic hideaways in places like Jackson Hole, Palm Springs and Santa Fe. In spite of this pedigree, it is not as elegant and stuffy as you might think. The rooms are large and comfortable with all the expected amenities, but they are still hotel rooms with thin walls. The size of the lodge means the pool is busy with teenagers and kids. There is no extra charge for tennis and use of bicycles and golf is a reasonable $16 per person for an entire day. The Avanyu Spa offering skin care, massages, body treatments, after-sun treatments, gentlemen's spa days, and a couples retreat, among other services. Scuba diving, boat rentals, parasailing, kayak rentals, beach cats, snorkeling, windsurfing and fishing excursions are all available. The famous "sand bar" party spot is only a mile away, so those inclined to youthful partying can easily paddle or motor out and congregate offshore.

Chesapeake Resort, *MM 83.4 OS, Islamorada,* ☎ *305-664-4662, 800-338-3395, www.chesapeake-resort.com, $$$.* Clean and very nicely appointed, the Chesapeake is located on a beautiful waterfront property right next to the Whale Harbor Inn. No pets. They have 44 guest rooms, eight suites and 13 villas with full kitchens. The views out to the reefs are some of the best. There is a swimming pool, tennis court, small marina, dive center and a modest selection of watersports equipment, including catamarans, kayaks, fishing poles and water bikes. No pets.

Coconut Cove Resort & Marina, *MM 85 OS, Islamorada,* ☎ *305-664-4055, www.coconutcove.net, $$$*. A classic Keys motel with thin, frayed, postage stamp-sized towels gracing the bathrooms, this 50s-style (or maybe 40s) spot is clean and the air-conditioning works. With 10 efficiencies (full kitchens) and a marina, Coconut Cove is a good base for divers and boaters, but the rooms are overpriced for the area. Many other motels of similar or better quality are half the price. Nonetheless, the resort's 11 acres are right on the Atlantic and there is a decent, if small, marina. All types of watersports – Jet Skiing, kayaking, fishing, diving, windsurfing and sailing – are catered to from the marina. The owners also offer ultra-light flying lessons. A new building, a pool and Tiki bar were finished in late 2003.

Conch Key Cottages, *MM 62.3 OS, Walker's Island,* ☎ *305-289-1377, 800-330-1577, www.conchkeycottages.com, $$$$*. A lodging with plenty of Keys charm, Conch Key surpasses most of the competition with its well-appointed individual cottages, pool and marina. Guests can dock their boat for no extra charge. The cottages are set on an island by themselves. No pets.

Days Inn Suites, *MM 82.7 OS, Islamorada,* ☎ *305-664-3681, fax 305-664-2703, $$$$*. Not like the mass-market Days Inns you find all over the US, this one has only deluxe rooms and suites. Some have kitchens and multiple bedrooms. There's also a good marina. No pets.

Gilbert's Resort, *MM 107.9, BS, Key Largo,* ☎ *305-451-1133, 800-274-6701, fax 305-451-4362, GILBERTSPI2@aol.com, www. gilbertsresort.com, $$$*. You can seemingly do it all from Gilbert's Resort. The motel-style property is loaded with Keys charm, but probably the best thing about it is the full-service marina, which offers docking for boats up to 125' and has a complete scuba service (NAUI & PADI). The restaurant has a great view of the Intracoastal Waterway and serves steaks, seafood and "authentic German cuisine."

Hampton Inn, *MM 80 OS, Islamorada,* ☎ *305-664-0073, 800-426-7866, www.keys-resort.com, $$$.* Much like other Hampton Inns, this one guarantees clean, well-appointed rooms in a well-managed operation. Shallow-draft docking is available for guests.

Hawk's Cay Resort, *MM 61 OS, Duck Key,* ☎ *305-742-7000, 888-443-6393, fax 305-743-3805, www.hawkscay.com, $$$-$$$$.* This is a big resort with golf nearby, tennis courts, five pools (one for adults only), several restaurants, a spa, boating, diving, fishing, a lagoon with dolphin encounters and all the amenities. The exclusive villas offer luxury and privacy. Standard rooms are well appointed and closer to most of the facilities than the more remote villas and suites. There is a small beach and marina, and you can snorkel right in front of the resort. Kids can be entertained by staff all day, if you wish. No pets are allowed. The resort was developed by successful and sometimes maligned real estate developer Pritam Singh (formerly Paul LaBombard) and is the largest in the Keys.

Hawk's Cay is host to a new fly-fishing academy that offers fly-fishing techniques, tackle and fly-tying lessons for beginners and advanced anglers.

Holiday Isle Resort and Marina, *MM 84 OS, Islamorada,* ☎ *305-664-2321, 800-327-7070, fax 305-664-2703, www. holidayisle.com, $$$$.* If you really want a lively time, the Holiday Isle has something for all ages, especially the younger set – shopping, bars, nightlife, fishing, diving are all here. Holiday Isle is actually four hotels – Holiday Isle, Howard Johnson's, El Capitan and Harbor Lights – in one large resort complex. Holiday Isle itself is the nicest of the four, with better views and the most facilities. El Capitan is made up of small cottages and is a bit older, but with more character. No pets.

Holiday Inn Resort, *Key Largo, MM 100 OS, Key Largo,* ☎ *305-451-2121, 800-465-4329, fax 305-451-5592, www. holidayinnkeylargo.com, $$$.* While unfortunately much like other down-market Holiday Inns in the US, there is at least plenty to do here. Playground, bars, restaurant and a large marina with extensive watersports possibilities keep guests occupied. The marina also makes for a pleasant evening stroll along the docks before dinner. Coconuts Lounge, nearby, has live enter-

Upper Keys

tainment every night – blues nights are Tuesday. The *African Queen* docks right at the hotel and can be hired for a cruise. Snorkeling, diving and fishing trips all leave from in front of the hotel.

Howard Johnson's Resort Hotel, *MM 102 OS, Key Largo,* ☎ *305-451-1400, 800-947-7320, fax 305-451-3953, $$$.* Pet-friendly and appealing to huge groups of Europeans, this is a straightforward Howard Johnson's like any other. It's relatively clean and neat, with medium-size, motel-style rooms.

Kelly's On The Bay & Aqua-Nuts, *MM 104.2 BS, Key Largo,* ☎ *305-451-1622, 800-226-0415, fax 305-451-4623, www. aqua-nuts.com, kellysmo@aol.com, $$$.* This is a full-service dive resort with dive shop (Aqua-Nuts) and charter boats in its own marina. The 34 motel-style rooms and heated pool are modest, comfortable and clean. They appeal mostly to a diver crowd, although non-divers come for eco-tours and sunset cruises. No pets allowed. The dive shop offers PADI and NAUI instruction from novice to Divemaster level. Of course, the Key Largo location is prime for visits to John Pennekamp. Diving starts at around $50 for a fully equipped, two-tank dive. Ask about package deals. All the boats in their fleet were purchased new, designed as dedicated dive boats, and are fast and roomy. This is a serious dive operation.

☆ **AUTHOR'S PICK** - **Kona Kai Resort**, *MM 97.8 BS, Key Largo, 97802 Overseas Highway,* ☎ *305-852-7200, 800-365-7829, www.konakairesort.com, konakai@aol.com, $$$$.* With plenty of privacy, shade, sand and quiet (it's adults only and has no phones), Kona Kai seems an oasis of calm after the drive from Miami. The beautiful grounds host only 11 small, luxury cottages and have a lovely pool and small wading beach, as well as a lighted tennis court. This is one of the nicest, if quietest, hotels on Key Largo. If you're looking for action and activity, go elsewhere. If you want a nice place to relax and retire after a hard day doing the Keys thing, then you'll love the Kona Kai. Rooms are spacious, cool and modern. Some have kitchens and come with books, videotapes and CDs by local artists. The owners, Joe and Veronica Harris, live on the property, which is listed in *Distinctive Luxury Hotels of the World*. Everglades National Park is only a half-mile from the hotel dock and Caribbean Watersports will pick you up at the dock to take you into the mangrove islands just a few minutes from Kona Kai's luxury. The wonderful Ballyhoo's (see *Where to Eat*) is right across the street, so you can roll home after stuffing yourself at one of the very best places to eat seafood in the Keys. No phones, no pets, no kids, but plenty of peace and quiet.

La Jolla Resort Motel, *MM 82.3 BS, Islamorada, lajollaresv@ aol.com,* ☎ *305-664-9213, fax 305-664-4201, $$*. The nice pool, small dock and old Keys motel architecture make this a timeless budget classic. The grounds have hammocks, BBQ facilities and a sports-oriented lounge The resort is owned and managed by Tony and Elizabeth Nobregas, who have attracted a crowd of regulars, mostly anglers with their families. Captain Tony operates as a guide for bonefish, tarpon, snook and permit. The rooms are like small apartments in six villas scattered around the property. Most of the rooms have fully-equipped kitchens. The location is quiet, fronting directly onto beautiful Florida Bay.

Lime Tree Bay Resort, *MM 68.5, BS, Long Key,* ☎ *305-664-4740, fax 305-664-0750, www.limetreebayresort.com, $-$$$*. Lime Tree's 35 renovated motel-style rooms have one of the best views of the Florida Bay. You can watch the sun set without leaving your room or take it all in from a hammock or poolside. All of the rooms are large and some have kitchens. The location is convenient to both Marathon and Islamorada. The resort has a full watersports facility right next door, with sunset cruises, boat and kayak rentals, fishing charters, and scuba and snorkeling trips. Lessons, including sailing and windsurfing instruction, are available. There is a tennis court across the street. Dockage for guests is free. Check the website or call for discounts. No pets allowed.

Lookout Lodge Resort, *MM 87.9 BS, Islamorada,* ☎ *305-852-9915, 800-870-1772, fax 305-852-3035, www.lookoutlodge. com, $$$*. Small, clean and neat, this pet-friendly hotel has quiet charm. The suites are a bargain, starting at $136. There is no pool, but you can swim in the bay.

☆ **AUTHOR'S PICK** - **Marina Del Mar Oceanside Resort**, *MM 99.5 OS and BS, Key Largo, 527 Caribbean Drive,* ☎ *305-451-4107, 800-451-3483, fax 305-451-1891, www.marinadel-markeylargo.com, $$$$*. An older, midrise-style hotel, the Marina del Mar is not on the ocean. It has a pool for swimming, but can't offer an ocean view. However, all the diving, snorkeling, fishing,

Upper Keys

parasailing and other watersports action you could want are based at the marina. There are also tennis courts, a professional dive operation and a first-class marina with beautiful yachts by the score. The well-maintained resort is convenient to John Pennekamp State Park and is close to Key Largo action, although far enough from the main highway to be quiet. Local Internet access numbers (AOL, Earthlink, MSN, etc.) are printed on a card next to your in-room phone, so connecting is a breeze. Small pets are allowed – they even have dog biscuits in a bowl at the front desk.

☆ **AUTHOR'S PICK** - **Marriott Key Largo Bay Beach Resort**, *MM 103.9, BS, 103800 Overseas Highway,* ☎ *305-453-0000, 800-228-9290, fax 305-453-0093, www.marriottkeylargo.com, $$$$.* The 153 oversized rooms at this Marriott include 20 two-bedroom suites with balconies. All units have full kitchen and living room with breathtaking waterfront views and data ports. There's a lagoon pool, fitness center, full-service spa and children's' facilities. The PADI dive center and charter fishing options are prime attractions, and the location offers good access to both bay and ocean fishing and diving.

☆ **AUTHOR'S PICK** - **The Moorings Village & Spa**, *MM 81.6 OS, Islamorada,* ☎ *305-664-4708, fax 305-664-4242, Moorings123@ aol.com, www.themooringsvillage.com, $$$$.* The Moorings offers tennis courts, a beach, windsurfing and kayaking. Accommodations come in the form of rooms, cottages or beach houses, some of which are available only with a minimum stay of one week. This beautiful hotel has a beautiful setting, with 18 acres of coconut palms and tropical plantings. It is one of the nicest places to stay in the Keys.

Ocean Pointe Suites, *MM 92.7 OS, Tavernier,* ☎ *305-853-3000, 800-882-9464, www.oceanpointesuites.com, $$$.* This is another hotel that seems to have everything. The rooms are all large, and some feature two bedrooms and a kitchen. A pool, tennis courts, a marina and playground are a few of the amenities. No pets. The marina is convenient to John Pennekamp Coral Reef State Park. Fishing and diving trips can be arranged.

Pelican Cove Resort, *MM 84.5, OS, Islamorada,* ☎ *305-664-4435, 800-445-4690, fax 305-664-5134, www.pcove.com, $$$.* The Pelican is a full-service resort with tennis, boating, fishing charters and a small outdoor restaurant. Accommodations range from standard oceanfront rooms to efficiencies and one- and two-bedroom suites with hot tubs. The rooms are a bit dated, but are comfortable, with small refrigerator, phone and cable TV. All have balconies looking out to the Gulf Stream. From the upper floors you can see freighters and container ships plowing their way along the horizon. The resort buildings sit right on the edge of the ocean and are tall enough to need elevators, with great views from the upper floors. The water in front of the property is deep enough for swimming. The resort offers all watersports, from belly boarding to big time offshore fishing charters. Rental equipment is available for windsurfing, kite boarding, kayaking and Jet Skiing. While the latter race off to the other side of the marina, kite surfers entertain directly in front of the resort. Every afternoon the various watercraft congregate on a sand bar about a quarter-mile offshore for watery partying and sandy social activities.

A basic breakfast is included in the room rate and is served by the pool. The resort is located behind the jumping dolphin show at Theater of the Sea, but far enough from the highway so you don't hear the traffic. You can, however, hear the seals next door barking at night.

Port Largo Villas, *MM 100 OS, Key Largo*, ☎ *305-451-4847, www.portlargovillas.com, $$$*. This is a timeshare operation that rents units on a nightly and weekly basis. The units are large, furnished and all have full kitchens. Although the property is not actually on the seaside, it does front a canal and have full-service boating facilities, a huge pool and tennis courts. They offer fishing charters and are a PADI Five-Star dive operation. One of the few gambling boats in the Keys (they go outside US waters to preserve a modicum of legality) docks right at the hotel. No pets.

Ramada Inn Key Largo, *MM 99.7, OS, Key Largo, 99751 Overseas Highway*, ☎ *305-451-3939, fax 305-453-0222, www. ramadakeylargo.com, $$$*. Right next to the Holiday Inn and the Marina del Mar, the Ramada Inn shares many of the same facilities and is somewhere between the two adjacent resorts in quality and pricing. There is a small swimming pool.

Rock Reef Resort, *Mile Marker 98 BS, Key Largo*, ☎ *305-852-2401, 800-477-2343, fax 305-852-5355, rockreefr@aol.com,* *www.rockreefresort.com, $-$$$*. A quiet bayside hotel with only 21 units, a small beach and nice dock, the Rock Reef is a good choice for relaxing and soaking up Old Keys atmosphere. A dock and small boat ramp are available for guest use. The view out over the flats towards Everglades National Park (a half-mile away) is stunning. Spend an hour or so gazing out over Florida Bay and you'll likely see an impressive array of marine life, including sharks, stingrays, horseshoe crabs and tarpon. I woke up early one morning and, while enjoying my coffee at the end of the dock, watched a solitary manatee browsing along the edge of the flats.

Standard rooms, efficiencies, suites and cottages are available. Some units have multiple bedrooms and are connected by a door that can be unlocked for large families. The cottages have kitchen facilities. If a group of friends are down for a diving or fishing trip, multiple beds can be placed in one room. There is a large picnic and BBQ area and a new pool should be in by the time you read this. The four-acre property is dotted with hammocks.

Owners Dave and Linda Adams have spent the last 14 years steadily adding and improving. This is one of the last few "Mom & Pop" hotels in the Keys. Try to get Dave to give you a tour of the grounds where he maintains an impressive collection of citrus and tropical plants, including tamarind, banana, guava and, of course, Key limes. His collection of roses and bonsai has to be seen to be believed. Parrots Bogie and Peaches add a raucous note to the overall laid-back Keys atmosphere. No pets. Ask about AAA and AARP discounts.

Sea Isle Resort & Marina, *MM 82 OS, Islamorada,* ☎ *305-664-2235, fax 305-664-2093, $$-$$$*. Sea Isle has villas as well as two- and three-bedroom houses with all the trimmings.

Topsider Resort, *MM 75.5 BS, Islamorada,* ☎ *305-664-8031, 800-262-9874, fax 305-664-9337, www.topsiderresort.com, $$$*. All 20 units in this timeshare property are large, with family-style with kitchens, washer and dryer. This is an older property but most rooms have been well restored. Each is a separate octagon-shaped house on stilts that can sleep six and has dock space for one boat. There are pool, spa, tennis court and boat ramp. Rates start at $700 per week.

Tropical Reef Resort & Marina, *MM 85 BS, Islamorada,* ☎ *305-664-8881, 800-887-3373, fax 305-664-4891, ike500@aol. com, www.tropicalreefresort.com, $$-$$$*. Although I rate this as one of the more expensive hotels in the area they do have some rooms at basic prices. Aging a bit, the hotel still has much to offer in the way of luxury. They have three pools and do not allow pets.

☆ **AUTHOR'S PICK** - **Sheraton Beach Resort Key Largo**, *MM 96.9 BS, Key Largo,* ☎ *305-852-5553, fax 305-852-8669, www.keylargoresort.com, $$$$*. This is a class act. A full-service, luxury hotel, the Sheraton Key Largo (once a Westin) has everything, including fine restaurants, a beauty salon, a pool and marina, and tennis courts. Guests can dock their boats here with no extra charge. The hotel is just off the highway in a quiet, tree-shrouded, waterfront site with great views of Florida Bay and the less-frequented side of Everglades National Park. Try to get a room on the upper floors to enjoy the views of the bay and the spectacular sunsets. They describe their beds as "insanely comfortable." Surely they're using hyperbole here, but the beds are very good with plenty of fluffy pillows. No pets.

White Gate Court, *MM 76 BS, Islamorada,* ☎ *305-664-4136, 800-645-4283, www.whitegatecourt.com, $$$*. An older property that has been nicely restored, the White Gate has more charm and Keys flavor than most places in the Upper Keys. Some units have kitchens. Pet-friendly.

■ Camping

Throughout the Keys, camping rates tend to start around $20 for a tent with no hook up and $40 for a RV with full hookup. Waterfront locations can cost more. Watch for mosquitoes at campgrounds near mangroves.

America Outdoors, *MM 97.5 BS, Key Largo,* ☎ *305-852-8054, $$*. Laundry, beach, grocery, 155 sites, bait shop, boat ramp, bathhouses. Sites are shady and well maintained. Tent sites start at $55 per day and RV sites with full hookups start at $85.

Fiesta Key Resort KOA, *MM 70 BS, Long Key,* ☎ *305-664-4922*, has 350 tent and RV sites with pools bar, game room, marina and boat ramp. Some pets allowed. Tent sites start at $42 per night and RV sites at $60.

Florida Keys RV Resort, *MM 106 OS, Key Largo,* ☎ *305-451-4615.* Cable TV, pets OK. Its 116 RV sites (no tents) start at $40 per night.

Key Largo Kampground & Marina, *MM 101 OS, Key Largo,* ☎ *305-451-1431, 800-526-7688.* Oceanfront RV and tenting with two beaches, pool, boat ramp, dock, picnic area, BBQ, laundry bathhouses and playground. Pets OK. Tent sites start at $33 per night and RV sites with full hookups start at $42.50.

Long Key State Recreation Area, *MM 67.5 OS,* ☎ *305-664-4815, $.* Sixty tent and RV sites with picnic facilities, fishing, beach, nature trails, electricity at each campsite and shower rooms. No pets. All the sites are $22 per night, with an extra charge for electricity.

■ Vacation Rentals

 Be sure you know what a vacation rental house offers in the way of furnishings and equipment before you plunk down a deposit. Many vacation properties have websites that offer a look at the facilities. I recommend that you request to speak with previous renters to get a better idea about what you are getting into. You may be expecting a sandy beach with umbrellas, when all that's offered is a seaweed-choked dock with a beat up rowboat. Make sure you know how many distinct "bedrooms" the house has. Some claim to sleep six and do so with three of those people on futons in the living room.

Most vacation rentals are freestanding single-family homes ranging in quality from very nice to luxurious. Expect to pay anywhere from $1,200 to $4,000 per week for a two- to three-bedroom, modern home either on the water or near it. Nicer homes with docks and direct frontage on the bay or ocean command the highest rents. Houses usually come furnished with everything you need except sheets and towels, but be sure to check the details of each property before making a reservation.

> **AUTHOR TIDBIT:** Houses in the land-starved Keys are almost always close together, so if absolute privacy is important to you find out how the house is situated before you commit.

Several agencies represent vacation properties in the Upper Keys.

Houseboat Vacations of the Florida Keys, *MM 85.9 BS, 85944 Overseas Highway,* ☎ *305-664-4009*. Modern and newish 40- to 44-foot houseboats rent from $600 for three days to $1,600 for a week.

Island Villa Rental Properties, *MM 81.6 OS, Islamorada,* ☎ *305-664-3333*. Long- and short-term rentals of over 50 properties.

Vacation Properties in the Florida Keys, *MM 99 OS, Key Largo,* ☎ *305-453-9062, ghoward@keysconnection.com.*

Ocean Reef Rentals, *Key Largo,* ☎ *305-367-4280.*

Where to Eat

 The price symbols for each listing consider the average cost of main courses listed on the menu.

RESTAURANT PRICE CHART	
$	Under $8
$$	$8-12
$$$	$12-20
$$$$	Over $20

Alabama Jack's, 58000 Card Sound Road, Key Largo, ☎ 305-248-8741, $. This open-air seafood joint with beer and wine (in plastic cups, Keys-style), shrimp, conch fritters and more has been run by "Alabama" Jack Stratham since 1953. It has reliably good food live music on the weekends. Mosquitoes close the place down every night about 7:30 so come early. This is a good stop on your way south since it is not too far past Homestead. Take the toll route ($1) from Homestead over Card Sound instead of the usual, more direct route down Highway 1.

■ Recommendations

☆ **AUTHOR'S PICK** - Ballyhoo's, *MM 97.8 in the Median, Key Largo,* ☎ *305-852-0822, $$$.* Set in a conch house dating from the 1930s, Ballyhoo's is an authentic Keys restaurant preparing fresh fish in almost any way you can imagine. Pick your fish – yellowtail, grouper, mahi, tuna or whatever – then select the way you want it prepared, either broiled, pan-fried, blackened or with one of Ballyhoo's interesting Caribbean sauces. In season, all-you-can-eat stone crab claws are a bargain at $25. Beer and wine selections are good. The atmosphere is definitely Keys and no real effort at making the place fancy has ever taken place, but the food is a real treat and the prices are good.

☆ **AUTHOR'S PICK** - **Bentley's Restaurant & Raw Bar**, *MM 82.8 OS, Islamorada,* ☎ *305-664-9094, $$$.* Big portions of lobster, crab, fish and raw bar offerings vie with the popular happy hour to pack in the hungry and thirsty. There is a decent wine selection. Cioppino is served as a big pile of shellfish and crustaceans in a tomato broth with linguini. The ambiance is that of an upscale fish joint.

> **AUTHOR TIDBIT:** Bentley's has been voted the Best Overall Restaurant and Best Seafood in the Upper Keys for 11 years in a row by the *Miami Herald*.

☆ **AUTHOR'S PICK** - **Denny's Latin Café**, *MM 100, BS, Key Largo,* ☎ *305-451-3665, $.* No relation to the chain of the same name, Denny's is a real rootsy Cuban spot with roast pork, chicken, huevos rancheros and other "muy autentico" Cuban and Mexican dishes. The waitstaff bring you two or three plates of sides (beans and rice, plantains, bread, etc.) with every order. The plates are huge oval-shaped platters and the portions are gargantuan, despite the low prices. Bring your appetite. I recently had a lunch of *masas de puerco* (chunks of pork) with mounds of rice and beans, an imported beer and café con leche for a grand total of $9. Try the duck quesadillas.

AUTHOR TIDBIT: Caffeine junkies will appreciate the fantastic brew served at Denny's. Notice the little window in the side of the building where Cuban men walk up and buy coffee "shots" for 50¢. This is the real thing and a bargain.

☆ **AUTHOR'S PICK** - **Fish House**, *MM 102.4 OS, Key Largo,* ☎ *305-451-HOOK, 888-451-4665, www.fishhouse.com, $$$*. The décor is typical seaside, with fishnets hanging from the ceilings. You pick your fish from the glass-fronted refrigerated cases and can order it steamed, sautéed, fried, broiled – whatever. My preference is for the waitstaff to show me a selection of whole yellowtail; I pick my fish and have the cook broil it with little more than lemon. When I visited, the daily specials involved filleted fish with interesting sauces like Gorgonzola cream. This is one of the few places where I have ever seen cobia on the menu. This very tasty fish has a delicate texture. The Key lime pie is justly famous. Open for lunch and dinner every day, but closed September.

☆ **AUTHOR'S PICK** - **Harriette's**, *MM 95.7 BS, Key Largo,* ☎ *305- 852-8689, $, no credit cards*. This breakfast and lunch-only, old-fashioned American café serves biscuits and gravy, steak & eggs, grits, hot cakes and hot coffee in heavy ceramic cups. It's a favorite with locals. Leave your Hawaiian shirt and Bermuda shorts at the hotel and squeeze through the crowd for some good chow. Don't miss the corned beef hash and dinner plate-sized biscuits – they are almost as good as the ones my wife makes.

☆ **AUTHOR'S PICK** - **Marker 88 Restaurant**, *MM 88 BS, Islamorada,* ☎ *305-852-9315, $$*. Opened in 1978 by André Mueller, Marker 88 has hosted such luminaries as George Bush Sr. Very popular and often crowded, it is open for dinner only every night except Monday. The chowder and bisque are quite good and the chef comes up with some imaginative and delicious ways to present Keys seafood. Marker 88 is a bit nicer than most of the seafood places in the area and the service is outstanding. The seemingly hundreds of waitstaff have obviously had some formal training. Steamed vegetables are served with some selections.

Upper Keys

The wine list is broad, with good selections of new and old world, including a couple of good Spanish and Chilean labels.

> **AUTHOR TIDBIT:** The *New York Times* selected Marker 88 as "Best Restaurant in the Keys."

☆ **AUTHOR'S PICK** - **Pierre's at Morada Bay**, *MM 81.6 BS, Islamorada,* ☎ *305-664-3225, $$$$*. This is one of the top two or three most elegant eateries in the Keys. Check the limit on your credit card before entering. Hubert Baudoin started this Euro-trendy upscale restaurant which relies heavily on traditional Florida food and fusion. Presentation is perfected, and dishes like shrimp bisque and snapper are well prepared. There is a great view of the bay and diners are entertained by a strolling guitarist on weekends. Don't miss out on the full moon party every month (check the solar/lunar tables or call). Open for lunch and dinner every day.

☆ **AUTHOR'S PICK** - **Snappers**, *MM 94.5 OS, Key Largo,* ☎ *305-852-5956, $$*. Crab cakes and Keys specialties (yellowtail, mahi, raw bar and burgers) are the deal here. A jazz band plays during the Sunday brunch and other live entertainment is usual on weekend nights. Arrive by boat if you like.

☆ **AUTHOR'S PICK** - **Tower of Pizza**, *MM 100 BS, Key Largo and MM 81.5 BS Islamorada,* ☎ *305-664-0634, 305-664-8246, $*. Both locations are open daily to serve Greek salads, pizza, antipasto and pasta dishes. They'll deliver free of charge to your hotel room (providing it is not too far away). If you're really hungry and are tired of paying the inflated tourist prices for pre-frozen seafood, you'll find the Tower of Pizza to be a refreshing change. For about $9 you will be served a large Greek salad, enormous pile of pasta with interesting topping (try the mussels) and garlic bread. There are also some seafood items on the menu. A decent Cabernet goes for a mere $2.50 per glass and a half-carafe is just $6.50. The restaurants are not all fancy, but the food is good, the prices honest and the service is snappy.

☆ **AUTHOR'S PICK** - **Whale Harbor Inn**, *MM 83.9 OS, Islamorada,* ☎ *305-664-4959, $$$*. For seafood lovers it is hard to beat the all-you-can-eat buffet at the Whale Harbor Inn. The buffet is legendary and includes much more than seafood, with a huge array of salad fixings, pasta, meats such as roast beef, ribs and chicken and desserts like an ice cream bar and the famous Key lime pie. This smorgasbord of delights doesn't come cheap, but your $22.50 gets as much shrimp, crab legs, yellowtail, oysters and crawdads as you can eat. Just be sure to bring an appetite. The owners have kindly placed curved, full-length slimming mirrors in the lobby so you can check out your improved figure when leaving satisfied.

No matter where you are staying in the Keys, it is worth the drive to load up at Whale Harbor. The dining rooms overlook the ocean and are more elegant than you might expect. Lobster and fish entrées start around $14. Reservations are a good idea on weekends or holiday evenings. The breakfast grill is open from 5:30 am, with a buffet running from noon to midnight; the Sunday brunch begins at 11 am.

■ The Best of the Rest

Anthony's Italian Restaurant, *MM 97.6 in the median*, ☎ *305-853-1177, $$*. The owner seems to have been sampling his own cooking. Mussels in marinara sauce are a spectacular signature dish. Live music is featured on the weekends.

Atlantic's Edge, *MM 82 OS in the Cheeca Lodge, Islamorada,* ☎ *305-664-4651, www.cheeca.com, $$$$*. Avocado ice cream and other fusion-like specialties make this a different experience. Although on the fancy side with white linen and fine wine glasses, the place does have an elaborate and thoughtful menu for children. Open for dinner only every night.

Café Largo, *MM 99.5 BS, Key Largo,* ☎ *305-451-4885, $$*. Dinner only is served in this Italian-style trattoria. This is a garlic-lover's paradise with great hand-tossed pizza pies. Smooth jazz plays in the background.

Coconuts, *MM 99.5 next to Marina del Mar Resort, Key Largo,* ☎ *305-453-9794, $$$*. Situated in the marina, Coconuts has outdoor or air-conditioned indoor dining. The usual Keys seafood is on the menu, with respectable (if a bit pricey) mahi and shrimp offerings. The house wines are mediocre, but the margaritas and daiquiris are good. The bar is crowded with locals for the 4-7 pm

Upper Keys

nightly happy hour, when drinks are two-for-one and good specials are offered on peel-and-eat shrimp and some other seafood. The live music is typical Keys Margaritaville-style cover artists, except for Tuesday nights when blues is the choice sound. You can catch some great blues bands here, including a Keys favorite: the Charlie Morris Blues Band.

Crack'd Conch Restaurant, *MM 105 OS, Key Largo,* ☎ *305-451-0732, $$$*. This pricey landmark restaurant has a rootsy Keys feel that's embellished by its setting in an old conch-style house. Of course, conch is on the menu in numerous forms: fritters, chowder, burgers. Over 100 types of beer are also on offer. Open for lunch and dinner; closed Wednesday.

Dino's Ristorante Italiano, *MM 81 OS, Islamorada,* ☎ *305-664-0727, $$*. This authentic Italian place offers pizza pies in half of the restaurant and more upscale, fine dining in the other. Mama is in the kitchen and Papa greets guests as they enter. Loud Italian voices can be heard when the kitchen door swings open. There are even grapes growing in back behind the parking lot! The salads are large and chock full of interesting vegetables. Pizzas are hand-tossed and the cheese stretches for two or three feet when you pull up a slice. The dessert cart is a large affair with many goodies, including tiramisu and cheesecake. The wine selection has a couple of good choices from Italy at reasonable prices. Open for lunch and dinner.

Frank Keys Café, *MM 100 OS, Key Largo,* ☎ *305-453-0310, www.frankkeyscafe.com, $$*. Situated in a gingerbread, faux conch-style building with linen, candles and subdued lighting inside, Frank Keys place feels like a fine dining emporium. The food is good, if a bit fancy. The maple leaf duck with an orange and mango sauce is interesting and good. Frank's is closed Monday and Tuesday, except in January, February, March and April.

Green Turtle Inn, *MM 81.5 OS, Islamorada,* ☎ *305-664-9031, $$$*. Turtle used to be the star on the menu of this over-dark piano bar/restaurant. The Green Turtle has been around since time began and is a Keys institution. It's in the only building left standing after the 1935 Labor Day hurricane. I can remember eating turtle burgers here as a kid. I could get into a "don't-eat-turtle-it's-not-politically-correct" rant but their turtle is now farm-raised freshwater turtle from Iowa instead of endangered salt-water turtle. They have a well-stocked, proper bar with all the trimmings. Most of the Keys specials are served here and they have a good variety of steaks and chops. Soft drinks are served from the bar in ice-choked wine glasses at $1.50 a pop. Refills are irritatingly also $1.50 a pop. Their chowders, conch, clam and seafood are quite good, but come in very small portions.

The Islamorada Fish Company, *MM 81.5 BS, Islamorada,* ☎ *305-664-9271, $$$.* Located right behind the World Wide Sportsman and Zane Grey Bar, The Fish Company used to be a funky fish market and Keys-type eating place. There is still a fish market with the appropriate smell, but the rest of the place has gone upmarket. The ambiance is touristy, but the food is fine, if a bit high-priced. Standard Keys seafood is here: yellowtail, grouper, shrimp, mahi and more. The steamed vegetables and limp salads are the same as served in so many tourist-oriented South Florida eateries.

> **AUTHOR TIDBIT:** Ask for a table overlooking the marina, where tarpon hang out. The tarpon show here involves about 20 or 30 tarpon weighing up to 100 lbs. They come to gorge on fish scraps from the back of the kitchen.

Kaiyo, *MM 82 OS, Islamorada,* ☎ *305-322-8745, $$$.* If you can handle the fusion thing, try this trendy attempt place that draws yuppie diners. Tempura grouper and clam and ginger soup are good eating, if a bit pretentious. Open for lunch and dinner, with no reservations (they are not usually crowded).

L'Attitudes Restaurant, *MM 87, Plantation Yacht Harbor,* ☎ *305-852-2381, $$$.* Open for dinner only, L'Attitudes gets good reviews from the big time critics that write for the Miami papers.

Lazy Day's Oceanfront Bar & Grill, *MM 79.9 OS, Islamorada,* ☎ *305-664-5256, $$.* Lazy Days offers casual lunch and evening dining overlooking the Atlantic. It's filled with ceiling fans, ferns and trade winds and offers the usual (nothing spectacular) seafood specials.

Little Italy Restaurant, *MM 68.5 BS, Long Key,* ☎ *305-664-4472, $$.* Do you wanna eat a great big piece of fish but you don't wanna pay twenty bucks? Little Italy serves very, very large portions of great fish for waaay less than the fancy joints.

Upper Keys

Where else can you get a 21-piece shrimp basket for $5.50? The huge portions of pasta and seafood are done in Italian style. As is usual in an Italian restaurant, most of the entrées are served with a side of pasta. The ravioli is particularly nice. Breakfast, lunch and dinner are served every day. (I'm afraid to eat breakfast here – I might need to take a nap afterwards.) Lines form in the evening even in low season, so call ahead for a reservation.

Lor-e-lei Restaurant & Cabana Bar, *MM 82, Islamorada,* ☎ *305-664-4656, www.loreleifloridakeys.com, $$$.* Located right on the water so you can watch the mullet schooling about while you eat, the restaurant offers the usual seafood and steaks served with modest salads and the same steamed vegetables you can find everywhere. Their onion-encrusted yellowtail is good. Next door, the bar opens at 7 am for early drinkers (or the late-night carousers who never made it to bed) and is one of the best live music venues in the Keys. It is popular (especially late) with locals and is a great place to watch them as they let down their hair. Unless you choose to dine inside in air-conditioned splendor, you can hear the music from the bar while eating in the restaurant.

Manny & Isa's, *MM 81.6 OS, Islamorada,* ☎ *305-664-5019, $$.* The plain atmosphere and good seafood keep the place crowded. Call ahead for reservations and expect lines on weekends. The food is supposed to be Cuban, but if you've ever been to Cuba, you'll know that nothing there tastes this good. The Key lime pie is famous and piled high with meringue. Manny was the cook for many years at the Green Turtle until he set up shop on his own. Baseball player Ted Williams was a regular and swore the food was the best anywhere.

Num Thai Restaurant & Sushi Bar, *MM 103.2 BS, Key Largo,* ☎ *305-451-5955, $$,* serves a blend of Asian cuisines dominated by Thai and Japanese specials. The sushi bar delivers the Japanese side of things, while hot curries represent Thailand. Num Thai is open for dinner every night and lunch during the week. The usual Asian beers and sticky-sweet plum wine are on offer.

Papa Joe's, *MM 79.9 BS, Islamorada,* ☎ *305-664-8109, $$.* Papa Joe's is another dockside restaurant/bar with all the usual Keys specials, including lobster, prime rib, coconut shrimp and Jamaican yellowtail. They will cook your catch for lunch and dinner every day. Reservations are not accepted, but you can call ahead and be put on the waiting list. The food is average and the service can be glacial. There is a ragged plastic hammerhead shark dangling from a rope in front of the Tiki bar.

Perry's Restaurant, *MM 102.5, Key Largo,* ☎ *305-451-1834*, is a prime example of a typical touristy, lame seafood place. For $14.95 you get five "shrimp in a sock" and a some frozen, crinkle-cut French fries. There are three Perry's in the Keys – all part of the same chain. Avoid them.

The Quay Key Largo, *MM 103.2 BS, Key Largo,* ☎ *305-451-0943, $$$.* Enjoy good views of the bay while dining on seafood or steak. There is an informal grill room, plus a fancy dining room with candles and all the big city restaurant stuff. You can arrive by boat, and sunset cruises through the mangroves are offered nightly. Serves lunch and dinner daily.

Smuggler's Cove Restaurant, *MM 85.5 BS, Islamorada,* ☎ *305-664-5564, smugglers@worldnet.att.net, $$.* Fish sandwiches, ribs and rib eye steaks make this a popular spot with the locals. It's not fancy, but it does offer good food at fair prices.

Snook's Bayside, *MM 99.9 BS, Key Largo,* ☎ *305-453-3799, www.snooks.com, $$$.* Fancy touches you see here – candles and white linen tableclothes – are not always a good sign for a seafood place. Yellowtail is prepared in several interesting ways and prime Angus beefsteaks keep meat-lovers happy. They actually have their own pastry chef (I've always wanted to have *my* own pastry chef), who prepares wonderful baked goodies. Live bands play most nights. Lunch and dinner are served every day, and there's a Big Brunch on Sunday. With a good waterfront location, you can arrive by boat if you wish.

Squid Row, *MM 81.9 OS, Islamorada,* ☎ *305-664-9865, $$$.* Squid Row serves a variety of fish and seafood dishes, including grouper and bouillabaisse. It's owned by a seafood wholesaler, so everything should be fresh. The food is good, the prices are fair. Open for lunch and dinner every day except Wednesday.

Sundowners on the Bay, *MM 104 BS, Key Largo,* ☎ *305-451-4502, www.sundownerskeylargo.com, $$.* Beautiful sunset views attract dinners who arrive by car and boat – park your boat in front, stroll down the dock and select a table. The yellowtail is a special treat that can be prepared at least seven different ways.

Uncle's Restaurant, *MM 81 OS, Islamorada*, ☎ *305-664-4402*, *$$$*. Uncle's offers fine dining under the stars (weather permitting) or inside in elegant, Keys-themed surroundings. Dishes are formal and traditional, such as rack of lamb and veal loin chop. Open for dinner only every day except Sunday.

Waters Edge, *MM 61 OS, Hawk's Cay Resort*, ☎ *305-743-7000*, *$$$$*. Conch chowder, stuffed crab, great stuffed lobster and a salad bar are featured. Dinner only is served throughout the year, except from March to November, when lunch is also an option.

Zane Grey Lounge, *MM 82, Islamorada*, ☎ *305-664-4244*, *$$$*. Upstairs at World Wide Sportsman, Zane Grey is an upscale spot with nice cigars, interesting martinis and a Big Game fishing theme. Black-and-white photographs of people you've heard of standing next to enormous fish line the walls. The menu includes jumbo Key West shrimp, Bahamian conch chowder, crab or yellowtail sandwiches, stone crab claws and other reasonable quality bar food. I like the lobster salad, even though it is a little pricey considering the small amount of lobster involved.

Ziggies's Gumbo and Crab Shack, *MM 83 BS, Islamorada*, ☎ *305-664-3391*, *$$*. Jambalaya, gumbo, red beans and rice, étouffée and other Cajun specialties may not compare with what is on offer in the Big Easy, but put your regional snobbism behind you and enjoy the food.

Nightlife

Nightlife is active, but limited to just a few Tiki bars and hotel lounges. There are no dance clubs or discos. The only place open after midnight is Woody's, a strip club. Since many visitors are here to dive or fish, they tend to go to bed early and get up early. For around-the-clock fun, you will be well served in Key West or back in Miami.

Breezers, *MM 103.8, Key Largo at the Marriott*, ☎ *305- 453-0000*. Occasional live "island" entertainment of the electronically-assisted sort is the best you can expect at this hotel Tiki bar.

Happy hour runs from 4-6 pm. Of course, frozen drinks are the specialty.

Caribbean Club, MM 104 BS, Key Largo, ☎ 305-451-9970. The house band at this big local hangout has been here for about 20 years. It's rumored that Humphrey Bogart's *Key Largo* was filmed here. For many years, the club had no doors because it never closed – they just hosed the place out every day at dawn. Although not open all night these days, the caribbean Club still draws a big late-night crowd. Happy hour runs from 4-6 pm.

Chilli Willie's Grill & Pub, *MM 86.7, Islamorada,* ☎ *305-852-8786.* With a large game room, Willie's claims to host the best singles scene in the Keys. I'm not sure how the word "pub" got in the name, but what are ya gonna do? The usual frozen blender drinks keeps things hoppin'.

Coconuts Lounge, *MM 100 OS, Key Largo in the Marina del Mar Resort,* ☎ *305-453-9794.* Tuesday night is blues night but there is some sort of musical theme every evening. Ladies drink for free from 9 to 11 on Wednesday, and their happy hour runs from 4-7 pm Monday through Friday.

Holiday Isle Resort and Marina, *MM 84 OS, Islamorada,* ☎ *305-664-2321.* This large resort has several bars. Live music is usual at Rum Runners Tiki Bar. Typical fare is a singer/instrumentalist set up with prerecorded backing music. Expect to hear Jimmy Buffet's *Margaritaville* several times each night. The blues on Sunday is usually okay.

Gilbert's Tiki Bar, *MM 107.9, Key Largo,* ☎ *305-451-1133.* Live music is played every night except Monday at this waterfront Tiki bar.

☆ **AUTHOR'S PICK** - **Lor-e-lei Bar**, *MM 82, Islamorada,* ☎ *305-664-4656, www.loreleifloridakeys.com.* One of the best live music venues in the Keys, the Lor-e-lei opens at 7 am for hard-core partiers who never made it to bed last night. I'm not sure when they close. Locals flock here very late and get rowdy after they get off work at nearby tourist places. The restaurant next door serves good seafood. The bar is an outdoorsy kind of place and you can wander around and look at the boats and birds while enjoying a tropical beverage and listening to the band. The Charlie Morris Blues Band plays here from time to time and re-ally rocks the joint. Although it still has a reputation as being funky and run-down, the Lor-e-lei (especially the restaurant) has actually become a tad yuppified lately.

Mandalay Tiki Bar, *MM 97.5, Key Largo,* ☎ *305-852-5450*. The restaurant and bar share the same live performers every night.

☆ **AUTHOR'S PICK** - **Snappers**, *MM 94.5 OS, Key Largo,* ☎ *305-852-5956*. Good food, especially the Sunday brunch with jazz, separates Snappers from the rest. Other live entertainment plays on weekend nights. Guests can arrive by boat.

Woody's Saloon & Restaurant, *MM 82 BS, Islamorada,* ☎ *305-664-4335*. The entertainment is totally nude strippers. Big Dick and the Extenders is a good house band that has been polishing their act here for years. I believe they close somewhere south of 4 am.

Zane Grey Lounge, *MM 81.5 BS, Islamorada, over Worldwide Sportsman,* ☎ *305-664-4244*. "Step back in time" is the house suggestion, but you'll need to be nearsighted to make this happen. The historic atmosphere is plastic and oriented toward posing yuppies, cigars and all, in spite of the solid mahogany bar. Drinks are overpriced and the exterior of chipped stucco with fake brick exposed makes me want to turn around and head for a real dive. In my humble opinion, this type of fake-front establishment is bringing the whole Keys experience down. You don't need to come to the Keys to drink in a place like this. Head on over to the nearby Lor-e-lei (see above) before it suffers the same fate. You can be sure Papa and Zane would run as fast as they could from a place like this.

Marathon & the Middle Keys

The Middle Keys are made up of the town of Marathon and several small keys to the east. Marathon is large enough to have a couple of top-quality restaurants and several excellent mom-and-pop eateries. Most of the fast-food chains are represented. The selection of lodging ranges from old-style motels with rooms for around $60 to high-end B&Bs and resorts going for several hundred dollars nightly. There is a Home Depot and a couple of large grocery stores. Bait shops, dive shops, charter operators and marinas appear by the dozen.

At a Glance

LARGEST TOWN: Marathon, population 10,255

ELEVATION: Three feet

AREA: 8.6 square miles

COUNTY: Monroe

MAJOR ROUTES: Overseas Highway (US 1)

NEAREST AIRPORTS: Marathon (0 miles); Miami International (98 miles)

ZIP CODE: 33050

AVERAGE TEMPERATURE: January 67.7°; August 83°

PRECIPITATION: January 2.1 inches; August 6.4 inches

Getting Here & Getting Around

The **Overseas Highway**, also known as US 1, is the only major road. It's also the only road in and out, so you must use it to drive from Miami (or fly into Key West and rent a car). Of course, you can also arrive by boat – the best way! There are a few side streets in Marathon, but other towns in the Middle Keys are little more than wide places in the road.

The **Florida Keys Marathon Airport**, *MM 52 BS, Marathon* ☎ *305-743-2155*, is large and modern. Is it used only by private planes and charter companies; sharp rent increases and various other fees have forced major airlines to take their business elsewhere. **Florida Coast Airlines**, ☎ *888-435-9322, www.flyfca. com,* offers flights from Ft. Lauderdale.

Several major **car rental** agencies have offices in the Marathon Airport, including **Avis**, ☎ *305-743-5428, 800-831-2847, www. avis.com;* **Budget**, ☎ *305-743-3998, 800-527-0700, www.budget. com;* and **Enterprise**, ☎ *305-289-7630, 800-325-8007, www.enterprise.com.*

Area History & Highlights

Marathon and the Middle Keys experienced the same periods of boom in sponging, wrecking and a little piracy but due to lack of freshwater and the area's inaccessibility, there were never more than a handful of settlers until the railroad was built. The Labor Day hurricane of 1935 did much less damage here than in the Upper Keys. Fishing and small market farming were the occupation of the few settlers that made the area their home.

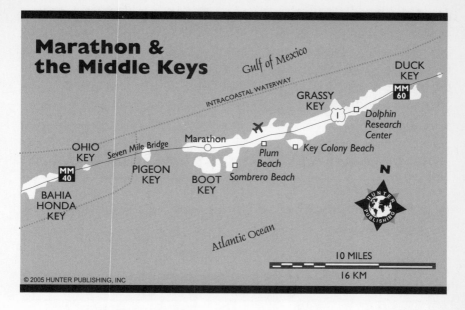

Marathon & the Middle Keys

AUTHOR TIDBIT: There is speculation that the town of Marathon was named after a railroad worker who expressed his opinion that the work was a "marathon." The settlement was originally known as "Cayo de Vacas" (Spanish for Island of Cows).

In 1814, a Spanish Land Grant awarded the island to Don Francisco Ferreira. In 1824, he sold it to Isaac Cox for the grand price of $3,000. The first town was called "Conch Town" and was located near what are now 109th and 112th streets. Pigeon Key was the site of a major railroad encampment and some of the original buildings still remain. During World War II the area advanced into civilization, with electricity, water and an airport.

In 1960 Hurricane Donna blasted directly across the island doing significant damage. Although Marathon does not have the romance created by the Humphrey Bogart movie *Key Largo*, *True Lies* does feature a few scenes from the area.

Most visitors come to the area for fishing, diving or other activities that involve sun and sea. The area is a good base from which to explore Florida Bay and some of the more remote parts of Everglades National Park. Spectacular coral reefs lurk just a few miles offshore. Tackle-busting game fish of various types can be

Marathon/Middle Keys

caught year-round. Other than the Hurricane (see page 172), a good blues bar, there's not much to do after dark except hang around in Tiki bars enjoying frozen concoctions with tiny cocktail umbrellas. If you want nightlife and action you need to head on down to Key West. But if outdoor delights are more your style, then the Middle Keys are great.

Information Source

Marathon Chamber of Commerce, *MM 53.5 BS*, ☎ *305-743-5417, 800-262-7284.*

Sightseeing

■ Suggested Itineraries

If You Have One Day

 It's a little too much to go to the Middle Keys from Miami and have enough time to be able to appreciate what makes this area special. If you drive down very early and back very late at night, you can squeeze in a half-day fishing, diving or backcountry exploring.

Leave Miami early and, where the Overseas Highway splits just past Homestead, take Card Sound Road, stop at **Alabama Jack's**, ☎ *305-248-8741*, for refreshments. Continue on Card Sound Road until it joins back up with the Overseas Highway on Key Largo. If you need a kick, stop at **Denny's Latin Café**, *MM 100*, for a cup of Cuban coffee then enjoy the view out over Florida Bay and the Gulf Stream as you head toward Marathon. If you arrive in the early afternoon, spend a few hours **kayaking** with **Marathon Kayak**, *MM 50 OS, Marathon at Sombrero Resort*, ☎ *305-743-0561, www.marathonkayak.com*. If you still have time after kayaking, take a walk out on the old Seven Mile Bridge, MM 47 BS. Park in the lot at then end of the bridge.

Have a seafood dinner at **Castaway's**, *MM 47.8, 1406 Oceanview Ave., Marathon,* ☎ *305-743-6247, 305-849-0472.* If you need a shot of coffee for the drive back, stop again at **Denny's Latin Café**, *MM 100*, for a cup of Cuban coffee.

If You Have Three Days

3 DAYS Three days is long enough to properly appreciate the fishing, diving and wildlife viewing opportunities. These activities can be booked as half-day trips. Everglades National Park is not far out into the bay and backcountry touring and fishing is a good way to see some of the more pristine areas of the Keys. Since a three-day trip means you probably have only one full day in the Keys, a half-day trip to the reefs for diving or snorkeling would be a good way to spend the first afternoon.

Day One should be planned as above.

Start Day Two with an early breakfast at the **Wooden Spoon**, Marathon, ☎ *305-743-8383*, then head for **Adios Charters**, Marathon, ☎ *305-289-9892*, for a day fishing with **Captain Bob Tittle** (get the Wooden Spoon to pack you a lunch). If you are lucky enough to catch your dinner, head to the **Hurricane Grille**, *MM 49.5 BS, Marathon,* ☎ *305-743-2220*, where they will prepare your catch. That night, take in the blues show at the **Hurricane Lounge**, *MM 49.5 BS, Marathon,* ☎ *305-743-2220*. The best bands usually play on weekend nights starting at about 10. Call ahead to see if the Charlie Morris Band will be playing.

On Day Three you should check out a few interesting things to do in the Upper Keys on your way back north. Everglades National Park is only a mile into the bay and guides offer backcountry fishing, birding and eco-touring near mangrove islands and over the fascinating turtle grass and sand flats. Reserve several weeks in advance with **Florida Bay Outfitters**, *MM 104, Key Largo,* ☎ *305-451-3018,* for a morning guided kayak tour in Florida Bay through the Everglades.

Head back to Miami stopping in Homestead at **Shivers**, *28001 Dixie Hwy,* a great BBQ joint on the right as you go north.

Marathon/Middle Keys

If You Have a Week

 A week gives you plenty of time to enjoy the best of what the area has to offer and still leaves time for a day in Key West and a day in Everglades National Park.

On Day One, check out the beaches and bridges, which offer a decent chance to view birds and sea life up close. Good **beachcombing** can be found on **Coco Plum Beach** at the east end of Marathon. The best bridge in the Keys for seeing turtles, sharks, rays and horseshoe crabs is the old Overseas Highway bridge at the west end of the **Seven Mile Bridge**. It's a nice ride across the bridge and a spectacular walk over the flats.

For Day Two, I suggest a full day with a fishing guide in the backcountry (reserve in advance), allowing you to get a good look at birds and remote mangrove keys. **Captain Diego** with **Flat-Out Sport Fishing**, *Marathon,* ☎ *305-743-7317, www. floridakeysflats.com,* will show you more than just the fishy delights of the area.

The morning of Day Three can be spent diving or snorkeling at Sombrero Reef. The *Reef Runner* in *Marathon,* ☎ *305-289-9808, 800-332-8899, www.floridadivecharter.com*, will pick you up at your hotel. You should be back in time for lunch at **Keys Fisheries**, *Gulf View Ave., Marathon, no phone* (just past the Stuffed Pig). Spend the afternoon in more leisurely pursuits such as beachcombing at Coco Plum Beach (see above), an almost deserted stretch of sand, mangroves and scrub with some of the best birding in the Keys.

As the day winds down, lounge around the pool until sundown, then head to the **Barracuda Grill**, MM 49.5 BS, Marathon, ☎ 305-743-3314, for one more seafood dinner. Catch the blues show at the **Hurricane Lounge** (see *Three-Day Itinerary,* above).

Day Four is the day to catch sailfish, amberjack or mahi mahi during a day of offshore fishing. **Captain Frank Waters**, with **Pursuit Fishing**, *Marathon,* ☎ *305-743-2816, www. pursuitfishing.com,* knows where they live and will put you on them. **Island Tiki Bar & Restaurant**, *MM 54 BS, Marathon,* ☎ *305-743-4191,* will cook your catch and serve obligatory end-of-the-day cocktails. If you didn't see the show last night, head over to the **Hurricane Lounge** for late-night blues.

Try a sailing charter with snorkeling, eco-touring in Florida Bay and birding on Day Five. Contact **Mike's Sailing Charters**, *35 Sombrero Road, Marathon,* ☎ *305-743-3017, www.mikes-charters.net.* Their comfortable trimaran is a stable platform for an enjoyable day out. Head to **Burdine's**, *MM 48 OS, Marathon,* ☎ *305-743-5317,* for dinner.

Depending on traffic, **Key West** can be reached from Marathon in an hour or two. This gives you plenty of time to soak up the sights and nightlife. So plan on spending all of Day Six in Key West.

The architecture of Old Key West is a big draw.

Get an early start and stop at **Baby's Coffee Bar** close to Key West at *MM 15 OS,* ☎ *800-523-2326,* for coffee just before getting into town. Parking in the Old Town Parking Garage on the corner of Caroline and Grinnell streets is a good move. Take the shuttle to Duval Street. Walk up and down Duval watching people. Do your souvenir shopping and take the shuttle back to your car to stash your purchases in the trunk. Avoid most of the cheesy restaurants on Duval for anything other than a drink. Have a lunch

Marathon/Middle Keys

of conch fritters at **Johnson's Café**, *306 Petronia Street/801 Thomas Street*, ☎ *305-292-2286*, and while away the afternoon walking the back streets of Old Town admiring the Caribbean architecture, shopping or simply people watching. Spend time with cooling beverages in a bar like **Mangoes**, *700 Duval Street*, ☎ *305-292-4606*, which has a great view of Duval Street. Stroll along the waterfront by **Mallory Square** at sunset checking out the street theater, musicians and other entertainers and, after the sun goes down, head to **Sloppy Joe's**, *201 Duval Street* ☎ *305-294-5717, www.sloppyjoes.com*, to catch Pete and Wayne's childish adult comedy act. Mixed drinks can be foul here, so stick to beer.

Splurge on dinner at **Café Marquesa**, *600 Fleming Street*, ☎ *305-292-1244*, then go to the **Green Parrot**, *601 Whitehead Street*, ☎ *305-294-6133, www.greenparrot.com*, for blues. Check their website to see who is playing. If the Charlie Morris Band is playing one night during your stay, that is the night you should go to Key West so you can catch his show. With your designated driver driving, drag yourself back up the Overseas Highway to your hotel.

Day Seven is a good day to sleep late. On the way back to Miami, treat yourself to a hangover-curing breakfast of bacon, eggs and biscuits at **Harriette's**, *MM 95.7 BS, Key Largo*, ☎ *305-852-8689*. If you have time, take a tour of **Indian Key** from **Robbie's Marina**, *MM 77.5 BS*, ☎ *305-664-4815*. They also rent kayaks.

Head northeast up the Overseas Highway toward Miami in the early afternoon, with a stop for a huge fish sandwich dinner at **Alabama Jack's**, ☎ *305-248-8741, Card Sound Road*.

> **AUTHOR NOTE:** Be sure you keep going straight ahead as the Overseas Highway splits off to the right in Key Largo heading toward Jewfish Creek. Take the alternate route straight to Card Sound Road and take the toll bridge back to Homestead.

■ Beaches

These are rare in the Keys as a whole, but the Middle Keys actually have a couple of nice, sandy beaches. They are not on par with Daytona or Marco Island, but they are sandy.

Coco Plum Beach, *MM 54.5 OS,* is a bare-bones but pleasant county-owned public beach near then end of Coco Plum Drive. It offers no facilities other than a dog bag dispenser (clean up after your dog) and a trash can, but the sand manages to attract nesting turtles in the season, April 15-Oct 31. There are not many houses or hotels in the area and it's far enough away from the highway so you don't hear the traffic noise. Osprey and wading birds abound along the water and up from the beach where there is a festering mangrove swamp. The water is shallow and the sand changes quickly to turtle grass. You might find some interesting critters hidden in the seaweed if you snorkel slowly. The beach is often deserted. Open 8 am to dusk.

Key Colony Beach, *turn at MM 54 OS, Marathon.* The beach is good for swimming and is near restaurants and bars so you recoup your energy after toasting in the sun.

Sombrero Beach Park, *turn off the main highway at MM 50 OS, Sombrero Road, Marathon,* ☎ *305-743-0033.* This park was being completely renovated in 2003 and features a playground, covered picnic areas and some sports facilities. The beach here is one of the best in the Keys. The park is open daily, 8 am until sunset; there is no charge for entry.

■ Parks

Small **Curry Hammock State Park**, *MM 56.2 OS, 8 am-sunset, $2 entry fee*, has covered picnic tables with BBQs and a playground. The water is very shallow, with no beach to speak of. Although there is no boat ramp this is a good place to park in the shade and launch a kayak or canoe. The mangroves at the edge of the hammock are not a far paddle and are rarely visited. Birds nest by the zillions. You can walk along a narrow path through parts of the hammock itself, but be sure to douse yourself with bug repellent.

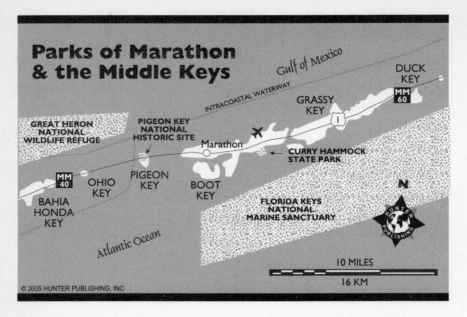

Pigeon Key, *MMS 47 OS, Marathon,* ☎ *305-289-0025, www.pigeonkey.org, 9 am-5 pm, $8.50.* As you cross Seven Mile Bridge you'll see this small (five-acre) key and its funky old buildings. The key has its own off-ramp from the old bridge. You can arrange for access at the base of the new bridge on the ocean side at the old railway car. The entire key is a National Historic Site. It features a picnic area, restrooms, very good snorkeling and tours run by the on-site marine biology camp (see *Nature & Adventure Tours & Walks*, below).

Adventures

■ On Foot

There is really only one beach to walk on in the area, but it is a good one. Fortunately, it is hard to beat walking on the old Overseas Highway bridges, used mostly as fishing piers since the highway was put out of use and a new highway constructed.

Beachcombing

Sombrero Beach Park (see *Beaches*, above) allows access to adjacent **Boot Key** by boat. If you can manage to get there, Boot Key is a good place for roaming up and down the beach and in and out of the mangroves looking for treasures.

More accessible and rarely visited by more than a few birds is **Coco Plum Beach** (see *Beaches*, above), at the other end of Marathon. Here you can get in a good half-mile walk.

Birding

Water birds galore can be seen from almost anywhere in the area, but I prefer a bridge walk for serious viewing. Near-deserted **Coco Plum Beach** has stretches of sand, mangroves and scrub, making for some of the best birding in the Keys. The small lagoon just up from the beach is almost always swarming with nesting birds. Wear bug spray.

Bridge Walks

Walking along the abandoned bridges of the Overseas Highway over sand flats, turtle grass and winding tidal channels is one of the more rewarding and peaceful activities to be had for free. Put on your hat and sunscreen and head out on the old **Seven Mile Bridge** toward Pigeon Key for a good view of the sea bottom and probable views of turtles, stingrays, sharks, horseshoe crabs and maybe even a tarpon or two. The bridge starts at the west end of Marathon and has a parking lot at its base. You will almost always find a few fishermen set up on the bridge itself. Stop for a chat to find out what they've been catching, if anything. The far end of the old Seven Mile Bridge is also open to the public and is, in my opinion, the best bridge for fishing or wildlife viewing in the Keys (see next chapter).

Golfing

Other than a small miniature golf course at Crystal Bay Motel, the **Sombrero Country Club**, *4000 Sombrero Road in Marathon,* ☎ *305-743-2551*, is the only 18-hole course. The club also has tennis, a restaurant and pro shop. **Key Colony**, *MM 53.5 OS,* ☎ *305-289-1533*, has a nine-hole public course.

Marathon/Middle Keys

Nature Walks

Crane Point Hammock, *MM 50.5 BS, Marathon,* ☎ *305-743-9100, Monday-Saturday 9-5, Sunday noon-5*. There are two museums at this site, the **Museum of Natural History of the Florida Keys** and the **Florida Keys Children's Museum**. The area covers 63 acres of undisturbed palm hammock with trails and educational tours run in association with the museums.

Pigeon Key Marine Biology Camp, *MMS 47 OS, Marathon,* ☎ *305-289-7178, www.pigeonkey.org*. This historic property on Pigeon Key operates daily tours and has a program of day and overnight marine biology camps. Some are aimed at students from ages nine to 16, while others are available to adults. The schedule and offerings change, so call for details. Most of the classes are fairly basic, appealing to the average Keys visitor. Snorkeling, beachcombing field trips and eco-tours of surrounding areas are featured.

■ On Wheels

 Service roads and bike paths can get you through the Middle Keys off the main highway. The bridges are just wide enough for experienced cyclists.

■ OUTFITTERS

Mama Joe's Cycles and Stuff, *MM 49 BS, Marathon,* ☎ *305-743-1932, www.mamajoescycles.com*, rents Harley Davidson motorcycles for $185 per 24-hour period and their bikes are new and sparkling clean. Check out their website for Internet specials.

Equipment Locker Sport & Bicycle, *MM 53 BS, Marathon,* ☎ *305-289-1670*, rents bicycles by hour, day, week or month.

All Aqua Adventures, *MM 48 OS, behind Hampton Inn and Suites, Marathon,* ☎ *305-743-6628*. These guys rent bikes as well as watersports equipment.

■ On Water

The Middle Keys are a boater's paradise. The offshore reefs and nearby Florida Bay offer calm waters, solitude, excellent fishing and diving. There are public **boat ramps** at Indian Key Fill, MM 79 BS, in Marathon at MM 54 BS, and at the Marathon Yacht Club, MM 49 BS.

Boat Tours

If you want to see the best reefs you have to get offshore. If you don't dive or feel uncomfortable about snorkeling, a glass-bottom boat is the way to go.

> **AUTHOR TIDBIT:** Dramamine prevents seasickness for almost everyone if taken at least two hours before leaving shore. It can cause drowsiness.

The Glass Bottom Boat, *MM 58 OS, Marathon at Rainbow Bend Resort,* ☎ *305-289-9933, www.seethereef.com.* The aptly named Glass Bottom Boat visits over 40 locations, most of them fairly close-in patch reefs alive with multiple varieties of flashy fish and colorful coral. Proprietor Donna Browning offers NAUI certification courses, but you can also enjoy their four-hose hookah system or snorkel with no certification whatsoever and get down where all those pretty fish live. They specialize in taking beginners. Call for departure times and costs.

Sailing

Hobie Cats and larger boats can be rented by the hour, day or week. Most resorts can arrange for sailing excursions or lessons.

Mike's Sailing Charters, *35 Sombrero Road, Marathon,* ☎ *305-743-3017, www.mikescharters.com.* Mike takes from two to six people on custom eco-tours, sunset sails, scuba diving or snorkeling trips aboard a new 38-foot trimaran. Trips begin at $45 per person.

Canoeing & Kayaking

Channels winding through mangroves lure paddlers to both the **Booth Key** area and the lagoons behind **Coco Plum Beach** in

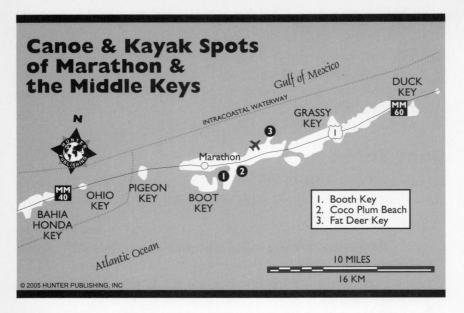

Canoe & Kayak Spots of Marathon & the Middle Keys

Gulf of Mexico

DUCK KEY

MM 60

GRASSY KEY

INTRACOASTAL WATERWAY

N

Marathon

MM 40

OHIO KEY

PIGEON KEY

BOOT KEY

BAHIA HONDA KEY

Atlantic Ocean

1. Booth Key
2. Coco Plum Beach
3. Fat Deer Key

10 MILES

16 KM

© 2005 HUNTER PUBLISHING, INC

Marathon. You could easily paddle inside channels and shallow flats from Key Colony all the way along Grassy Key to Long Key. For the most part, the small keys in Florida Bay are a little far from the main keys for casual kayaking.

> **WARNING:** Currents through the channels, especially near bridges, can be extreme and can change direction quickly at tide changes.

■ OUTFITTERS

Marathon Kayak, *MM 50 OS, Marathon at Sombrero Resort,* ☎ *305-743-0561, www.marathonkayak.com*, is the most complete kayak center in Marathon, offering guided tours, instruction, rental and sales. Their kayak tours include a red mangrove eco-tour and a sunset tour. Tours can be customized. Kayak rental prices start at $30 for a half-day. Guided tours are $40 and are suitable for people with no previous kayaking experience.

Dolphin Encounters

If you must swim with the frisky and wise dolphins whether just for fun or for possible therapeutic or scientific reasons, be sure to book well in advance and have your pocket book ready. Rates run well over $100 for a program of less than an hour.

The **Dolphin Research Center**, *MM 59 BS on Grassy Key,* ☎ *305-289-0002 (reservations), 305-289-1121 (offices), www.dolphins.org, general admission $17.50/adult, $11.50/children,* is where the whole *Flipper* movie originated. It is a not-for-profit facility, but there is a charge of $155 for the "Dolphin Encounter" where you spend a half-day learning about dolphins and 20 minutes in the water with some. You can touch them. Other less-expensive activities include the "Play With Dolphins" (one hour, $40) and "Paint a Dolphin" (30 minutes, $55). The latter allows kids over age five to meet a dolphin, then hold a t-shirt that the dolphin paints; you get to keep the shirt. Children under 12 must pay for activities and must swim with an adult, who must also pay. Reservations are essential.

Fishing

In an earlier chapter I said Islamorada is the sportfishing capital of the Keys and perhaps North America. Anglers loyal to Marathon and the Middle Keys would argue. The same subtropical conditions with miles of reefs, Gulf Stream and turtle grass flats exist all along the Keys. While there are more charter boats in the Upper Keys the Middle Keys certainly hold their own for excellent fishing opportunities.

■ FLATS, BACKCOUNTRY & LIGHT TACKLE GUIDES

Flat Out Sportfishing, *Marathon,* ☎ *305-743-7317, www.floridakeysflats.com.* Captain Diego Cordova is a classic flats fishing guide. He specializes in spinning and fly-casting for bonefish, tarpon, permit, shark, barracuda and jack for old salts as well as relative beginners.

Little Native Sport Fishing, Inc., *Marathon,* ☎ *305-731-3512, 305-743-1946, www.bonefishcentral.com.* Captain Ray Rhash has been fishing the area for over 40 years. He specializes in bonefish, tarpon and permit on light tackle.

Marathon/Middle Keys

■ OFFSHORE CHARTERS

Adios Charters, *Marathon*, ☎ *305-289-9892, www. adioscharters.com*. Captain Bob Tittle has been catching sailfish, grouper, mutton snapper and tarpon for the past 30 years. His equipment is excellent. He has three boats and covers flats fishing in the backcountry as well.

Family Fun Charters, *Crystal Bay Resort, Marathon*, ☎ *305-743-4691, www.FamilyFunCharters.com*. Specializing in family fishing trips, Captain Jeannie Simmons on the 37-foot *Anticipation* charges only $375 for a five-hour trip. "No rock & roll" is their promise.

Pursuit Fishing, *Marathon*, ☎ *305-743-2816, www. pursuitfishing.com*. Pursuit fishing claims you'll go home with a "good catch" under your belt after a day out with them. They charge $450 for a half-day (four hours) and $650 for a full day (eight hours). Captain Frank Waters is based at the Holiday Inn Marina.

Two Conchs Dive & Fishing Charters, *Marathon*, ☎ *305-743-6253, www.twoconchs.com*. Captain Jack Carlson fishes a custom 31-foot Contender and has graced the cover of *Florida Sportsman* at least six times. He is well known for his serious pursuit of trophy-size wahoo, sailfish, grouper and other offshore and near-shore species. He offers the usual offshore trips at $475 for a half-day (four hours) and $650 for a full day (eight hours). He also offers full-day trips into Florida Bay for $700.

■ PARTY BOATS

Marathon Lady, *MM 53, Marathon*, ☎ *305-743-5580, www.marathonlady.com*, charges $30 for morning trips and $37 for night runs. The boat leaves at 8:30 am and 1:30 pm. The 6:30 pm night trips are offered during summer only. This is one of the oldest and most popular party boats in the Keys. The price includes bait but, if you don't have your own, you'll need to rent a rod and reel from them for $3. That's still a pretty good deal.

Sea Dog Charters, *MM 47.5 BS, Marathon, next to the 7-Mile Grill*, ☎ *305-743-8255*. Morning, afternoon and night fishing trips go for $60 per person, everything included. This isn't as crowded as most party boats and it goes out a bit farther for more interesting trips.

Bridge & Shore Fishing

As in most of the Keys, fishing from shore is hard to do since much of the shoreline is developed and the water is shallow. There are several good bridges where you can fish in peace and quiet for no cost and still find yourself in good, fishy water. You can set up on any of the fishing bridges, but my favorites are those by **Tom's Harbor**, where I've caught some nice grouper under the east side of the bridge at Vaca Cut, in the middle of Marathon. The current rips on through this area and there is a lot of boat traffic, but the water is deep and the bridge pilings attract some good-sized fish. A small dirt path leading off the highway immediately east of the bridge takes you to a shady parking area under the bridge. This spot is easy to get to, comfortable and fishy.

There are hundreds of guides and charter boats lining up to take visitors out for a day or half-day. Those I list above have a reputation for giving customers a fine day out.

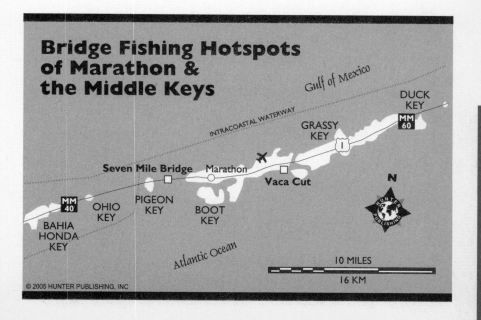

Bridge Fishing Hotspots of Marathon & the Middle Keys

© 2005 HUNTER PUBLISHING, INC

Marathon/Middle Keys

HOUSEBOAT RENTAL

Florida Keys Sportsmen Charters, *Faro Blanco Marina, Marathon,* ☎ *321-626-3117.* Divers or fishermen can rent the newly refurbished 80-foot houseboat *Dream Believer* for use as a mother ship. It comes with a 17-foot outboard tender, two kayaks and snorkeling gear. Use it to find a good spot away from the crowds, anchor and enjoy the nearby reefs or fishing spots without having to travel back and forth each day and without the crowds. The boat sleeps up to 12 in four staterooms and foldout beds in the lounge. Rentals start at three full days for $1,500 and are ideal for a family or group of friends. Figure it up: four hotel rooms for two nights and boat rental for three days alone will cost more than the same period on *Dream Believer*.

Scuba Diving

Even though there is no famous underwater park like Pennekamp in the middle Keys, there are miles and miles of reefs that are just as interesting and slightly less visited, in addition to wrecks and artificial reefs. Marathon has several dive and snorkeling charter operators who take visitors out to the nearby reefs, such as **Hen & Chickens**, and farther out to **Sombrero Key**, with its boxcar-sized coral heads, and **Delta Shoals**. Most of the trips offered from Marathon go to the shallow reefs about two miles offshore, like **East Washerwoman Shoals**. These are interesting, shallow "patch" reefs and are great for beginners and good for the dive boat owners since it doesn't take much gas to reach them. Operators can work in two, back-to-back two-tank dive trips in one day, the first at 8 am, returning at 12:30, and another at 1 pm, returning at 5 o'clock. If you are comfortable in water over 40 or 50 feet deep, make sure you get on a boat going to the more developed reefs farther offshore along the Gulf Stream edge. Wrecks like the ***Thunderbolt*** lure more advanced divers.

■ DIVE SHOPS & CHARTERS

Aquatic Adventures Dive Center, *Key Colony Beach, Marathon,* ☎ *305-743-2421, www.aaquaticadventure. com.* Located behind the Holiday Inn, Aquatic Adventures is a small dive shop with their six-pack dive boat tied up nearby. The NAUI training facility takes small groups out to the patch reefs and, if the qualifications of the divers are sufficient, to deeper sites like the *Thunderbolt*. The boat is roomy and well set up for divers, with a freshwater shower. Be sure you are aware of the types of dives planned since newer divers are taken to shallower reefs that may be less interesting to experienced divers. With demand, the boat makes two trips daily, with night dives a possibility. Ask about their snorkeling trips.

Captain Hook's Marina & Dive Center, *MM 53 OS, Marathon,* ☎ *305-743-2444, 800-278-4665, www. captainhooks.com.* Jan and Lou Vasel operate this well-run PADI Five-Star dive facility that offers full training, two dive and snorkel-only trips daily, night dives, sunset cruises and dive/motel packages. They sell a full complement of dive gear as well as resort wear. Their two boats have freshwater showers and take only small groups.

Discount Divers, *MM 52 BS, Marathon,* ☎ *305-743-2400, toll-free 866-743-6054, fax 305-743-2221, www.DiscountDiversBandB.com.* Longtime ecology activist Ed Davidson runs a full-service dive shop and divers' hotel right behind Walgreens and just before the airport. He generally works with *Reef Runner* (see below), but has less-expensive options as well. His rooms, aimed primarily at dive groups (see *Where to Stay*, page 163) are a bargain.

Reef Runner, *Marathon,* ☎ *305-289-9808, 800-332-8899, www.floridadivecharter.com.* Captain Sam Watson has been offering custom dive charters on the *Reef Runner* for many years, specializing in groups of no more than six divers. The *Reef Runner* is a bit nicer than most other Keys dive charters. Of course, Captain Sam charges more, but you get what you pay for. Pick-up at your hotel can be arranged. Sam makes only one trip per day, usually leaving at a comfortable 9:30 and returning whenever you like. Four or five sites are visited during the day and each person can use up to four tanks per

Marathon/Middle Keys

person. Top-quality US Divers equipment is used. The 33-foot boat was specially designed to be a dive charter and features full galley, head and air-conditioning. PADI resort course instruction and Nitrox training are available. If you're tired of the cattle boats and not being able to decide what types of dives to go on, the *Reef Runner* may be the answer. Call and discuss what type of diving or snorkeling interests you; Captain Sam will customize the trip to fit the skills and desires of your group. Wreck, drift and wall dives as well as runs to shallow reefs for snorkeling extend the usual options of deep reef or shallow patch reef. To give some idea of the cost, he charges $365 for four people with four tanks each. Captain Sam is a young 70 years, but will probably be able to out-dive anyone on the boat. No credit cards, please.

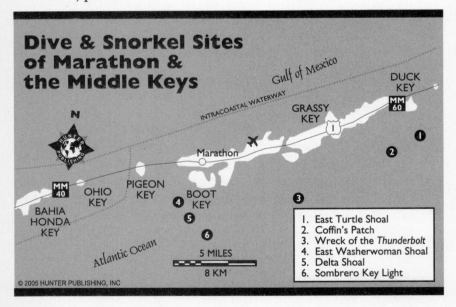

Dive & Snorkel Sites of Marathon & the Middle Keys

1. East Turtle Shoal
2. Coffin's Patch
3. Wreck of the *Thunderbolt*
4. East Washerwoman Shoal
5. Delta Shoal
6. Sombrero Key Light

© 2005 HUNTER PUBLISHING, INC

Snorkeling

For the most part, snorkeling from shore in the Middle Keys area is poor. But just a mile or two offshore is a wonderland of snorkeling delights. You can access the reefs only by boat, so either rent a boat, go in your own or a friend's, or join with one of the many dive boats. The majority of the boats focus on scuba diving, which is usually done in deeper water than snorkeling. For the best snorkeling, be sure you sign up for a snorkeling-only trip. If you are new to the sport, get together with an operator that works with beginnings.

Sunset Cruises

Keylypso Catamaran, *MM 53, Marathon at the Marathon Lady Docks,* ☎ *305-743-7655, www.keylypso.com*, offers sunset sails and two three-hour snorkel trips aboard a 47-foot catamaran.

Sombrero Reef Explorers, Sombrero Resort, Sombrero Blvd., Marathon, ☎ 305-743-0536, offers a sunset cruise every night.

Watersports

For under $50 even complete greenhorns can parasail high above the flats without even getting their feet wet. Of course if you *want* to get wet (called "dipping"), that can be arranged.

■ EQUIPMENT RENTALS

Aloha Parasail, *MM 54 BS, Marathon at Island Tiki,* ☎ *305-289-9412,* runs single or double parasailing. There is no need to make reservations – just show up with your courage.

■ In the Air

Viewing the land from high up is a unique way of looking at this part of Florida. The Middle Keys has some interesting options.

■ OUTFITTERS

Fly A Fighter-Jet, *MM 52.2 BS at the Marathon Airport,* ☎ *305-289-0007.* If you've always wanted to blast into the wild blue yonder in a real fighter jet but didn't want to join the Air Force to do it, here's your chance. No license is needed. Instruction is part of the deal, so you can actually take the controls for a moment or two, even if you have never flown before. Don't do this after a big meal. Prices start at $800 for 15 minutes; $1,200 for a half-hour.

Grantair Service Inc., *MM 52 BS, Marathon,* ☎ *305-743-1995,* rents aircraft and offers flightseeing tours of the reefs and Florida Bay. Call for rates.

Where to Stay

■ Ratings & Prices

 All the room prices in this book are for two people staying in a double room during high season. Taxes and meals are not included unless so mentioned. Hotels and lodges marked "Author's Choice" are my personal favorites, offering top quality lodging and services but, more importantly, something of particular interest or charm.

ACCOMMODATIONS PRICE CHART	
$	Under $100
$$	$100-200
$$$	$200-300
$$$$	Over $300

■ Hotels & Resorts

HOTEL **Banana Bay Resort**, *MM 49.5 BS, Marathon,* ☎ *305-743-3500, 800-226-2621, www.bananabay.com, $$$.* Banana Bay sits on a quiet 10 acres directly on Florida Bay but within walking distance of Marathon. They have a pool, tennis, lounge, Tiki bar, marina, diving and fishing facilities and watercraft rentals of all sorts. A good breakfast buffet is included in the price. The 65 rooms are modern and billed luxurious.

Blackfin Resort Motel & Marina, *MM 49.5 BS, Marathon,* ☎ *305-743-2393, 800-548-5397, www.blackfinresort.com, $$$.* The Blackfin offers simple motel-style rooms, two-bedroom apartments and almost everything in-between. Some units have kitchens and all have been remodeled recently. There is a full-service marina on the premises, along with a pool, a very nice beach, kayak rentals, fishing (Captain Bob Tittle) and diving services. Pet-friendly. The nearby Hurricane Grill (see page 169) is one of my favorite places in the Keys for seafood, blues and beer.

Cocoplum Beach & Tennis Club, *MM 54.5 OS, Marathon,* ☎ *305-743-0240, 800-228-1587, fax 305-743-9351, www.coco-plum.com, CocoPlum1@aol.com, $$$$.* Located right on the very quiet and sandy Coco Plum Beach, the hotel has all two-bedroom villas with fully equipped kitchens and laundry facilities in each unit. All are particularly nice, two-story raised buildings with sports equipment storage underneath. The bedrooms are upstairs, high, light and breezy and the rooms are well furnished with good-quality appointments. There's a tennis court, Jacuzzi and heated pool. Located in a quiet part of Marathon, the club is close to restaurants and all the tourist services you could possibly want, yet far from the bustle of Highway 1. The beach here is one of the best in the Keys and is sandy enough to be popular with turtles from April until October. The swimming is shallow enough for beginner snorkelers to practice, with a sandy bottom changing to turtle grass as you swim farther out. Sombrero Key (my favorite dive spot in the Keys) is directly offshore. The tropical lushness of over 50 kinds of palm trees and four types of limes surround the buildings. You are welcome to pick a few Key limes to use in cooking or to mix drinks. There are only 20 units but Allen Levitt, the owner, also has holiday rental houses sleeping up to 12 people, available in the same neighborhood (see *Vacation Rentals*, below). Call or check their website for seasonal specials.

Crystal Bay Resort & Marina, *MM 49.0 BS, Marathon,* ☎ *305-289-8089, 888-289-8089, fax 305-289-8189, www.crystal bayresort.com, $$-$$$.* The recently remodeled rooms range from basic to large and luxurious with full facilities. The amount of tender loving care that has been lavished on the resort since the new owners took over has to be seen to be believed. Every little detail of this formerly forlorn property has been carefully daubed with paint or been replaced by something newer and better. At night, the grounds are a wonderland of fairy lights. There is a pool and a small miniature golf course.

Discount Divers, *MM 52 BS, Marathon,* ☎ *305-743-2400, fax 305-743-2221, www.DiscountDiversBandB.com, $.* Captain Ed Davidson runs the dive shop of the same name and, around back, has four large, clean rooms suitable for up to six people in each room. All have a full kitchen, washer and dryer, fluffy pillows, big towels and large, comfortable bunk beds. These are ideal for a group of divers or anglers down for a weekend or week-long orgy of their favorite watersports. Rooms start at a bargain $89.50, with an additional $10 per person. Ed also offers packages that include room and diving. He works closely with the much-better-than-average *Reef Runner* for dive trips (see page 159).

Faro Blanco Resort, *MM 48.5 BS, Marathon,* ☎ *305-743-9018, 800-759-3276, www.spottswood.com/faroblanco.htm, $$$$*. This property was recently remodeled and now has small, freestanding cottages as well as large rental condos. The on-site marina offers all services. They have live music in the bar on weekends.

Ocean Beach Club, *MM 53.5 OS, Marathon in Key Colony Beach,* ☎ *305-289-0525, 800-321-7213, fax 305-289-9703, www. oceanbeach-club.com, $$$$*. This place offers good fishing from the dock right in front of the hotel. The accommodations are all new, and there are more suites with kitchens than regular rooms. No pets allowed.

Sea Dell Motel, *MM 50 BS, Marathon,* ☎ *305-743-5161, 800-648-3854, fax 305-743-9395, $*. Clean with good air-conditioning, the Sea Dell is an Old Keys-style motel right in the middle of town, a short walk from the Hurricane Grill (see *Where to Eat*). Units are small, but clean and comfortable. With a pool, coffee in the morning, in-room phones and refrigerators, this is a real bargain if you need a quiet, comfortable place to hang your hat in the evenings. Pet-friendly.

☆ **AUTHOR'S PICK** - **Seascape Ocean Resort**, *MM 50.5 OS, Marathon,* ☎ *305-743-6455, 800-332-7327, fax 305-743-8469, www.seascaperesort.us, $$$*. The Seascape is a small, laid-back place with only nine rooms, some with kitchens. The place has a B&B feel with plenty of privacy. The breakfasts are amazing, with a good selection of fruit, interesting breads and three types of gourmet coffees. Wine and snacks are served in the evening. Commercial photographer Bill Stites and his artist wife, Sara, feel attention to detail and tasteful elegance are a big part of the atmosphere. Rooms are well appointed (but without phones) and comfortably decorated in tropical style, with Sara's artwork on the walls and bowls of fresh fruit. There is a pool and dock for fishing. Several kayaks are available for guest use. The resort is located in a good kayaking area and Bill can be easily cajoled into leading a kayak tour through the mangroves and over the flats. Allegra (the dog) has a pleasant manner and greets guests with an inquisitive bark followed by extensive wagging. No kids under age 12, and no pets.

Sombrero Resort & Marina, *MM 50 OS, Marathon,* ☎ *305-743-2250, 800-433-8660, fax 305-743-2998, www.sombreroresort.com, $$$*. Sombrero Resort offers rental condominiums and smaller units, all with kitchens. Their four tennis courts see constant use, and there is a small exercise room, a sauna, a full-service marina and a large, heated pool. The resort is a bit off the main drag so it is relatively quiet. The poolside Tiki bar has the usual frozen tropical drinks and the restaurant is well known for pizza. You are close to a large assortment of good places to eat in town, so you are not stuck eating in the same place every night. No pets.

White Sands Inn, *MM 57.5 OS, Grassy Key,* ☎ *305-743-5285, fax 305-743-2032, www.whitesandsinn.com, $$$*. There are just eight efficiencies on this very quiet and beautiful parcel of waterfront property. The rooms are all different and have been tastefully modernized. All the usual Keys activities are catered to, but this is also a very good place to just chill out and slowly wade the flats in front of the rooms. The website gives a good feel for the ambiance and what to expect in the rooms.

■ Camping

Knights Key Campground, *MM 46.5 OS, Marathon,* ☎ *305- 743-4343, 800-348-2267, fax 305-743-2907*. Set right on the water at Seven Mile Bridge, Knights has facilities for tents and RVs. There is a nice beach and marina with boat ramp. There are some pet restrictions.

■ Vacation Rentals

Expect to pay anywhere from $1,200 to $4,000 per week for a two- or three-bedroom, modern home either on the water or near it. Nicer homes with docks and direct frontage on the bay or ocean command the highest rents.

Coco Plum Holiday Rentals, *MM 54.5 OS, Marathon,* ☎ *305-743-0240, 800-228-1587, fax 305-743-9351, www.cocoplum.com, CocoPlum1@aol.com.* The owners of Coco Plum Beach & Tennis Club have a top-quality, luxury home available for daily or weekly rentals. It is just around the corner from Coco Plum Club on a quiet street with long water frontage at the east end of Bonefish Bay. Snook and tarpon are caught right off the 200-foot dock, which is suitable for deep-draft boats up to 85 feet long. The area is super for kayaking, with backcountry mangroves almost at your doorstep. With four very large double bedrooms, each with its own bath, plus a full gourmet kitchen with granite counter tops and stainless steel appliances, the home is ideal for hosting several couples while allowing for plenty of privacy. There is enough covered parking for eight vehicles. When I visited, the owners were planting palm trees and creating a tropical landscape. A pool was about to be added. This is a very large, comfortable house on a very large, choice lot. The rent runs between $300 and $600 per night, depending on season, length of rental and number of people.

Exit Realty Vacation Rentals, *MM 50 BS, Marathon,* ☎ *305-743-0235, 888-440-0235, fax 305-743-4227, rentals@ exitrealtyfloridakeys.com.* Exit Realty offers vacation rentals in Marathon, Islamorada, Duck Key, Grassy Key and Key Colony Beach.

Where to Eat

 The price symbols for each listing consider the average cost of main courses listed on the menu.

RESTAURANT PRICE CHART	
$	Under $8
$$	$8-12
$$$	$12-20
$$$$	Over $20

■ Recommendations

☆ **AUTHOR'S PICK** - **Barracuda Grill**, *MM 49.5 BS, Marathon,* ☎ *305-743-3314, www.barracudagrill.com, $$$$.* The Barracuda has big steaks and other fine dining menu items, as well as a good selection of wines (overpriced as usual). They also offer up an imaginative children's menu. The food is consistently good, but there is little ambiance other than a bit of leftover funky Keys atmosphere. Open for dinner only; closed on Sundays.

☆ **AUTHOR'S PICK** - **Captains Three**, *MM 54.5 OS, Coco Plum Drive, Marathon,* ☎ *305-289-1131.* Not a restaurant, but a little seafood market in a shack on a canal where locals head to get good, fresh seafood at low prices. I recommend calling ahead to see what they have on hand. The boats come in at odd times and they often sell out of the good stuff pretty quick. They also have a tasty Key lime pie.

☆ **AUTHOR'S PICK** - **Castaway's**, *MM 47.8, 1406 Oceanview Avenue, Marathon,* ☎ *305-743-6247, 305-849-0472, lobster-crawl@aol.com, $$$.* John & Arlene Mirabella left California in their trimaran and somehow ended up in Marathon owning a classic Keys restaurant and running it well. This is the oldest restaurant in Marathon and has been open since 1951. These guys don't waste time or money on frills – they focus on good, fresh seafood and quick service. The owners are almost always behind the bar or in the kitchen sipping a Corona and making sure things are done properly. The specials are usually snapper or grouper prepared in interesting ways. They offer more big, plump steamed shrimp than most people can eat in one sitting for a mere $11.95. What a deal! Plus, you won't find the same old steamed vegetables that are served at all the other restaurants. The chefs take regular fish and groceries and cook them the way somebody's seafood-loving mother would. The best seafood joint in a town full of seafood joint wannabe's. It is set right next to a fish house and is a bit hard to find. Turn toward the Oceanside at MM 47.8 OS and keep going to the end; look for the sign.

☆ **AUTHOR'S PICK** - **Island Tiki Bar & Restaurant**, *MM 54 BS, Marathon,* ☎ *305-743-4191, $$.* This is one of my favorites, even though it can get overrun with kids at times; children love it here. The bar food – nachos, tacos, etc – are great. With a water-front location, a great view and a full bar, the Island specializes in interesting seafood dishes, such as oysters Moscow (on the half shell with sour cream, horseradish and red caviar) and shrimp and scallop burritos (ugh!). Try the chef's salad, which is excellent. Steamed shrimp and she crab soup are my favorites. Be sure to peer down over the edge of the dock at night to see the group of resident lobsters waving their feelers around. Open daily for lunch and dinner.

■ The Best of the Rest

7 Mile Grill, *MM 47 BS, Marathon,* ☎ *305-743-4481, $.* The open-air, authentic Keys kind of place serves good Keys-type seafood along with occasional Mexican specials, chili dogs and even a decent spaghetti plate. This is a good place to eat reasonably- priced steamed shrimp. The women behind the counter seem to run the place in a cheeky, confident manner and serve a good variety of draft and bottled beers. Save room for the Key lime pie, one of the best on the planet. The 7-Mile Grill is located at the beginning of Seven Mile Bridge. It closes at strange times, so be sure to call before you head out the door.

Blond Giraffe, *MM 51 OS, Marathon,* ☎ *888-432-MATE, www. blondgiraffe.com, $.* As much as I hate to give the prize for the best Key lime pie to such a commercial and sterile place, Blond Giraffe has absolutely wonderful pie. You can buy whole pies for $24.95 or single slices in individual plastic containers for a mere $3.50. They only use Key limes, eggs, flour and sugar. The crust is slightly crunchy and the meringue is piled high. Their website offers all kinds of Key lime goodies, such as Key lime cookies, Key lime rum cake and even a frozen Key lime pie on a stick. The Blind Giraffe also has two locations in Key West and one in South Miami.

Burdine's, *MM 48 OS, Marathon,* ☎ *305-743-5317, $$.* This old-style seafood-in-a-basket joint also offers up blackened mahi sandwiches. It is open for lunch and dinner with bands on weekends at night. If you have trouble finding the place and think you've gone too far, just keep going a bit farther – it's at the end of the road past a bunch of trailer homes. This is a good place to drink and have bar snacks, but the main restaurant dishes are uninspired.

Cabot's, *MM 47 OS*, ☎ *305-743-6442, $$$*. Although several restaurants (including Shucker's, which used to inhabit this space) have tried and failed in this excellent sunset view location, Cabot's has made a proper go of it and even serves reasonable food. Many people I meet swear it is the best place to eat in Marathon, but I have had a few unfavorable reports. Personally, I found the food well prepared but nothing out of the ordinary, and the atmosphere a little bit snooty. With so many good seafood places in town with lower prices, I'm not sure I'll go back.

> **AUTHOR NOTE:** I'm sad to say that **Deadhead George**, once a Marathon institution, is no longer in business.

Don Pedro's Cuban Restaurant, *MM 53.5 OS, Marathon,* ☎ *305-743-5247, $*. The great food is more innovative than authentic and I can forgive the inclusion of some interesting menu items like sangria, yellowtail and Argentinean steak. Sandwiches on "Cuban" bread are great and economical. Lunch is served Monday through Friday and dinner through Saturday.

Grassy Key DB Seafood Grille, *MM 58.5 OS, Grassy Key,* ☎ *305-743-3816, $$*. The DB used to be a dairy bar and although you can still get a glass of milk here, broiled fish and Mexican or German dishes are the specialty. Sometimes there is live music. It is best to call ahead and get your name on the waiting list. Open for dinner only except from May through November, when lunch is also served; closed Sunday and Monday.

Herbie's, *MM 50 BS, Marathon,* ☎ *305-743-6373, $$$*. Herbie's is a very touristy place that draws a crowd of locals slamming down beers during the Wednesday evening happy hour, which features live music and dancing. The drinks are big, the food is fried and the atmosphere is tourist funky.

Hurricane Grille, *MM 49.5 BS, Marathon,* ☎ *305-743-2220, $$$*. A Keys landmark, the Hurricane has good Italian and seafood dishes. Yellowtail, grouper and other usuals are served nicely. There are saltwater aquariums in the dining room with interesting reef fish and moray eels – don't stick your hand in.

Check for dinner specials and wine promotions. The Key lime pie is just okay. The bar sits alongside he restaurant and features bands with some notable blues names. It is a bit of a local hangout. I was lucky enough to catch Rock Bottom here one evening. If the Charlie Morris Blues Band is playing, come early and stay late.

Island City Fish Market Eatery, *MM 53 OS, Marathon,* ☎ *305-743-9196, $$*. Though plain in appearance, this is a good place to honk down a big pile of fresh seafood at reasonable (but still not cheap) prices. Closed on Tuesdays.

Keys Fisheries, *Gulf View Avenue just past the Stuffed Pig, Marathon,* ☎ *305-743-6727, $$*. Look carefully for the sign that indicates the turn for this excellent seafood joint. This fish heaven is right on the water in a marina. You order food at one window and drinks at another, wait for your celebrity name to be called (you have to pick a celebrity name – you can't use your own unless you are one) and pick up your chow at the first window. All the usual Keys seafood items are here, with a few notable and delicious specials, such as lobster Reuben sandwiches and all-you-can-eat golden crab. It can get crowded on weekends, but the wait is worthwhile.

Marathon Liquor and Deli, *MM 51, Marathon,* ☎ *305-743-6350, $$*. You can't miss the huge signs for cheap liquor as you drive through town, but don't be fooled – the booze is the most expensive in town. Locals buy their rum at Walgreens and stop in the Marathon Liquor and Deli for their wonderful sandwiches.

Mike's Hideaway Café Restaurant, *MM 57.7 OS, Grassy Key, Located at Rainbow Bend Resort,* ☎ *305-289-1554, $$$*. Mike's features fine dining and big portions of roast duck and the usual seafood specials. The views of the water are superb, as is the food. The service is stately; allow plenty of time to enjoy your meal at a leisurely pace. The restaurant is open every day for lunch and dinner. They offer early bird specials from 4:30-6 pm.

Porky's Bayside, *MM 47.5 BS, Marathon,* ☎ *305-289-2065, $*. A low-down (translate: authentic) BBQ joint open for lunch and dinner. No credit cards.

The Quay, *MM 54 BS, Marathon,* ☎ *305-289-1810, $$*, has a great pre-dinner bar scene with good views and ambiance. The gigantic menu has seemingly everything, including gator, frog legs, pasta, seafood, steaks and more. An overly large menu usually means the kitchen staff cannot spend much time making any one dish with special care, and the Quay seems to be no exception to the rule. The food is okay, but the best reason to come is to hang out in the crowded bar before you eat and stroll along the boardwalk looking in shop windows afterward. Lunch and dinner are served daily.

Wooden Spoon, *MM 51, Marathon*, ☎ *305-743-8383, $*. Grab a seat at the counter, pick up the morning paper, and eat breakfast with charter captains, police and other locals. The biscuits are fluffy and the corned beef hash tasty. Omelets, French toast, hot cakes and seafood lunch specials keep the Wooden Spoon crowded. The walls are decorated with – guess what? – wooden spoons.

The Wreck & Galley Grill & Sports Bar, *MM 59 BS, Grassy Key,* ☎ *305-743-3816, $$*. With two ampersands in the name I would expect this to be a mish-mash, but it is actually a decent spot for a beer and some wings. They offer full meals, if you can stand the loud sports bar atmosphere with too many TVs.

Nightlife

There is a little nightlife in the Marathon area if you look hard and are not too picky.

Angler's Lounge, *MM 48.2 BS, Marathon in the Faro Blanco Resort,* ☎ *305-743-9018,* has weekend bands in a regular old marina bar.

Brass Monkey Lounge, *MM 52, Marathon,* ☎ *305-743-4028*, in a strip shopping center at the end of the Kmart building. More or less a neighborhood bar, the Brass Monkey is best known as a late-night haunt where everyone goes after the Hurricane Lounge (see below) closes. It is used almost exclusively by locals and service personnel – most tourists aren't ready to start partying at 2 am.

Dockside Lounge, *MM 53 OS, Marathon, Sombrero Road,* ☎ *305-743-0622*, has live entertainment every night, including a big jam session on Sundays.

☆ **AUTHOR'S PICK** - **Hurricane Lounge**, *MM 49.5 BS, Marathon*, ☎ *305-743-2220*. The bar and restaurant of the same name are famous for their good food, good music and funky Keys atmosphere. Live bands on the weekends include some popular Florida regulars like the Charlie Morris Band and Rock Bottom. The beer is cold and the margaritas tasty. You can eat bar food or go next door for a proper sit-down dinner. The fish sandwiches are good. Some locals hang here for the late-night sounds and happy hour specials.

Lower Keys

The Lower Keys are the least-developed and least-visited part of the Keys. Lodging and dining choices are limited but, as a direct result, the surrounding environment is more pristine. Key West is close by, which means you can take advantage of the relative quietness and still enjoy the sometimes-raucous pleasures of the biggest party town in the US.

AUTHOR TIDBIT: Key West cops often set up road blocks in the evening on the Overseas Highway just outside town looking for drivers who have been too liberal with the sauce; select a designated driver.

At a Glance

LARGEST TOWN: Big Pine Key, population 5,032

ELEVATION: Five feet

AREA: 9.8 square miles

COUNTY: Monroe

MAJOR ROUTES: Overseas Highway (US 1)

NEAREST AIRPORTS: Marathon (22 miles); Miami International (98 miles); Key West (29 miles)

ZIP CODE: 33043

AVERAGE TEMPERATURE: January 69.1°; August 83.7°

PRECIPITATION: January 2.2 inches; August 5.9 inches

Getting Here & Getting Around

The **Overseas Highway** (US 1) is the only road of any consequence in the area. Most visitors come by car from the Miami area via this road, although some fly into Key West, rent a car, and make the short drive to the Lower Keys.

Key West International Airport, *Roosevelt Boulevard,* ☎ *305-296-5439*, is served by **American Eagle,** ☎ *800-433-7300*, **Cape Air,** ☎ *305-293-0603*, **Delta,** ☎ *800-221-1212*, **Continental Connection,** ☎ *305-294-1421*, and **USAir Express**, ☎ *800-428-4322*. **Sugarloaf Lodge**, *MM 17 BS, Summerland Key,* ☎ *305-745-3211*, has a private 3,000-foot strip.

There are no **car rental** agencies in the Lower Keys, but Key West has plenty. Most of them have offices at the airport (see *Rental Car Companies*, page 204).

Area History & Highlights

There were few settlers in the area before World War II. The 1870 census lists only one family living on Big Pine Key. Little wrecking was carried on since most wreckers preferred to be based in nearby Key West. The few settlers that stayed here relied on charcoal making and small market farms for a living. A 1966 census lists 181 residents of Big Pine Key, making it one of the slowest areas in the Keys to develop. In the 1970s the Big Pine Key Bottle Works was established and provided a limited amount of manufacturing jobs. Big Pine Key, still relatively undeveloped, now has one stoplight.

Because of its laid-back atmosphere and nearness to the delights of Key West, the Lower Keys are almost always the destination of choice for me and my family. We like to rent a vacation home and small boat for a month in the winter, enjoying watersports as well as dining and nightlife in Key West. Using the area as a base, we spend time doing all the usual tourist and outdoor sports things throughout the Keys. We fish out of Islamorada and dive off Key Largo, just a short drive away.

Information Sources

Key West, *Mallory Square, Key West,* ☎ *305-294-2587, 800-648-6269*

Lower Keys, *MM 31 OS, Big Pine Key,* ☎ *305-872-2411, 800-872-3722*

Sightseeing

■ Suggested Itineraries

If You Have One Day

1 DAY Trying to enjoy the Lower Keys in only one day from Miami is almost out of the question unless you are a speed-tourist. It can easily take four hours to get to the area from Miami if the traffic is heavy. The drive down and back is spectacular, but you won't have time to dive, fish or enjoy watersports. However, a half-day **scuba dive** or **snorkeling** trip to **Looe Key**, one of the most interesting area attractions, is possible. Book a couple of weeks in advance with **Reef Divers**, *MM 21 OS at Cudjoe Gardens Marina,* ☎ *305-515-2750, 877-886-6621, www.reef-divers.com.* Check in at 8 am or 1 pm for a four-hour, two-tank dive.

If You Have Three Days

3 DAYS Besides the wonderful scenery, undersea life is the main attraction of the Lower Keys. On Day One, if you are driving down from Miami, there are several great places to stop for a snack or lunch. I usually stop at **Denny's Latin Café**, *MM 100*, for a cup of Cuban coffee. Don't leave a dive or snorkel trip until your last day, when you may have checked out of your hotel and wind up salty and tired for the trip home. I suggest you check into your hotel and immediately head out to **Looe Key** for a two-tank scuba dive or snorkeling trip. Reserve at least two weeks in advance with **Reef Divers** (see above). Back at the hotel, shower and refresh yourself before heading to the **Geiger Key Smokehouse**, *MM 10.5, Geiger Key,* ☎ *305-296-3553,* for dinner and a few beers. With luck there will be some live entertainment.

On Day Two zoom up to **Baby's Coffee Bar** (close to Key West at MM 15 OS) for coffee and a muffin before going for a day of backcountry fishing with **Captain Eric Bonar**, **Back Country Guide Service**, *Ramrod Key,* ☎ *305-872-1819.* Depending on how tired you are at the end of the day, you could either drive into Key West for a night of people-watching, beer, conch fritters and live music or spend another pleasant evening at the Geiger Key Smokehouse. I love the place and have no problem going back again and again. But you are close to **Key West**; if the pleasures of the dining table or nightlife attract you, make the short drive.

Key West is a wonderful place to simply wander around so you could easily walk around town in the morning, have a great lunch and then head back for a half-day fishing and wildlife viewing in the backcountry or walking the interesting beaches around Bahía Honda State Park.

Start Day Three off right with another cup of good coffee from Baby's Coffee Bar and spend the morning fishing for billfish, amberjack and shark with **Captain Mark André**, **Grouch Charters**, *MM 21.5, Cudjoe Key,* ☎ *305-745-1172, www.grouch-charters.com.*

Head back toward Miami with stops at both ends of the **Bahía Honda bridge** to stare slacked-jawed at the amazing construction. Head out on the old bridge as far as you can from the Bahía Honda State Park (eastern) end. You can sometimes see tarpon moving through the channel far below. Stop in Homestead for at late BBQ dinner at **Shivers**, *28001 Dixie Hwy,* on the right as you go north.

If You Have a Week

7 DAYS A week is enough time to indulge in your particular passions (fishing, diving, viewing wildlife) in depth. On the drive from Miami there are several great places to stop for a snack or lunch. On Day One I suggest a stop at **Ballyhoo's**, *MM 97.8, in the median, Key Largo*, ☎ *305-852-0822*, for a seafood lunch or **Denny's Latin Café**, *MM 100 OS*, for a cup of Cuban coffee. As soon as you arrive in the area, check into your hotel and head out to **Looe Key** for a two-tank scuba dive or snorkeling trip (reserve at least two weeks in advance with **Reef Divers**, see above). Have dinner and enjoy live entertainment at the **Geiger Key Smokehouse**, *MM 10.5, Geiger Key,* ☎ *305-296-3553*.

A good way to spend Day Two would be to walk some of the old bridges over the flats and sand channels looking for turtles, sharks, rays and other exotic sealife. Both ends of the Bahía Honda bridge are well worth a stop. **Bahía Honda State Park** is on the eastern end of the bridge and has a great beach for beachcombing. Lunch at the **No Name Pub**, *MM 31 BS, North Watson Boulevard, Big Pine Key,* ☎ *305-872-9115*, is a requirement. I suggest another lazy evening at the Geiger Key Smokehouse (I love this place), but if you see another place that takes your fancy, give it a try.

Since the reefs are one of the most glorious sights in the Keys, Day Three can be well spent diving or snorkeling on **Looe Key**, if you haven't done this on Day One. Once again, book well in advance with **Reef Divers** (see above). Lunch at any of the interesting eateries you see, and follow it with a lazy afternoon by the pool. For a mouth-watering change from seafood, head to **Raimondo's Ristorante**, *MM 21, Cudjoe Key,* ☎ *305-745-9999, for proper Italian food.*

Set aside Day Four for a full day offshore fishing for sailfish, dorado or marlin (some of the best in the country) with **Captain Mark André**, **Grouch Charters**, *MM 21.5, Cudjoe Key,* ☎ *305-745-1172, www.grouchcharters.com.* Half-day trips are less expensive but if you are hoping for a billfish, a full day is best. Save some energy and drive to Key West for an elegant dinner at the **Café Marquesa**, *600 Fleming Street,* ☎ *305-292-1244.* After dinner, find a spot at the bar at the **Green Parrot**, *601*

Whitehead Street, ☎ *305-294-6133, www.greenparrot.com,* for the best blues in the Keys. If you have been sampling the city's famous refreshing beverages, take a cab back to your hotel.

Day Five. Backcountry guides can show you the pleasures of more than just fishing. There are seemingly thousands of remote mangrove keys around Big Pine Key and they teem with birds. Everglades National Park is just about out of reach from this area, but you can see most of the same wildlife in Florida Bay from a shallow-water fishing skiff. Book at least two months in advance with **Captain Eric Bonar** of Back Country Guide Service (see above). After a day fishing you are required to hang out and brag about your fishy exploits at the **Geiger Key Smokehouse**. If you can put your money where your mouth is, and if you ask nicely, you can hand your fish over to the chef who will cook it for you.

Classic Old Key West architecture.

Zip up the road to **Key West** for sightseeing, dining or partying, or take a sunset cruise and get back to your hotel with little trouble. Depending on traffic, Key West can be reached from Marathon in an hour or two. This gives you plenty of time to soak up the sights and nightlife. Spend all of Day Six in Key West. Stop on the drive at **Baby's Coffee Bar** at MM 15 on the way into town, then park in the Old Town Parking Garage on the corner of Caroline and Grinnell streets. Take the shuttle to Duval and walk that street leisurely, checking out the weirdoes who will be checking you out. If you need souvenirs, but them as you wander around and take the shuttle back to your car to put your purchases in the trunk.

Most of the restaurants on Duval Street are tourist traps good for little more than having a drink and resting your feet. The best conch fritters on the planet come from **Johnson's Café**, *306 Petronia Street/801 Thomas Street,* ☎ *305-292-2286,* so stop there for lunch. Pass the afternoon walking along the back streets of Old Town admiring the Caribbean architecture, shopping or simply people watching. Enjoy soothing alcoholic beverages in a bar with a good view of Duval Street, such as **Mangoes**, *700 Duval Street,* ☎ *305-292-4606.* In the late afternoon, walk along the waterfront by Mallory Square for the sunset celebrations, checking out the street theater, musicians and other entertainers. After the sun goes down, **Sloppy Joe's**, *201 Duval Street,* ☎ *305-294-5717, www.sloppyjoes.com,* is the place to see Pete and Wayne's childish adult comedy act. They usually start at 5 and do two sets, so you should have plenty of time. Mixed drinks can be lame here, so stick to beer at Sloppy Joe's.

Sloppy Joe's is a Key West institution.

Have a seafood dinner at **Seven Fish**, *632 Olivia Street, Key West,* ☎ *305-296-2777, www.7fish.com* (look for the bullet holes), then go to the **Green Parrot**, *601 Whitehead Street,* ☎ *305-294-6133, www.greenparrot.com,* for blues. Check their website to see who is playing. If the Charlie Morris Band is up, try to catch them. With your designated driver in the seat, drag yourself back up the Overseas Highway to your hotel.

On Day Seven check out of your hotel at a reasonable hour and start your drive home. Head northeast up the Overseas Highway toward Miami with stops for a short bridge walk at the western end of the **Seven Mile Bridge**. Have lunch in Marathon at the **Island Tiki Bar & Restaurant**, *MM 54 BS, Marathon*, ☎ *305-743-4191*, and stop in Homestead for at late BBQ dinner at **Shivers**, *28001 Dixie Hwy*, on the right as you go north.

■ Beaches

In an area not known for great sandy beaches there are, in fact, two nice ones.

Bahía Honda State Park (see below) has by far the nicest beach in the Keys. The sandy stretch that extends for a mile or so at Bahía Honda is shallow and calm enough for children. There are picnic tables nearby and plenty of parking. While there is not much shade, the park has showers so you can cool off after your swim. Wade along the sandbar just a few yards offshore at low tide to check out the sea life. I've seen rays, sharks, conchs, lobsters and thousands of colorful reef fish. Near the marina is an enclosed snorkeling and swimming area that, while not as nice as the sandy beach, is a good place to practice your snorkeling skills.

Little Duck Key Beach, just after the Seven Mile Bridge at MM 39 OS, is part of a small park with bathrooms and picnic tables. The area offers little shade, but there is a parking area and boat ramp on the other side of the highway. There is a small wading beach. The old Seven Mile Bridge is one of the very best bridges for walking out over the flats and viewing interesting sea creatures. Little Money Key is close offshore and is a good kayaking destination.

■ Parks

Bahía Honda State Park, *MM 37 OS, Big Pine Key*, ☎ *305-872-3210, www.bahiahondapark.com, $2.50 per person*. Known to have the nicest beach in the Keys,

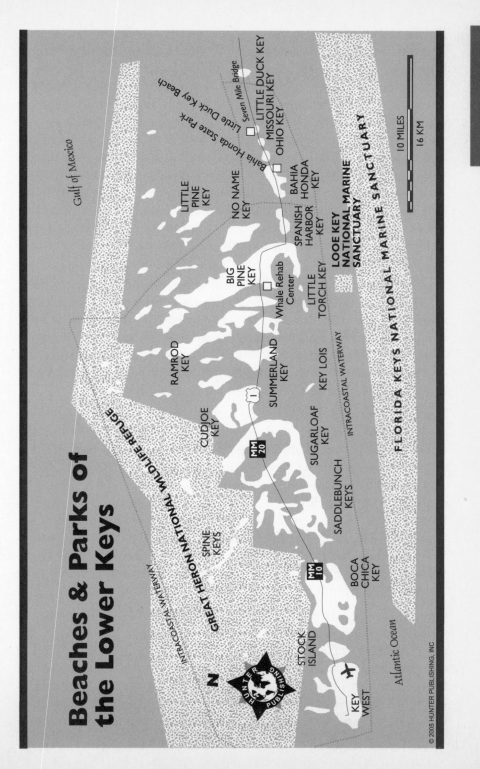

Beaches & Parks of the Lower Keys

Gulf of Mexico

Atlantic Ocean

INTRACOASTAL WATERWAY

GREAT HERON NATIONAL WILDLIFE REFUGE

SPINE KEYS

CUDJOE KEY

RAMROD KEY

LITTLE PINE KEY

NO NAME KEY

BIG PINE KEY

Whale Rehab Center

SUMMERLAND KEY

SUGARLOAF KEY

KEY LOIS

LITTLE TORCH KEY

SPANISH HARBOR KEY

BAHIA HONDA KEY

OHIO KEY

MISSOURI KEY

LITTLE DUCK KEY

Seven Mile Bridge

Bahia Honda State Park

Little Duck Key Beach

SADDLEBUNCH KEYS

INTRACOASTAL WATERWAY

BOCA CHICA KEY

STOCK ISLAND

KEY WEST

MM 20

MM 10

LOOE KEY NATIONAL MARINE SANCTUARY

FLORIDA KEYS NATIONAL MARINE SANCTUARY

10 MILES

16 KM

N

HUNTER PUBLISHING

Bahía Honda (Spanish for "deep bay") also offers a full-service marina, shady camping and RV sites, three duplex cabins, kayaking, a concession with food and equipment rentals, a half-mile bicycling trail, picnic area and a gift shop. Plus, the most spectacular bridge in the Keys, old Bahía Honda Bridge, looms over the park like Henry Flagler's ghost. You can walk out on it far enough to get an excellent view of the surrounding flats and channels. This is a short hike and is one of the best bridge walks in the Keys. I felt thrills down to my toes one afternoon walking on the bridge as I watched a procession of gigantic tarpon swimming along the edge of the channel. In the near distance I could see perhaps a dozen bored-looking fishing boats anchored, loaded with anglers who had visions of these fish dancing in their heads.

The sandy beach is long, clean and good for swimming, wading, snorkeling and just hanging out. If you keep walking east you'll run into one of the Keys' better eco-trails. It runs along the edge of the mangroves and provides opportunities to view thousands of wading birds and nesting sites in the trees. When I was a child on vacation in the area, Bahía Honda was impossible to drive by. Splashing around in the shallow sand was a highlight.

National Key Deer Wildlife Refuge, *managed from Big Pine Key,* ☎ *305-872-3329*. Combined with the adjacent protected marine waters, this park and Great White Heron park (below) cover approximately 300 square miles. The Key Deer refuge centers around Big Pine Key and No Name Key, which can be accessed by a bridge from Big Pine. No Name Key is by far the best place to spot the tiny little deer; drive or walk very, very slowly to see them. Most sightings are in the early morning or just before sunset, although I've seen them along the side of the Overseas Highway during the heat of the day. Turn off the Oversea Highway at the Big Pine Shopping Center.

Great White Heron National Wildlife Refuge, *managed from Big Pine Key,* ☎ *305-872-3329, http://southeast.fws. gov/GreatWhiteHeron/*, is accessible only by boat and most of the islands within the reserve are closed – you cannot set foot on them, camp or otherwise disturb the environment. Parts of Upper and Lower Sugarloaf Keys have areas through which you can drive, but there is not much to see for the casual visitor other than birds and crabs. The flats and channels around the remote keys teem with strange sea creatures.

Looe Key National Marine Sanctuary. Looe Key is not much more than a sand bar surrounded by impressive coral reefs. It is almost never above the water's surface and not really deserving of the name "key." The 5.3-square-nautical-mile sanctuary, six miles offshore opposite Ramrod Key, was set up in 1981. It features a tongue-and-groove reef system just to the south of the shallow sandy area is one of the more spectacular reefs in the Keys. When the water is calm, this is the best place for snorkeling you can ever hope to find. The protected reefs teem with colorful fish just like the Jacques Cousteau TV shows. The coral is still in good condition and even inexperienced snorkelers can easily see all the joys of the reef since it is so shallow. If you are going to do only one snorkeling or diving trip on your Keys visit, head to Looe Key. Several companies bring divers and snorkelers here (see *Adventures On Water* for dive and snorkel outfitters). Since it is a popular spot, some of the dive operators have fallen into the "cattle boat" mentality and seem more interested in shearing tourist sheep than in providing good service. I recommend Reef Divers and suggest staying away from Looe Key Reef Resort (unless you're just going to their fun Tiki bar).

Adventures

The Lower Keys has plenty of all the good things people come to the Keys to do. Florida Bay is chock full of small keys and mangrove clumps that can be explored by boat. Fishing and diving are superb – perhaps the best in the Keys.

■ On Foot

Bridge Walks

It's hard to beat a stroll along one of the old bridges that have been converted to fishing piers. These are restricted to foot traffic only and are a good way to get out over the flats and tidal channels without a boat. Stroll for a mile or so down any of these fishing piers and you are sure to see sharks, stingrays birds and diving ducks. Both ends of **Seven Mile Bridge** offer access to long fishing piers that used to be the old Overseas Highway. Another good spot is at the far west end of the **Bahía Honda Bridge**, which has a proper parking area.

Bahía Honda Bridge.

Flats Wading

Much of the Overseas Highway passes through very shallow water with sand or turtle grass on the seabed. Quite a bit of sea life can be seen by simply wading out through the flats and looking in the seaweed. Crabs, lobsters, small colorful fish, stingrays and sometimes turtles can be found if you wade out for a quarter-mile or so.

> **AUTHOR TIDBIT:** Anglers learn how to spot the elusive bonefish on the flats by using polarized sunglasses.

A good spot to wade is at the **Veteran's Memorial Park**, on the ocean side, west end of Seven Mile Bridge. The park has picnic tables, toilets and a little bit of sand.

■ On Water

Almost all of the water in the Lower Keys is shallow and lots of props get chewed up here. A few channels separate the keys. Newfound Harbor and Coupon Bight get up to eight feet deep in places, but are littered with shallow flats that can be difficult to see when the wind has stirred things up. There are a few areas of coral heads to watch out for about a half-mile off Newfound Harbor, Saddlebunch and Boca Chica Keys.

A couple of **public boat ramps** with trailer parking can be found at the bridges. On the bay side, at the far end of Seven Mile Bridge, is a paved parking area used by picnickers and anglers. It has a ramp. Fishing around the old bridge can be good. Another free boat ramp is on the bay side at the far end of Bahía Honda Bridge. There are no facilities other than the ramp and parking for trailers. Same thing is true for a couple of ramps close to Key West at MM 5 OS and MM 11 OS.

Canoeing & Kayaking

The Lower Keys has a plethora of small mangrove islands in Florida Bay that are easily accessible to paddlers. The flats around **Little Duck Key** and **Missouri Key** cover acres and acres and are great for viewing shallow-water sea creatures. You can launch at **Bahía Honda** and paddle either on the ocean or bays side back toward them.

> **WARNING:** The currents between the keys are almost always pretty strong. I don't recommend messing around with the formidable Bahía Honda Channel.

Big Pine Key has dozens of places to explore. I particularly like to mess about on the flats and channels around **Long Beach** and **Newfound Harbor Keys**. The sea is almost always calm on the ocean side and the backside of the keys are very shallow. The cuts between the keys can barely be called "channels" since they are so shallow, but boaters can make it through them during high tide and paddlers can get through at any time. These passages are lined with mangroves and host all sorts of interesting birds and sea life. If you are experienced and very confident, you may be comfortable heading to the patch reefs about a half-mile directly off **Big Munson**, clearly marked by buoys. Don't head out there unless it is very calm. These reefs are in five to 10 feet of water. They sit in a protected area, so no fishing and no lobstering!

Sugarloaf Key and **Saddlebunch Key** have a large interior "lagoon" that is shallow and protected. Most of both keys are relatively undeveloped and offer wonderful opportunities for wildlife viewing. **Sugar Loaf Creek** separates the two keys and is an interesting place to explore all by itself. You can launch from the end of the small bridge that crosses over the creek. The current is almost always swift at Lower Sugarloaf Sound, but plan your trip to take advantage of the tidal change and you can float through to the ocean side and back again with little effort.

Similar Sound is too shallow and salty to have much in the way of observable sea life, but **Saddlebunch Harbor** gets more tidal action and is worth a look. **Saddlehill Key** and **Big Key**, surrounded by very shallow water, are both full of bird life. There is a small interior lake at the northeast end of Saddlehill Key that can be accessed by groping your way through mangroves. It's worth the effort as you'll get to see the thousands of birds that make the trees around the lake their home.

> **AUTHOR TIDBIT:** Plan carefully for currents. If you are heading to the many small keys out in Florida Bay, don't allow yourself to drift too far from your launch spot or you'll be fighting a current to get back.

■ OUTFITTER

Reflections Nature Tours, *MM 30, Big Pine Key,* ☎ *305-872-4668, www.FloridaKeysKayakTours.com.* Reflections is a small eco-tour company that focuses primarily on kayaking. They rent kayaks and conduct guided group tours daily. Their basic three-hour tour costs $50 per person and roams through turtle grass flats and mangroves around Big Pine Key. Custom backcountry tours can visit Great White Heron National Wildlife Refuge. Some of the more involved excur-

Canoe & Kayak Spots of the Lower Keys

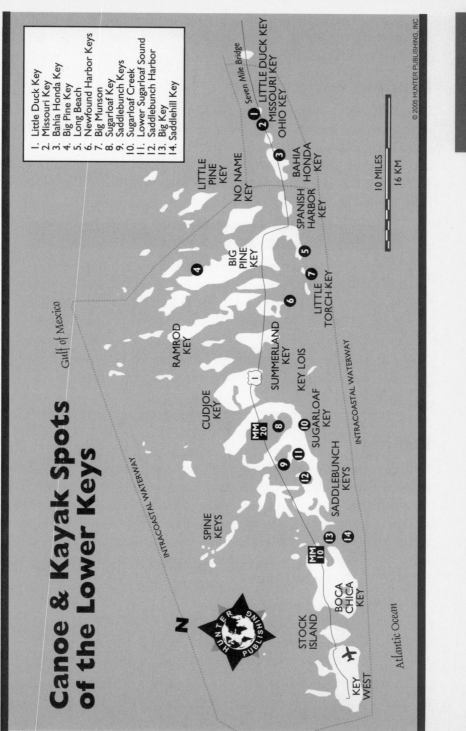

1. Little Duck Key
2. Missouri Key
3. Bahia Honda Key
4. Big Pine Key
5. Long Beach
6. Newfound Harbor Keys
7. Big Munson
8. Sugarloaf Key
9. Saddlebunch Keys
10. Sugarloaf Creek
11. Lower Sugarloaf Sound
12. Saddlebunch Harbor
13. Big Key
14. Saddlehill Key

Gulf of Mexico

INTRACOASTAL WATERWAY

INTRACOASTAL WATERWAY

Atlantic Ocean

10 MILES

16 KM

LITTLE PINE KEY

NO NAME KEY

BIG PINE KEY

RAMROD KEY

CUDJOE KEY

SUMMERLAND KEY

KEY LOIS

SUGARLOAF KEY

SADDLEBUNCH KEYS

SPINE KEYS

SPANISH HARBOR KEY

BAHIA HONDA KEY

LITTLE TORCH KEY

Seven Mile Bridge

LITTLE DUCK KEY

MISSOURI KEY

OHIO KEY

MM 20

MM 10

BOCA CHICA KEY

STOCK ISLAND

KEY WEST

N

HUNTER PUBLISHING

© 2005 HUNTER PUBLISHING, INC

sions require traveling to remote locations by powerboat and then setting out in kayaks. Sunset and full moon tours are available.

Dolphin Encounters

Currently free from tacky dolphin roadside attractions found in other parts of the Keys, the Lower Keys stands out for the **whale rehabilitation** activities on Big Pine Key. Subsequent to the stranding of 28 pilot whales in 2003, seven of these mammals were brought to a small cove at the west end of Big Pine Key for rehabilitation. Several are still there.

GIVING TIME

Volunteers are welcomed to help in this rehab program. For information on how to volunteer, contact Dolphin Research Center, Middle Keys, ☎ 305-289-1121; Florida Keys Marine Mammal Resue Team, Lower Keys, ☎ 305-745-8785; Marine Animal Resue Society, Upper and Middle Keys, ☎ 305-919-5503; or Dolphins Plus (Marine Mammal Rescue Foundation), Upper Keys, ☎ 305-451-1993.

Fishing

Fishing opportunities abound in the Lower Keys. The extensive flats in **Florida Bay** attract anglers shooting for bonefish, permit, redfish, tarpon and spotted weakfish. Also here is the best spot on the entire US Atlantic coast for marlin. **The Wall** is a few miles out in the Gulf Stream opposite Saddlebunch Keys. Additionally, the area has some great **fishing piers**, formerly bridges for the old Overseas Highway.

> **AUTHOR TIDBIT:** Because the area is less developed than other parts of the Keys, the selection of charter boats and guides is smaller. Make your reservations as far in advance as you can.

The Florida Bay area north of the Lower Keys teems with sea life and lures anglers from around the world. The shallow flats area covers hundreds of square miles.

■ BACKCOUNTRY & LIGHT TACKLE GUIDES

Back Country Guide Service/Captain Eric, *Ramrod Key,* ☎ *305-872-1819, $285 half-day, $400 full day.* Captain Eric Bonar will launch his flats skiff from any point in Key West or the Lower Keys. He knows where the big fish are and will pole you across the flats in search of bonefish, tarpon, permit, grouper and other shallow-water species.

Helicon Backcountry Charters, *Cudjoe Key,* ☎ *305-745-2800, www.heliconfishing.com, $300 half-day, $400 full day.* Captain Michael Vaughn is a fly fishing guru with a light flats skiff. He is environmentally aware, encouraging catch and release practices unless the fish will be served for dinner. With his boat on a trailer, his coverage ranges as far as the less-frequented Marquesas.

■ OFFSHORE CHARTERS

This is prime marlin country. Sailfish, dolphin and kingfish with the occasional wahoo make up the bulk of the area catch.

DoFish Charters, *Big Pine Key,* ☎ *305-872-4894, $550 half-day, $750 full day.* Fishing nut Captain Doug Lutz charters his 45-foot Viking Sportfisherman out of Big Pine Key and heads offshore in pursuit of trophy billfish. He can take up to six passengers. Doug is active in tournaments and this may be your chance to participate in some of exciting ones. Live bait and kite fishing are specialties.

Grouch Charters, *MM 21.5, Cudjoe Key,* ☎ *305-745-1172, www.grouchcharters.com,* $350 half-day, $500 full day. Captain Mark André fishes a 34-foot Luhrs Tournament Sportfisher out of Cudjoe Key.

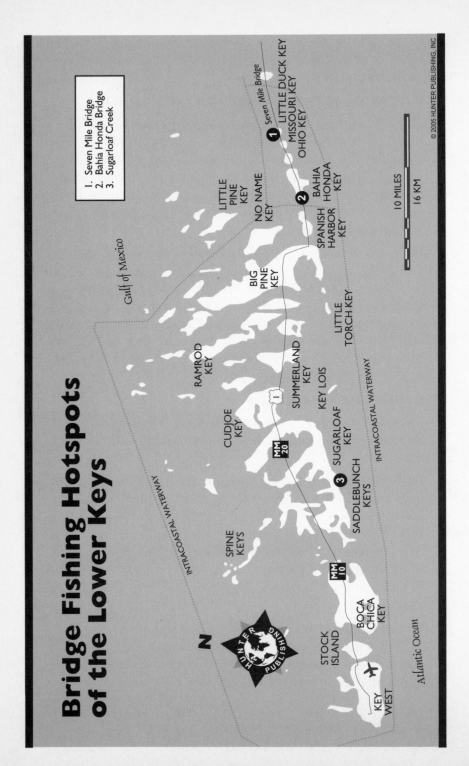

Bridge Fishing Hotspots of the Lower Keys

1. Seven Mile Bridge
2. Bahia Honda Bridge
3. Sugarloaf Creek

© 2005 HUNTER PUBLISHING, INC

Bridge & Shore Fishing

There are interesting angling spots at the ends of almost every bridge in the area. Some are better than others, due to bridge configuration and currents. My favorite locations are at the west ends of **Seven Mile Bridge** and **Bahía Honda Bridge**. There is good parking at both spots. I've seen schools of huge tarpon moving through the channel at the park end of the Bahía Honda Bridge, but have yet to hook one there.

The old **Overseas Highway bridges** maintained for anglers are good, too. Just walk out over the flats and channels looking for the right spot to drop a hook. Local families will camp out for entire weekends on these bridges, fishing around the clock. The trick is actually *landing* anything big you might catch. Remember, you're a good 30 feet or so up in the air.

Here's another one of my secret fishing spots: **Sugarloaf Creek** is a small channel separating the ocean sides of Saddlebunch and Sugarloaf Keys. To get to it, turn south off the Overseas Highway at the east end of Sugarloaf Key and follow the road all the way along the coastline until you get to a small bridge that crosses over the creek. The area is quiet and rarely visited. The current runs pretty quickly under the bridge, but the fishing can be good. Tarpon cruise along the creek's edges almost under the mangroves looking to pick off the weak or slow. I suggest plopping live mullet on a heavy one- or two-ounce sinker along the edge of the channel. It's shallow, so if you are paying attention you will see the tarpon coming. Try to control your excitement. Unfortunately, the creek is loaded with barracuda that sometimes decide they should share in your catch. If you try to walk your catch along the bridge to shallow water for easy picking, you may find yourself with only half of a fish.

Scuba Diving

Because the Lower Keys see fewer visitors, the environment is less spoiled. Looe Key is a famous protected reef ecosystem with superb diving and snorkeling. Several interesting areas of patch reefs are within a mile or two of land and in only 15 feet of water. **American Shoals** is another frequently visited reef system west of Looe Key. The wreck of the 210-foot *Adolphus Busch* is halfway between the two in over 100 feet of water.

Looe Key is a couple of acres of sand and reef about six miles off Ramrod Key. The word "key" is a little misleading, since the land almost never shows above water. Between the sandy shallows and the dropoff to the Gulf Stream is one of the most beautiful barrier reef systems. It runs from very shallow water to deep, with fingers of coral creating channels that can be navigated by snorkelers and divers. Rainbow-colored fish swarm in their gazillions around bright coral and sea fans. Exotic-looking invertebrates and tiny crabs lurk in their tiny crevices. The back side of the reef is shallow sand, with thousands of acres of turtle grass running off away from the reef area. Barracuda lurk in the hundreds waiting for the weak, sick, or slow to make a false move before being devoured. Because Looe Key is so popular, you'll almost always see other divers here. Fortunately, there are several mooring buoys and one is almost always available. The "Deep Balls" site just south of the main reef area in about 50 feet of water does not see nearly as much traffic as the fingers do.

There are only a few dive operators in the Lower Keys, and some rank solidly in the cattle boat category. If you want a more personalized experience, select a "six pack" or smaller trip that is going to the type of places you want to go to. Call around to different dive shops and ask where they are going that week, how much they charge and how many people are on the trips. If you have your heart set on diving deep wrecks, join a trip with like-minded participants so you don't end up on shallow patch reefs.

■ DIVE SHOPS & CHARTERS

Looe Key Reef Resort & Dive Center, *MM 27.5 OS, Ramrod Key,* ☎ *305-872-2215, 800-942-5397, www. diveflakeys.com.* The hotel is cheap and ratty, but the bar is a fun place. The dive operation is a bit on the shaky side. My brother visited the Keys recently and told me about his Looe Key dive experience. Just before he was about to board the boat, the dive master told him that because he had not been diving recently he would have to have a companion with him at a cost of $100. Fortunately, my brother holds Advanced Open Water certification and has been diving for 20 years. He left and went down the road to Reef Divers at Cudjoe Key (see below).

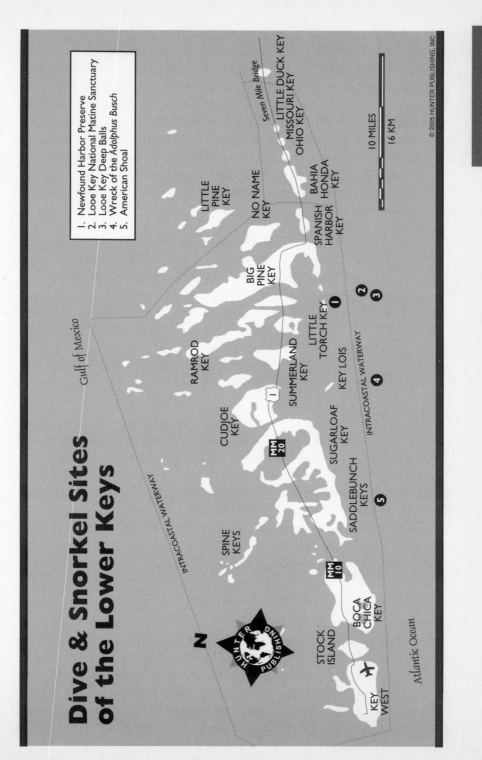

Dive & Snorkel Sites of the Lower Keys

1. Newfound Harbor Preserve
2. Looe Key National Matine Sanctuary
3. Looe Key Deep Balls
4. Wreck of the Adolphus Busch
5. American Shoal

Gulf of Mexico

INTRACOASTAL WATERWAY

SPINE KEYS

CUDJOE KEY

RAMROD KEY

LITTLE PINE KEY

NO NAME KEY

BIG PINE KEY

SUMMERLAND KEY

LITTLE TORCH KEY

SPANISH HARBOR KEY

BAHIA HONDA KEY

OHIO KEY
MISSOURI KEY
LITTLE DUCK KEY

Seven Mile Bridge

KEY LOIS

SUGARLOAF KEY

SADDLEBUNCH KEYS

INTRACOASTAL WATERWAY

MM 20

MM 10

STOCK ISLAND

BOCA CHICA KEY

KEY WEST

Atlantic Ocean

N

HUNTER PUBLISHING

10 MILES
16 KM

© 2005 HUNTER PUBLISHING, INC

Reef Divers, *MM 21 OS at Cudjoe Gardens Marina,*
☎ *305-515-2750, 877-886-6621, www.reef-divers.com*.
Operated by the thoroughly experienced Jim Wyatt,
Reef Divers offers only six-pack dives and has a fully
equipped dive shop. Two-tank dives with tanks and
weights run $59. The crew here is fully PADI certified
and offer all levels of training, including Nitrox and
Trimix certification courses. Most of their trips go to
Looe Key, but they also have three-tank dives to local
wrecks: *Aldolphus Busch* and the *Thunderbolt*. This is a
class operation.

> **AUTHOR TIDBIT:** It's hard to miss the white
> radar blimp known as "Fat Albert" that is sus-
> pended from a cable over Cudjoe Key and used
> by the Drug Enforcement Agency to look for un-
> savory activities in the Straits of Florida be-
> tween the Keys and Cuba. The blimp is also
> used by the US government to broadcast TV
> Marti, a Spanish-language television station
> aimed at a Cuban audience.

Snorkeling

This area has probably the best snorkeling spot in the entire
Keys – Looe Key – and even offers some reasonably good snorkeling close to shore. But like the rest of the Keys, the very best stuff
is a few miles offshore and you have to get there by boat. **Bahía
Honda State Park** (see *Parks*, above) has a couple of protected
snorkeling areas where you can see coral, brightly colored fish,
sea fans and more. If you are a strong swimmer you can reach
some interesting sand and grass ledges off the main beach on the
south side of Bahía Honda Key in about 10 feet of water. Watch
for the strong currents near the bridge.

The finger reefs of **Looe Key** are among the most wonderful
coral reef systems I've seen. Snorkelers can swim from channel to
channel following the reef as it changes from elkhorn coral in
shallow water to brain corals, giant sea fans and barrel sponges
in deeper water. On a calm day, Looe Key is a snorkeler's dream
but when things get rough, the waves break over the coral and
sweep onto the sand behind, making for tough conditions in the

shallow water. In such weather, head instead for a series of coral heads and smallish patches of coral in less than 10 feet of water just off **Newfound Harbor Keys** near Ramrod Key. The coral comes very close to the surface in places, posing a serious hazard to boaters, but creating a superb spot for snorkelers. You can see the giant red balls used to mark the corners of the protected area from far away. More coral heads are spread over many acres to the east.

For experienced snorkelers chasing the elusive spiny lobster, I'll break down and tell where one of my honey holes is (this is why I get paid the big bucks). Off the western tip of **West Summerland Key** near the old Boy Scout camp is a series of sand and turtle grass ledges in about 10 feet of water. They run for a mile or more on both sides of the channel and on both the ocean and the bay side of the bridge. The ledges are packed with lobsters. Within an hour, I almost always catch my fill at this spot. You need to have a boat or kayak as the current is almost always running briskly – that's what makes the ledges. As you drift along, dive down from time to time to tickle lobsters out of their hiding places. Watch out for sea urchins – the large black kind with very long spines are packed thickly in the same holes where lobsters hide out.

■ In the Air

If you're looking for a thrill out of the water and up in the air, head over to Sugarloaf Key.

■ OUTFITTER

Sky Dive Key West, *MM 17, Sugarloaf Key,* ☎ *305-745-4FUN, 800-968-5867, www.skydivekeywest.com.* You can't miss the big airplane by the side of the road on Sugarloaf Key. The operator caters to both experienced and first-time skydivers. The jumps start at 10,000 feet (almost two miles!), with a 40-second free fall and five-minute glide. Of course, jumpers sign lengthy disclaimers before their flights. I'm not sure you could call this a sightseeing opportunity since, unless you are particularly jaded, the experience may be so overwhelming you won't really think too much about whether you are falling through the air over the Keys or over Ardmore, Oklahoma. Prices are advertised as starting at $25. Although "Key West" appears in the name, they are actually 17 miles east on Sugarloaf Key.

Where to Stay

Accommodation choices are more limited here than in other, more developed parts of the Keys.

■ Ratings & Prices

 All the room prices in this book are for two people staying in a double room during high season. Taxes and meals are not included unless so mentioned. Hotels and lodges marked "Author's Choice" are my personal favorites, offering top quality lodging and services but, more importantly, something of particular interest or charm.

ACCOMMODATIONS PRICE CHART	
$	Under $100
$$	$100-200
$$$	$200-300
$$$$	Over $300

■ Hotels & Resorts

 Barnacle Bed & Breakfast, *Long Beach Drive, Big Pine Key,* ☎ *305-872-3298, 800-465-9100, www.thebarnacle. net, $$*, is small and quiet as befits a B&B. It has only four nicely appointed rooms. The atrium, which features a hot tub, is where a full breakfast is served.

Big Pine Resort Motel, *MM 30.5 BS, Big Pine Key,* ☎ *305-872-9090, fax 305-872-2816, www.bigpinekeymotel.com, $$*. This motel's 32 recently remodeled rooms appeal to budget divers.

There is a pool and plenty of parking for boat trailers. The location is great for trips to Looe Key. No pets.

Caribbean Village, *MM 10.7 BS, Big Coppitt Key,* ☎ *305-296-9542, fax 305-296-9503, $$*. This place is clean, neat and very close to Key West, but out of the hustle and bustle. The 32 rooms start at $35 per night, which is not bad for being so close to Key West. It is actually a little "village" of three small cottages and a couple of houseboats on the waterfront with a boat ramp and small beach. Some rooms have full kitchens.

Little Palm Island, *MM 28.5 OS, Little Torch Key,* ☎ *305-872-2524, 800-343-8567, fax 305-872-4843, www.littlepalm-island.com, $$$$+*. Rates are about $1,000/night for two people, all-inclusive, at the finest tourist property in the Keys. You have to take a boat to get here. All rooms are in separate, thatched, Pacific island-style huts raised off the sand to catch the trade winds. The restaurant is world-famous for fine cuisine prepared and presented with style and care. No TVs or phones make this a quiet, quiet, quiet place to relax and soak up luxury. The resort is very well located to take advantage of the fishing and diving in the Looe Key area. The dock is suitable for even the largest motor yachts. Presidents Roosevelt, Kennedy, Nixon and Truman have all stayed here. No children are allowed in either the hotel or restaurant.

Looe Key Reef Resort & Dive Center, *MM 27.5 OS, Ramrod Key,* ☎ *305-872-2215, 800-942-5397, www.diveflakeys.com, $$*. Set on a canal and with a boat ramp, marina services and PADI dive center, the Looe Key Reef Resort offers basic, motel-style rooms. The property is run-down and cheesy, but provides a basic place to stay and the air conditioning works. There is a pool. The cattle boat dive operation is in need of customer service training (see above).

Parmer's Resort, *MM 28.5 BS, Little Torch Key,* ☎ *305-872-2157, fax 305-872-2014, www.parmersplace.com, $$$*. Parmer's is an old Keys-style property with rooms spread out over several acres. Some units have kitchens. There is a pool and some dock space. No pets.

Sugarloaf Lodge, *MM 17 BS, Summerland Key,* ☎ *305-745-3211, 800-553-6097, fax 305-745-3389, $$*. The lodge has its own 3,000-foot airstrip, so if you arrive by small plane you can park it practically at the door to your room. The rooms are motel-style and face the water. There is a tennis court, pool and marina.

■ Camping

 Bahía Honda State Park, *MM 37 OS, Big Pine Key,* ☎ *305-872-3210, www.bahiahondapark.com, $.* The RV and tent sites at historic Bahía Honda State Park are some of the best in the Keys. Most have some shade, which is a rarity in the Keys. All sorts of water activities are catered to at the full-service marina. The park has what is probably the top beach in the Keys (see *Beaches,* above). The website gives a good idea of the activities and services they offer but, mysteriously, has no information about camping or an e-mail address to contact them. You'll have to call for details and reservations.

KOA - Sugarloaf Key, *MM20 OS, Summerland Key,* ☎ *305-745-3549, 800-KOA-7731, fax 305-745-9889, $$.* Close to Key West but quiet enough to enjoy, the campground offers tent and RV sites with a pool, beach and marina. Pet-friendly.

■ Vacation Rentals

 As is the case throughout the Keys, vacation homes rent for anywhere from $1,200 to $4000 per week for a two- or three-bedroom, modern home either on the water or near it. Nicer homes with docks and direct frontage on the bay or ocean command the highest rents.

Keys Rentals, *MM 23 OS, 22815 Port Royal Lane, Cudjoe Key,* ☎ *305-745-1919.*

Waterfront Realty, *MM 23 BS, 22966 Overseas Highway, Cudjoe Key,* ☎ *305-745-3911, fax 305-745-3951.*

Where to Eat

The price symbols for each listing consider the average cost of main courses listed on the menu.

RESTAURANT PRICE CHART

$	Under $8
$$	$8-12
$$$	$12-20
$$$$	Over $20

■ Recommendations

☆ **AUTHOR'S PICK** - **Geiger Key Smokehouse**, *MM 10.5, Geiger Key,* ☎ *305-296-3553, $$$.* Tucked away at the end of the road leading from Big Coppitt Key, Geiger Key is little more than a Tiki bar at a remote marina. This is a good thing. It is a hangout in the true sense of the expression. The quiet location makes this a nice place to simply sit in the shade, drink beer and eat fresh seafood. Blues music wafts through the air. They get my vote as the good place for the gainfully unemployed to go to seed, as well as for the best fish sandwich, which consists of two slabs of fresh fish fried, blackened or broiled with a choice of cheese, sautéed onions, lettuce, tomato and the usual sides of pickle slice, fries and slaw. If you want to actually pick this up and eat it like a sandwich, you will need to take about half of the fish off the sandwich and eat it separately before making the attempt. They have smoked fish and BBQ specials on the weekends, along with live entertainment. Because it is hard to find (turn on Boca Chica Road) and serves good food, the Smokehouse is a hangout for locals; few tourists make it here. Some locals never leave; some tourists become locals after a visit.

☆ **AUTHOR'S PICK** - **Little Palm Island Resort & Spa**, *MM 28.5 OS, Little Torch Key,* ☎ *305-872-2551, www.littlepalm-island.com, $$$$.* World-renowned Little Palm Island resort allows non-guests to enjoy the magnificent, gourmet-quality restaurant food at lunch and dinner. You must, however, reserve in advance. To get to the resort, guests are loaded on a small, elegant launch and taken across a mile or so of water to the island – there are no bridges. All this means the resort is extremely exclusive. The food is superb, but pricey, and the Sunday brunch is legendary. Refreshingly, no one under 16 is allowed in the dining room. Diners call ahead to arrange to be picked up by the launch that docks at Little Torch Key. This is probably the fanciest, most exclusive and expensive place to dine or stay in the Keys.

☆ **AUTHOR'S PICK** - **Raimondo's Ristorante**, *MM 21, Cudjoe Key*, ☎ *305-745-9999, $$*. A proper Italian restaurant with veal Marsala and scampi fra diablo.

■ Best of the Rest

Baby's Coffee Bar, *MM 15 OS, just north of Key West*, ☎ *800- 523-2326, www.babyscoffee.com, $*. The secret to great coffee is fresh roasting, and Baby's roasts theirs every day. Not far outside Key West, this is a must-stop for a delicious cup of Joe and a muffin or bagel. If you're not in the mood, buy a bag o' beans for later. You can find Baby's coffee on the menu at a few eateries in the Keys and, when you do, you know you are going to have a good cup.

Bay Point Pizza, *MM 15, just north of Key West*, ☎ 305-745-2149, $$. Pizza, subs, salads, pasta and real Philly cheese steaks. Delivered!

Bobalu's Southern Café, *MM 10 BS, Big Coppitt Key*, ☎ *305-296-1664, $*. If the place is good enough for Jimmy Buffet, I steer clear. Just joking! Bobalu's plain but good, solid food is popular with locals and drags many of them in from as far away as Key West. The parrot head himself is said to come by for a burger from time to time. Pizza, blackberry cobbler, fried chicken and other hardy fare is on offer. Open for lunch and dinner every day, except Monday. Beer only.

Mangrove Mama's, *MM 20 BS, Sugarloaf Key*, ☎ *305-745-3030, $$*. Mama serves lunch and dinner daily. Only good, fresh shrimp are used – nothing frozen here. There is a pretty good wine list. Bring your sunglasses as the paint job is extremely bright.

Montego Bay, *MM 30.2 BS, Big Pine Key*, ☎ *305-872-3009, $*. Serves steaks, shrimp and big salads for lunch and dinner every day.

Monte's Restaurant & Fish Market, *MM 25 BS, Summerland Key*, ☎ *305-745-3731, $*. This really is a fish market, but it also serves wonderful seafood on open-air picnic tables. Good seafood is not cheap anywhere in the Keys, but at least at Monte's you know you're getting the really fresh stuff. And prices are not bad, considering what you pay for a few frozen, breaded shrimp at the touristy spots in Key West. If you want to pig out on seafood, this is a good spot.

No Name Pub, *MM 31 BS, North Watson Boulevard, Big Pine Key,* ☎ *305-872-9115, $*. If you can take the time to look for it (it's just before the bridge to No Name Key), the No Name Pub is a small bar that serves pizza and seafood baskets. There are autographed dollar bills stuck up all over the walls and the atmosphere is definitely Keysey. Lots of locals hang around at lunch and in the evenings.

The Sandbar, *MM 28.5 BS, Little Torch Key,* ☎ *305-872-9989, $$$*. You can't miss it. The huge sign on top of the two-story Sandbar can be seen from the bridge as you approach from the east. The bar serves the usual, not-very-memorable fried and broiled seafood. Other than the huge sign, there is nothing to set the Sandbar apart from the thousand or so other Keys bars serving mediocre seafood and over-priced beer. There's nothing really wrong with the place, I just couldn't see any reason to go back.

Nightlife

Due to the lack of commercial development in the Lower Keys, there are few nightlife options. If you're serious about your evening out, I suggest rounding up a designated driver and heading down to Key West where the choices for nighttime dissolution are staggering.

Looe Key Tiki Bar, *MM 27.5 OS, Ramrod Key at the Looe Key Resort,* ☎ *305-872-2215*. Reasonable blender drinks and draft beer make this an oasis for the thirsty. They have live entertainment on the weekends and sometimes during the week. You could spend an evening here keeping a bar stool from blowing away in the trade wind. Happy hour is 5-7 pm, Monday through Friday. Wings, shrimp and the usual bar snacks can be had.

The Sandbar, *MM 28.5 BS, Little Torch Key,* ☎ *305-872-9989*. Otherwise a boring choice, the Sandbar has special event evenings for occasions like the Superbowl and the Kentucky Derby.

Occasionally, they have some live music. The drinks are ho-hum and the atmosphere is a bit down-market. Once was enough for me.

Key West

Key West is without doubt a tourist town. Go with the flow: put on your shorts and fanny pack, drape your camera around your neck, buy a loud shirt, suck down a few piña coladas and get in the mood. Take a trolley or the **Conch Train** to get a feel for the whole island on your first day. Besides being one of the premier party towns in the US, Key West is

a center for a wide variety of outdoor adventures you just can't duplicate elsewhere. When I am here I spend my first day wandering around Old Town admiring the period homes. The rest of the time I fish, dive, explore the surrounding aquatic environment and get myself out to the Dry Tortugas for birding. One of the best things about Key West is the large number of excellent restaurants – both high- and low-priced – that serve mountains of fresh seafood. I'm not much of a bar person; I'm usually ready for milk and cookies at about 8 o'clock. But I love going to **Sloppy Joe's** to catch some of the best live entertainment in the Keys. Don't miss the childish adult comedy act **Pete & Wayne** at Sloppy's if it is on when you are here.

At a Glance

LARGEST TOWN: Key West, population 25,478

ELEVATION: Eight feet

AREA: 5.9 square miles

COUNTY: Monroe

MAJOR ROUTES: Overseas Highway (US 1)

NEAREST AIRPORTS: Key West (0 miles); Marathon (52)

ZIP CODE: 33040
AVERAGE TEMPERATURE: January 70.3°; August 84.4°
PRECIPITATION: January 2.2 inches; August 5.4 inches

Getting Here & Getting Around

All roads in the Keys (there's really only one) lead to Key West. The **Overseas Highway** heads past Marathon and ends up, well, at the end. When you initially arrive in Key West the road splits, going either left or right around the island in both directions. Baseball legend Yogi Berra once said, "When you come to a fork in the road, take it." I suggest checking your map and figuring out where your destination is before you get to town to avoid confusion when you reach this particular fork in the road. Traffic in Key West is usually intense but slow and it helps if you have a clue before you are subsumed. Left takes you toward the airport, the beach and, eventually, Old Town. Right takes you past shopping centers and the harbor area to Old Town.

Key West International Airport, *Roosevelt Boulevard,* ☎ *305-296-5439*, is on the southeastern part of the island and is served by **American Eagle**, ☎ *800-433-7300*, **Cape Air**, ☎ *305-293-0603*, **Delta**, ☎ *800-221-1212*, **Continental Connection**, ☎ *305-294-1421*, and **USAir Express**, ☎ *800-428-4322*. Connections can be made through Miami, Atlanta and Fort Lauderdale, although cities with direct flights change frequently – check the Web for the latest routes.

The airport is probably where you will be when needing a **rental car**, but most agencies will deliver to your hotel if you ask. The following agancies can be found at the airport: **Alamo**, ☎ *305-294-6675, 877-252-6600, www.alamo.com*; **Avis**, ☎ *305-296-8744, 800-331-1212, www.avis.com*; **Budget**, ☎ *305-294-8868, 800-527-0700, www.budget.com*; **Dollar**, ☎ *305-296-9921, 800-800-3665, www.budget.com*; **Hertz**, ☎ *305-294-1039, 800-654-3131, www.hertz.com*.

Above: A seaplane lands at Fort Jefferson.

Below: A working boat sifts for emeralds.

Above: Dry Tortugas National Park.
Opposite: Colorful paintwork adorns many Key West buildings.
Below: Snorkeling can yield interesting finds.

Above: Sloppy Joe's, a well-known Key West landmark.

Below: Cypress hammock, Everglades.

Above: The Keys have plenty of secluded B&Bs.

Below: The region's spectacular water draws anglers, sailors and more.

Above: Tarpon in a feeding frenzy.
Opposite: Lighthouse.
Below: A beach that stretches as far as the eye can see.

Above: An alligator lurks among the reeds.

Below: Fort Jefferson makes a great day-trip.

Parking in Key West can be a problem when the city fills up with revelers. One neat solution is to park in the Old Town Parking Garage on the corner of Caroline and Grinnell streets and ride the free air-conditioned shuttle all over town.

> **WARNING:** Illegally parked cars are frequently towed. More than once I have heard a tourist shout "Hey! That's my car!" upon seeing a loaded tow truck creeping through the traffic down Duval Street.

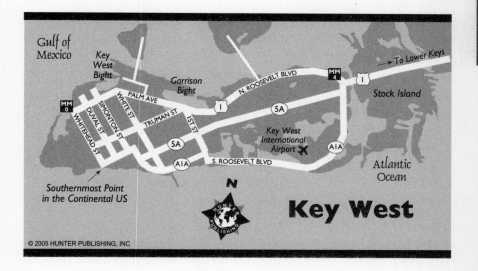

The Hilton Hotel near Mallory Square is easy to find and has a guarded parking garage convenient to the action. It's okay to use the parking garage even if you are not a guest. Take a ticket and pay (by the hour) when you leave.

Area History & Highlights

Early Spanish travelers referred to Key West as "Cayo Hueso" or "Key of Bones," perhaps because early visitors found enormous numbers of bones on the island. Speculation has it that the bones were the remains of shipwrecked sailors who died of thirst, starvation and exposure to the harsh climate. Since the key is one of the most westerly in the Keys and perhaps because of the similarity in sound of "hueso" and "west," the name was anglicized into "Key West."

Florida and the Keys became a part of the US in 1821 and Key West was a busy port for transshipment of goods between Havana and the Northern United States. Piracy in the early 1800s, wrecking, sponging and the tobacco trade gave Key West periods of prosperity that are reflected today in the hundreds of beautiful homes built with the wealth generated by these economic booms. Economic ups and downs, as well as a major 1846 hurricane with an eight-foot storm surge that almost flattened the town, slowed down growth at times.

By 1890 the population was 18,020. For a time it was Florida's largest city. The arrival of the railroad in 1912 made the town and its port even more strategic. The 1935 hurricane wiped out the railroad and, coupled with the Great Depression, caused Key West to suffer a period of lean times and an almost complete collapse of the new tourism industry. In 1938 the Overseas Highway was completed, allowing travelers to drive to Key West. This made a second tourism boom inevitable.

World War II also helped bring the city into a more prosperous time with a large Naval presence. By 1965 the civilian population was 26,000, with an additional 18,000 military and dependents. Shrimping further boosted the local economy. After the Cuban Missile Crisis the military presence was much reduced, but tourism continued to build.

In 1982, in an attempt to curb illegal immigration and drug smuggling, federal agents set up road blocks with inspection points discouraging visitors and angering residents. Due to the reduction in the tourism business this caused, Key West and the Keys declared independence and seceded from the US, forming the Conch Republic. They set up their own blockade and issued their own money and passports. Improvements in the Overseas Highway, a modern airport and cruise ship docking facilities ensured Key West's growth into a major tourism destination.

Services

■ Bookstores

Key West has a couple of good bookstores and one great one.

☆ **AUTHOR'S PICK** - **Key West Island Books**, *513 Flemming Street,* ☎ *305-294-2904.* For an unusual selection of great books, you can't beat Key West Island Books. They have a very eclectic range, with the best choice of Florida history and Keys guidebooks I've seen. They also sell a few used books. It's very hard for me to walk out of this place without spending more than I had planned.

Walden's Books, *2212 North Roosevelt Boulevard,* ☎ *305-294-5419.* The same old Walden's you'll find anywhere.

Valladares L and Son, *1200 Duval Street,* ☎ *305-296-5032.* This is the place to get your out-of-town newspapers and foreign magazines.

■ Public Library

Key West has a pleasant and quiet library at 700 Flemming Street, where you can read up on local history, architecture, birds, fishing or anything else. It has an excellent section on Florida history.

■ Film Processing

There are dozens of one-hour photo places around town. If you need something more complex or just want to be sure you get good service, head to **Pro Photo**, *1020 Duval Street,* ☎ *305-294-9908.* They offer complete professional development services and can put your film shots (negative or positive) on CD-ROM at a reasonable price.

Sightseeing

▪ Suggested Itineraries

Key West is a walking town, but it can be very hot during most of the year. As you walk around, keep to the shady side of the street and drink plenty of non-alcoholic liquids. You may want to plan your day so that mid-afternoon is spent by the pool, on the beach or inside someplace with air-conditioning. Mornings are cooler and the action on Duval Street starts in early evening. Sloppy Joe's cranks up at an early 5:30 pm.

> **AUTHOR TIDBIT:** If you indulge in luscious tropical drinks, or even beer, in the afternoon, try to drink a good amount of water (or other non-alcoholic liquid) before you head out for the evening to avoid early burnout.

If You Have One Day

Driving down from Miami to enjoy the delights of Key West and back again in the same day would be an exhausting and not particularly rewarding effort. You would get to see spectacular scenery form the Overseas Highway as you cruise down, but you'll want to be asleep in the back seat on the way back. If you fly in or arrive on a cruise ship for the day, you have enough time to enjoy town. To get a good overall feel for what Key West has to offer, take the **Conch Train**, even though it may be hokey or touristy. Hop on the 90-minute narrated tour at *601 Duval Street,* ☎ *305-294-5161, www.conchtrain.com.* Tours run from 9 to 4:30 pm every day of the year and cost $20. An alternate way to go is aboard the **Old Town Trolley**, ☎ *305-292-8906.* The $18 narrated tour leaves from Mallory Square and makes 10 stops as it goes through almost all of Key West; you can hop on and off as often as you like. If you want some exercise while you tour, **Lloyd's Original Key West Bike Tours**, ☎ *305-294-1882*, is a good way to soak up the history of

Old Town and have a chance to admire the unique Key West architecture.

A lunch of conch fritters or a fish sandwich at **Johnson's Café**, *306 Petronia Street/801 Thomas Street,* ☎ *305-292-2286*, is hard to beat. After your meal, check out either the **Key West Aquarium**, *Mallory Square at 1 Whitehead Street,* ☎ *305-296-2051, www.keywestaquarium.com*, or **The Little White House**, *111 Front Street,* ☎ *305-294-9911, www.trumanlittlewhitehouse.com*, before gravitating to the Duval Street tropical beverage emporiums for people-watching and refreshment towards the end of the day.

Just after watching the sun sizzle into the sea near Mallory Square, you'll probably be ready to fill your belly with food again. Key West has wonderful fine dining opportunities. If your credit cards have room, go to **Seven Fish**, *632 Olivia Street,* ☎ *305-296-2777, www.7fish.com*, for exquisitely prepared and presented seafood and a bottle or two of fine wine.

If you don't have to get back onboard your ship immediately after dinner, take in the wildlife on Duval Street. I suggest **Sloppy Joe's**, *201 Duval Street,* ☎ *305-294-5717, www.sloppyjoes.com*, for beer and the best live entertainment in town. If you have any of your day (night, at this point) left, go with the local music lovers to the **Green Parrot**, *601 Whitehead Street,* ☎ *305-294-6133, www.greenparrot.com*, for late-night refreshment and blues.

If You Have Three Days

3 DAYS Three days lets you enjoy the earthly delights of Key West and still have time for a solid day's fishing or a two-tank dive. On Day One, I recommend for people to take the **Conch Train** or the **Old Town Trolley** (see above for details on both). This way you can easily see the Little White House (details above); **Hemingway House**, *907 Whitehead Street,* ☎ *305-294-1575*; **Jimmy Buffet House**, *3624-3628 Sunrise Drive;* and check out some of the other attractions, restaurants and night spots you have heard about as you cruise by in comfort. Lunch at one of the people-watching spots on Duval Street (like **Margaritaville**, *500 Duval Street,* ☎ *305-292-1435*) is a good idea or you can act like a local and have wonderful, *muy auténtico* Cuban food at **El Siboney**, *900 Catherine Street,*

☎ *305-296-4184*. After lunch, take a nap or go on a bike tour with **Lloyd's Original Key West Bike Tours**, ☎ *305-294-1882*, through Old Town to find out about some of the interesting old houses.

I suggest stretching dinner out to an hour or two and taking it easy while enjoying the show. Get a seat with a view of the weirdness on Duval Street in a good restaurant like **Square One**, *1075 Duval Street*, ☎ *305-296-4300*. For nightlife, try the **Afterdeck Bar**, *700 Waddell Street in Louie's Backyard*, ☎ *305-294-1061*. Jimmy Buffett used to play here for drinks, or so the stories go. Tourists and locals hang out and listen to live music on weekend nights.

On Day Two, a long half-day sightseeing trip by seaplane to **Fort Jefferson** in the nearby Dry Tortugas is worth your time. Call ahead to **Seaplanes of Key West**, ☎ *305-294-0709 or 800-950-2FLY, www.seaplanesofkeywest.com*, to check departure times.

Fort Jefferson.

Try **Seven Fish**, *632 Olivia Street*, ☎ *305-296-2777, www.7fish. com*, for your evening meal. After-dinner fun for me starts at **Sloppy Joe's** (see above), followed by a casual walk down Duval Street for a mild mental shock provided by the other people walking casually down Duval Street. Buy the paper to find out what type of bands and live shows are on for the evening. There are lots of live entertainers in Key West, but the low pay and expensive lodging mean many are rather lame. Sloppy Joe's rarely has a stinker, and almost anything playing at the **Green Parrot** (see above) will be good. Barry Cuda is a good musician to look for. I try to end up in the Green Parrot for late-night refreshment. There is usually a local crowd and many musicians hang out here after their early sets.

On the last day of your visit, Day Three, a dive, snorkeling trip or anything else that involves getting salt water all over you may not be a good idea if you won't have access to a freshwater shower before putting on traveling clothes for the plane/car/boat trip back home. Instead, breakfast by the pool followed by a dash down Duval Street for last-minute trinket shopping is a good way to handle the leaving Key West blues.

If You Have a Week

7 DAYS A full week in Key West is plenty of time to enjoy the island and the associated watersports, as well as visit the Upper or Middle Keys. Some of the backcountry of Everglades National Park is also within reach. If you have a particular sporting interest you want to indulge extensively, such as fishing or diving, you can go for full-day charters.

Day One in Key West is best spent getting to know the basic layout of the island and what it has to offer. The **Old Town Trolley,** ☎ *305-292-8906*, and the **Conch Train,** ☎ *305-294-5161,* offer a good introduction in comfort and they even hand out fans on hot days. As you tour, be sure to give some thought to which of the various fine beverage emporiums on Duval Street you want to visit later in the day. Have conch fritters or a fish sandwich lunch at **Johnson's Café** (see above), do some casual walking around town in the afternoon, and catch the sunset action at **Mallory Square** at the end of the day. For dinner, taste the ribs at **The Meteor Smokehouse**, *404 Southard Street,* ☎ *305-294-5602,* for dinner. If you are a music fan, stop by **Sloppy Joe's** for early evening entertainment.

On Day Two you'll find the charms of wandering around Old Town are enhanced if you take a guided walking or bike tour. You

Key West

can ride with **Lloyd's Original Key West Bike Tours**, ☎ 305-294-1882, then go back on your own to the parts of town that seem most interesting. Have lunch at **Mangoes**, *700 Duval Street*, ☎ *305-292-4606*. Try to get a table with a good view of the crowd on Duval Street. After lunch, take your pick of touristy things. I suggest the **Little White House**, *111 Front Street*, ☎ *305-294-9911*, *www.trumanlittlewhitehouse.com*, and the **Key West Aquarium**, *Mallory Square at 1 Whitehead Street*, ☎ *305-296-2051*, *www.keywestaquarium.com*. For dinner, it's hard to beat **Square One**, *1075 Duval Street*, ☎ *305-296-4300*, *www.squareonerestaurant.com*. Stretching dinner out to an hour or two and take it easy while you watch the street show. For nightlife, head to the **Afterdeck Bar** (see above).

Traditional Key West architecture.

On Day Three, zap around town on a **moped**. I suggest doing a one-day rental and turning in the moped just after dinner. Mopeds are a great way to see town, but you certainly don't want to be driving a moped (or anything else) around town when you've got a buzz on. A moped will allow you to cruise around town and get to some of the out-of-the-way attractions, like **Smathers Beach**. Have lunch at **Alonzo's Oyster House**, *700 Front Street*, ☎ *305-294-5880*, followed by a drive through Old

Town and by the **Jimmy Buffet House**, *3624-3628 Sunrise Drive.* End up at **Margaritaville**, *500 Duval Street,* ☎ *305-292-1435,* just to keep the mood flowing. Have dinner at **Seven Fish**, *632 Olivia Street,* ☎ *305-296-2777, www.7fish.com.*

Day Four is spent in the **Dry Tortugas** soaking up history and sun. The most fun way to get there is by seaplane. Call ahead to **Seaplanes of Key West**, ☎ *305-294-0709 or 800-950-2FLY, www.seaplanesofkeywest.com.* When you get back, freshen up at your hotel and get dressed for a very special dinner at **Café Marquesa**, *600 Fleming Street,* ☎ *305-292-1244.* If you want to play late, head to the Green Parrot for drinks and blues. Or, for late, late action, try **Wax**, *422 Applerouth Lane,* ☎ *305-304-6988.*

Start Day Five with breakfast at **Pepe's Café**, 806 Caroline Street, ☎ 305-294-7192, then scuba dive, snorkel and shop. Book a reef trip at least two weeks ahead with **Blue Water Charters**, *Galleon Marina Slip #2,* ☎ *305-304-8888, 866-304-8666, www. bluewatercharters.com.* Back on land, enjoy an authentic Cuban lunch at **El Siboney**, *900 Catherine Street,* ☎ *305-296-4184.* Use the afternoon to stock up on souvenirs and presents. Stroll up and down Duval Street for the usual tourist purchases, take your loot back to your hotel, then rest up before heading to dine at **Café Solé**, *1029 Southard Street at Frances,* ☎ *305-294-0230, www.cafesole.com.* It's always safe to spend another evening at **Sloppy Joe's** and the **Green Parrot**, but if you see other places that appeal to you, head in and have a good time.

Start Day Six with breakfast at **Camille's Restaurant**, *703½ Duval Street,* ☎ *305-296-4811, www.camilleskeywest.com,* and get them to pack you a lunch for your day fishing offshore or backcountry with the **Lucky Fleet**, *Land's End Marina by Turtle Kraals,* ☎ *305-294-7988, 800-292-3096.* When you get back, you'll already be in the right place to have dinner at **Turtle Kraals Waterfront Seafood Grill & Bar**, *231 Margaret Street at Land's End Marina,* ☎ *305-294-2640.* I like to finish a Key West evening by strolling along Duval Street people-watching and listening for any interesting-sounding music in the bars. sure you know by now.

On Day Seven, check out of your hotel at a reasonable hour and start your drive back to Miami. Stop at **Baby's Coffee Bar** just outside Key West at MM 15 OS, for a cup of good coffee and a snack. Stop for a short walk at start of the Seven Mile Bridge. Park on the bay side (left) and walk out over the old Overseas Highway Bridge. Back in the car heading north, have lunch at the **Island Tiki Bar & Restaurant**, *MM 54 BS, Marathon,* ☎ *305-743-4191,* and stop in Homestead for at late BBQ dinner at **Shivers**, *28001 Dixie Hwy.*

■ Attractions

GETTING FROM A TO B

Old Town Trolley, ☎ *305-292-8906.* If you've never been to Key West before, take the Old Town Trolley before you do anything else. The $18 narrated tour leaves from Mallory Square and makes 10 stops as it goes through most of town. You can get on and off all you like. If you see something that grabs your interest, hop off at the next stop. When you're ready, jump on any of the trolleys going by. This will keep your feet from hurting.

Old Town Trolley guides are locals who point out their favorite restaurants and tell you who is playing at Sloppy Joe's. Trolleys can handle handicapped passengers.

The **Conch Train** is very touristy, but it's still a good way to get a comfortable introduction to the sights and sounds of the city. When I was a small child I thought this was the height of adventure. To enjoy your ride, remember who you are – a tourist – and go ahead and let yourself be an unembarrassed one. You don't have to tell your pals back in Carbondale you went on the Conch Train, but you'll be able to tell about some interesting Key West trivia you learned on the tour. Hop on the 90-minute narrated tour at *601 Duval Street,* ☎ *305-294-5161, www.conchtrain.com.* This is a good way to see parts of the city you would never find or hear about on your own. Tours run from 9 to 4:30 every day of the year and cost $20.

Any place where large numbers of tourists congregate tends to develop cheesy tourist attractions and Key West has its share. It also has some wonderful, historic and interesting things to see.

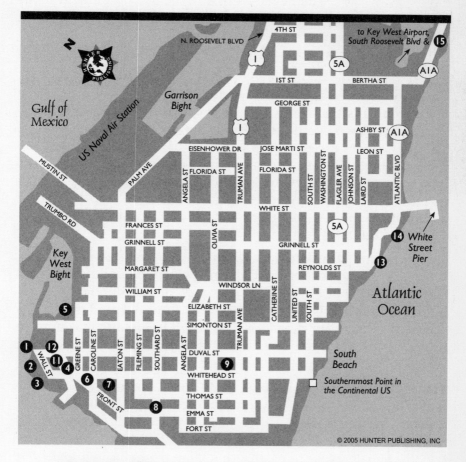

Old Town Key West

1. Sunset Pier
2. Mallory Square
3. Chamber of Commerce
4. Mel Fisher Maritime Museum
5. Historic Seaport & Boardwalk
6. Audubon House & Garden
7. Harry S. Truman Little White House
8. Fort Zachary Taylor Entrance
9. Hemingway House & Museum
10. Jimmy Buffet's Old House
11. Key West Aquarium
12. Key West Shipwreck Historuem
13. CB Harvey Rest Beach Park
14. Clarence S Higgs Memorial Beach
15. Smathers Beach

Audubon House & Tropical Gardens, *Whitehead Street between Caroline and Greene streets*, ☎ *305-294-2116*, is where John James Audubon lived and worked in the "Geiger House," dating from 1840. The house itself and the surrounding gardens are interesting. The antiques indoors and exotic garden plantings are the main points of interest. There is a self-guided tour. The museum is open from 9:30 until 5 daily, and your $10 entrance fee includes viewing the gardens.

Mallory Square is a small tourist trap-lined square near the waterfront. It's known for the lively crowds that gather in it every evening to watch the sunset and marvel at street performers. The performers range from a one-man-band, body painters and fire jugglers to the guy who has trained his cats to do circus tricks (you have to see this one to believe it). Most of the activity is not actually in Mallory Square itself, but takes place on the adjacent docks where there is a long promenade with a world-famous sunset view.

The historic **Hemingway House**, *907 Whitehead Street*, ☎ *305-294-1575*, is filled with all things Hemingway. A brick wall the writer had built to keep tourists out still surrounds the building. Now that he is dead, the tourists (and descendants of his cats) have the run of the place. The architecture and gardens are interesting and, if you are a Hemingway buff, the memorabilia inside is fascinating.

Jimmy Buffet's Old House, *3624-3628 Sunrise Drive*. While parrotheads know Mr. Buffett has given up on the Keys for greener pastures, they still get a kick out of driving by his old house. Recently on the market for a mere $2 million, the property has little on show for tourists, other than bushes and a roof – but that seems to be enough for hard-core fans. No doubt it will become a proper attraction like Hemingway's old house at some point.

Key West Aquarium, *in Mallory Square at 1 Whitehead Street*, ☎ *305-296-2051*, *www.keywestaquarium.com*, *10-6 every day*. Dating from 1932 and claiming to be the first tourist attraction in the Keys, the Key West Aquarium is still a "must see" for the first-time visitor. You can get close to some really big and ferocious fish. Giant sharks thrash around during feeding time in the outdoor pens and tiny colorful reef fish flit about in small tanks lining the walls inside. Although a major tourist trap, it actually has a decent display of things you can see if you were to snorkel on the reefs just offshore. I've paid my $9 entrance fee many times and hope to do so many more.

Key West Shipwreck Historeum, *Mallory Square*, ☎ *305-292-8990, www.shipwreckhistoreum.com, 9:45-6:45 daily, $9*. In a town full of tourist traps, this one takes the cake. The Historeum (whatever that means), is a small old warehouse filled with a few fake relics purportedly from shipwrecks. The idea is to present the history of the wrecking industry that made Key West, for a short while, the wealthiest town in the US. The results are weak, weak, weak. I feel sorry for the people who work here in their demeaning jobs as guides. A tower rising above the building gives a good view of the cruise ship dock and the area around Mallory Square, but your $9 entry fee would be better spent on, well, almost anything else.

Harry S. Truman Little White House Museum, *111 Front Street*, ☎ *305-294-9911, www.trumanlittlewhitehouse.com*. If you have any interest at all in US history, a visit to the Little White House is well worth your time. The building itself is listed on the National Register of Historic Places and is filled with authentic items owned and loved by the Truman family. Harry's fantastic, custom-made poker table is, in my opinion, the star of the show. In a phone call to Bess made just three days after my birthday, he said "... I've a notion to move the capitol to Key West and just stay." Sounds like a good idea to me. Fully narrated tours are led by extremely knowledgeable guides who are familiar with the smallest Truman trivia and they challenge you to stump them. They bring Truman and his era to life as you walk through the old house and examine the photographs and period furniture that the Trumans once used. This is one of the best attractions in Key West. Don't miss it.

When you are done with the tour you can walk up Front Street and see dozens of restored Key West homes controversially converted to time-shares and condos.

Drag Queens & Other Interesting People on Duval Street. Although not an actual "attraction" as such, the people-watching here can't be beat. After a few minutes spent strolling down Duval Street in the evening, both men and women visitors will likely find themselves admiring the beautiful people displaying large parts of their bodies in revealing outfits. Realize that some of the most attractive women you see may not be women at all. They may not be exactly men in women's clothing either. Be fore-warned that the more outrageous drag queens enjoy goofing on tourists by flirting outrageously and provocatively. You're not in Kansas anymore, so relax and enjoy the show or join in.

> **AUTHOR TIDBIT:** Key West is well known as a haven for people of all sexual flavors and toler-ance is the rule rather than the exception. While flamboyant clothing is common, during some of the more intense party periods like Fantasy Fest, the lack of any clothing is also noticeable. If you are with kids, or if nudity offends you, plan accordingly.

■ Beaches

Unlike the rest of the Keys, Key West actually has a few beaches in the true Florida sense of the word. The sand may be trucked in and the water shallow and wave-free, but there is a proper crowd of people sitting under umbrellas, stretched out on towels and doing all the things you would ex-pect. All beaches are on the Atlantic side.

C.B. Harvey Rest Beach Park, near the White Street Pier, has been nicely landscaped and has several picnic areas. It is small and fairly private, a good place for a romantic view of the sunrise if you are inclined to get up that early or have somehow managed to stay up all night.

Clarence S. Higgs Memorial Beach, or "County Beach," as the locals know it, is a long stretch of white sand with all sorts of things to do. There are six tennis courts, covered picnic spots, a walking/fishing pier, showers and restrooms, volleyball and handball courts, a playground and a kiddies' play area. Vendors selling things to eat, drink and rent line the road. It is on Atlantic Avenue at the end of White Street.

Smathers Beach, near the airport on South Roosevelt Boule-vard, lacks much in the way of shade, but it does have a picnic area, restrooms and volleyball. I used to come here snorkeling when I was a kid and would find hundreds of lost fishing sinkers and snagged lures. Fun!

■ Parks

Fort Zachary Taylor State Historic Site, ☎ *305-292-6713.* You must pass through the Truman Annex at the end of Southard Street to the historic Fort Zach. Although it has seen nothing that could be called "action," the fort was built by the Army during the 1850s over concerns of invasion by Spain. It was occupied by the Union during the Civil War and eventually turned over to the Navy. During the Spanish America War, it was deemed to be of strategic importance, but still saw no action. During the Cuban missile crisis, radar and other detection equipment was quickly upgraded and for once the fort actually was of strategic importance. The fort is on the National Register of Historic Places and is a National Historic Landmark. It's a peaceful place to walk and the beach is quite attractive. There are restrooms, showers and picnic/BBQ facilities. The fishing along the seawall can be good. Daily tours start at noon and 2 pm.

> **AUTHOR TIDBIT:** Dr. Mudd, who attended Lincoln's assassin John Wilkes Booth, spent four years in prison at Fort Zachary Taylor for his troubles.

Adventures

Adventures in Key West come in many categories – some not to be described in a family book. If you tear yourself away from the bars and entertainment emporiums around Duval Street, you'll find Key West has all the outdoor pleasures of the Keys close by – sailing, diving, fishing, flying in dubious-looking aircraft, birding, paddling and even golf. Some people actually spend a couple of weeks here doing adventurous things in the water and never even walk down Duval Street at all.

■ On Foot

 One of the very best things to do on foot is simply to wander around Old Town admiring the beautiful old homes and their tropical landscaping. It costs nothing and can soak up an entire morning or afternoon.

> **AUTHOR NOTE:** Realize that it can get very hot here. Bring a hat, water and try to stay on the shady side of the street as much as possible.

Birding

While you can see some interesting birds in Key West and on some of the surrounding mangrove islands, the **Dry Tortugas** are within easy reach and are one of the premier birding venues in South Florida, with over 200 varieties recorded. The remoteness of the area as well as its sub-tropical climate makes it a favorite for birders and nature enthusiasts. The **Marquesas** are closer to Key West, but they lack popular tourist activities and so fewer operators visit them. The Marquesas are a good place to observe water birds. For information on plane and boat charters to the Tortugas and Marquesas, see the list of operators in the *Adventures in the Air* and *Adventures on Water* sections.

SOOTY TERN SANCTUARY

As you step off the ferry or seaplane at Fort Jefferson, you can't help but notice thousands of sooty terns swirling about above their nests just a few yards away. The isthmus leading to the nesting grounds on Bush Key is blocked to casual visitors, and only accredited researchers are allowed to get within a couple of hundred feet from the site. This is the only sooty tern nesting site in North America and the clouds of birds are nothing less than magnificent.

Birds you can see in Key West, the Marquesas and the Dry Tortugas include black-throated blue warblers, ovenbirds, black-poll warblers, common yellowthroats, frigate birds, black skimmers, gulls, pelicans, northern gannets, masked and brown boobies, pomarine jaegers, American redstarts and many more.

Golf

The only golf course in Key West is a public facility on the east end of the island.

Key West Golf Club, *6450 East College Road,* ☎ *305-294-5232*. Rees Jones designed this 18-hole course. Green and cart fees run from $80 to $150, depending on the season. Call about their early bird and twilight specials. Key West can get very hot, so a very early tee time is a good idea.

■ On Wheels

Key West is littered with bike and motor scooter rentals and the city lends itself well to two-wheeled exploration. The only problem is the fierce and dangerous traffic. This leads some cyclists to use the sidewalks (not a good idea), sharing the danger with pedestrians. Afternoon drinking, and even morning or before-breakfast drinking, is almost the norm in this throw-your-cares-to-the-winds tourist town, which puts the two-wheeled tourist in even greater danger. Drinking only water while on two wheels is always good advice. Expect to pay about $12 per day for bicycle rental.

> **AUTHOR TIDBIT:** Bargain when looking for bike or scooter rentals; most of the agents are on commission and will "work with you" if you suggest you may try another agency.

Several agencies offer guided bike tours; ask ahead of time. Lloyd's, below, even specializes in tours that will keep kids happy and fascinated.

■ OUTFITTERS

Bike Key West Tours, *534 Flemming Street,* ☎ *305-294-8380*

Bike Shop, *1110 Truman Street,* ☎ *305-294-1073*

Conch Bike Express, *930 Eaton Street,* ☎ *305-294-4318*, will deliver bikes to your hotel and pick them up when you are through. They charge from $12 per day and have a selection of regular old fat-wheeled, six-speed and kids' bikes, as well as trikes.

☆ **AUTHOR'S PICK** - **Lloyd's Original Key West Bike Tours**, ☎ *305-294-1882*. Mr. Lloyd leads guided bike tours through the scenic back streets and popular tourist areas of Key West, specializing in keeping kids fascinated. He makes several stops to sample fresh fruit picked from trees growing along the route. Tours cost approximately $40.

Paradise Scooter Rentals, *112 Fitzpatrick Street & 430 Duval Street,* ☎ *305-293-1112,* rents both bikes and scooters. Rates are $25 per hour, $60 per day.

There are plenty of **taxis** and, if you are staying on the other end of the island from the action, you will probably find yourself using them. You can bargain with the drivers once you have a feel for what prices are like. Call **Mom's Taxi**, ☎ *305-852-6000*, or **All Island Taxi**, ☎ *305-664-4688*.

■ On Water

The end of the road is not the end of the Keys. West from Key West lie the less-frequented **Marquesas** and **Dry Tortugas**. The Marquesas are a group of islands separated from Key West by a few miles of flats and sand channels. They are easily reached by boat. The Dry Tortugas are a long one-day haul from Key West, but why try to do it in one day? There are facilities at Fort Jefferson for campers and a snug harbor for visiting boats. Fishing and diving in both the Marquesas and the Dry Tortugas is probably the best in the Keys due to their isolation and lack of facilities – there is simply less traffic than other, easier to reach parts of the Keys.

There are two public **boat ramps** in the Key West area. One is at the end of A1A (turn left at the split when you first get to Key West and keep going); the other is at the end of Simonton St. Stock Island Ramp.

Boat Tours & Sunset Cruises

Dry Tortugas Ferry, *240 Margaret Street, Key West Seaport,* ☎ *305-294-7009, 800-634-0939, www.yankeefreedom.com,* offers a full-day trip to Fort Jefferson in the Dry Tortugas aboard the *Yankee Cat.* The boat leaves at 8 am from Land's End Marina at the end of Margaret Street. There are parking garages on the corner of Caroline St. and Grinnel St ($8 all day, shaded) and at the parking lot on Caroline St ($10 all day, not shaded). The high-speed trip out and back is air-conditioned, comfortable and smooth with complimentary breakfast and lunch and a cash bar that's open all day. You'll likely see plenty of turtles, dolphins, stingrays and birds as you zip along, as well as views of the Marquesas and other keys. Included in the 4½ hours at Fort Jefferson is a 45-minute tour. Snorkeling equipment is provided. Both birding and snorkeling in the Dry Tortugas are the best anywhere in the Keys. The place has a peculiar, remote charm. Several people on the trip I joined said they wanted to go back in the next day or two. One guy even claimed he was going to try to get a job with the Park Service so he could stay there. It's really that captivating.

Dry Tortugas National Park.

Schooner *America*, *202 William Street, Schooner Wharf,* ☎ *305-292-7787, www.schooneramerica.com*. *America* is a replica of one of the most famous racing yachts in US history. She is available for scheduled sunset sails every day at 4:30 and will dip into blue water on private charters. Nautically appointed staterooms accommodate up to eight guests who can help sail or simply indulge in seagoing luxury for $75.

NOT AMUSED

In 1851 the original *America* defeated all challengers in the Hundred Guinea Cup Race, held in England. When Queen Victoria was told of the outcome, she asked who came in second. A seaman aboard the royal yacht responded, "Your Majesty, there is no second." The cup was taken by the winning team to the New York Yacht Club and was eventually renamed The America's Cup.

Schooner *Western Union*, *202 William Street, Schooner Wharf,* ☎ *305-292-1766, www.schoonerwesternunion.com*, is available for scheduled sunset sails and private charters in the waters around Key West, offering entertainment along with the sights and smells of the sea. Fore and aft rigged, the 130-foot boat uses sail power once it leaves the slip. It's big enough and the water is calm enough so the trips are smooth and relaxing. If you choose, you can work up a sweat by helping haul on halyards, pull on sheets or take a turn at the helm.

> **AUTHOR TIDBIT:** Read a little Hornblower or O'Brien before you go on *Western Union* so you can holler out authentic 18th-century nautical jargon.

Their "Stargazer Cruise" ($59) leaves at dusk and, while being serenaded by squeezebox and harp, the magic of the night sky is explained by your guide using a laser beam to point out each passenger's birth constellation. The beer flows freely. Bring a light jacket. Fifteen men on a dead man's chest. Yo ho ho and a bottle of rum. Sunset trips leave at 4:30.

Yankee Freedom II, *Land's End Marina,* ☎ *305-294-7009, 800-926-5332, www.yankeefleet.com, $95 adults, $60 children.* This large, comfortable catamaran zips you to the Dry Tortugas in a little more than two hours, leaving most of the day for you to explore Fort Jefferson, snorkel and birdwatch. The boat offers all modern amenities with free use of snorkeling equipment and showers. Breakfast and lunch are complimentary; the cocktail bar is open all day. The boat leaves the dock at 8 am and returns at 5 pm every day, weather permitting.

Schooner *Wolf, 201 William Street,* ☎ *305-296-9653, www. schoonerwolf.com.* The (sort of) tall ship leaves three times daily for sails around Key West reefs, sunset and starlight cruises. They offer a twee kids' pirate cruise. Aaargh matey! Sunset sails with complimentary beer and wine cost $40. Departure times vary with the season.

Sebago Watersports, *Key West Bright, Ocean Reef Resort, Sunset Pier,* ☎ *305-294-5687, www.KeyWestSebago.com.* Sebago sales booths can be found all over the more touristy areas of Key West. They have snorkeling/sailing trips every day, as well as sunset cruises and parasailing. Their large catamarans are favorites for special events. They rent kayaks, personal watercraft and all types of water toys.

Liberty Fleet of Tall Ships, *Hilton Resort & Marina,* ☎ *305-292-0332, www.libertyfleet.com.* Two tall ships, the *Liberty* and the *Liberty Clipper,* leave on daily tours around Key West. On the *Liberty Clipper* you can take advantage of sailing and seamanship lessons, especially when the boat makes its annual two-week trip to Boston and back. Two-hour tours leave at 11, 2:30 and 5 daily. The price ($45 adult; $35 children) includes complimentary drinks.

Discovery **Glass Bottom Boats Tours**, *251 Margaret Street, Land's End Marina,* ☎ *305-293-0099, $20 adults, $15 children.* A glass-bottom boat with a large underwater viewing area, the *Discovery* takes guests for a good look at the teeming fish and coral life on reefs near Key West. During rough weather or murky water conditions, the boat goes to shallower, and less interesting, sheltered reefs close to Key West harbor. The trip lasts two hours.

Pride of Key West, *2 Duval Street,* ☎ *305-296-6293, www.seathereef.com, $20 adults, $10 children.* This glass-bottom catamaran offers fair viewing of the reefs around Key West and in the harbor. Trips leave at noon and 2 pm every day; sunset cruises are offered in the evening.

Canoeing & Kayaking

Not all the wildlife in Key West is on Duval Street. Even though the island is quite developed with condos, hotels and military installations, there are some quiet areas of flats and mangroves that are definitely worth a look. The nearby Marquesas (too far to paddle there) offer superb paddling. If you're interested, hook up with Key West Kayak, Fishing & Eco-Tours, below.

■ OUTFITTERS

Island Kayak, *2400 N. Roosevelt Blvd*, ☎ *305-292-0059,* offers independent rentals and guided kayak tours. Their three-hour tours go for $40 and basic rentals start at $30 for a half-day. Unless you are hardy and have plenty of sunscreen, a half-day out in the subtropical sun is probably all your skin can handle.

Key West Kayak, Fishing & Eco Tours, *Geiger Key Marina*, ☎ *305-304-0337, www.keyskayakfishing.com.* These guys can get you to the Marquesas and some less-visited areas around the Lower Keys for some of the best kayaking in the Keys and you don't have to fish unless you want to. They specialize in getting their guests to some of the more remote and most interesting places near Key West. With all tackle, bait and fishing license included, they charge $85 for a half-day trip and will come and pick you up at your Key West hotel and drop you back there afterwards.

Fishing

Key West has more than its share of top-quality fishing guides and charter boats, as well as opportunities for casual anglers to enjoy wetting a line. You can get some vicarious thrills by heading down to the charter docks at Garrison Bight on Truman Avenue around five or six in the afternoon to see what they've brought in. Although Key West doesn't have much to offer the shore-based angler, the environments for backcountry flats, inshore reef and offshore trolling are all within a very short boat ride.

For **backcountry** lovers, tarpon start moving from Florida Bay through the channels toward deeper water in late April and early May, while grouper, snapper and cobia are found almost any time of year.

Offshore anglers already know that Key West is located strategically near a structure know as **The Wall**. Charter captains have learned the man in the blue suit (blue marlin) gather to feed here, where the powerful current of the Gulf Stream is interrupted by a ridge rising to within 950 feet from the surface and dropping down almost vertically to the normal bottom depth of closer to 2,000 feet. This causes an upswell of warmer water that attracts large amounts of biomass leading up the food chain to congregations of marlin and sails. The Wall runs from south of Key West down to Big Pine Key and attracts the bulk of the serious marlin anglers. Sailfish, dorado, tuna and kingfish are commonly found a little closer in and account for most catches, but the offshore techniques for these table fish are different than going after the big game. Peak season for marlin starts in late summer, with the bigger fish being caught in mid-winter. Sailfish can be caught year-round, but the best time is in the fall. Dorado tend to start running in late April or early May. Expect to raise no more than one marlin for every three days spent in their pursuit. If you want to wrestle with the man in the blue suit you need to be prepared to spend some serious money and perhaps as much as a week on the water. Your chances of catching a sailfish are much better – perhaps one hookup every two days.

◾ GUIDE LOCATOR & BAIT & TACKLE RESOURCES

Saltwater Angler, ☎ *305-294-3248, 800-223-1629, www.saltwaterangler.com,* arranges fishing charters and guide services working with a variety of the local guides. They specialize in fly-fishing and can arrange for flats, inshore or offshore trips. They are located at the Hilton Marina, but bookings can be made by phone; you don't need to actually go there unless you want to browse through their supply of "technical" fishing products.

Key West

Key West Bait & Tackle, *241 Margaret Street,*
☎ *305-292-1961*, has the biggest and best tackle shop on
the island. They have a good selection of all types of
tackle and live or frozen bait. They also have free parking, a rare commodity in Key West.

If you need to save money, **K-Mart** on North Roosevelt
Boulevard has a selection of frozen bait and tackle.

■ BACKCOUNTRY & LIGHT TACKLE GUIDES

Prices vary widely for different types of fishing, boat style and
choice of tackle. Guides that are in demand can charge more than
others. In general, you can expect to pay from $250 to $350 for a
half-day of flats fishing and $350 to $500 for a full day. Offshore
charters run from $500 to over $1,000 for a full day in air-conditioned fishing luxury.

☆ **AUTHOR'S PICK** - Simon Becker, ☎ *305-745-3565*.
Orvis-endorsed guide Captain Simon Becker is usually
booked solid for six months out; if you can get him, he is
one of the most respected names in the Lower Keys area.
He offers friendly fly-fishing instruction for the novice
and expert guide services for the experienced angler.

Doug Kilpatrick, ☎ *305-745-2824*, loves to fish for permit. He knows where they hang out and how to nab
them. If you're in the market for a grand slam (a tarpon,
a bonefish and a permit caught all in the same day), this
is the guide you want. Doug has led many anglers to significant tournament wins, but you'll need to book waaay
in advance.

☆ **AUTHOR'S PICK** - Tom **Rowland**, ☎ *305-294-
7447, www.bigblueflyfishing.com*, has probably won the
most tournaments of all anglers in the Keys. He grew up
in Chattanooga and has been fishing all his life. He has
been the focus of dozens of TV fishing shows and magazine articles and has guided hundreds of clients to pres-
tigious tournament wins.

☆ **AUTHOR'S PICK** - Michael **Pollock**, *Key West,*
☎ *305-296-4949,* is a well-regarded flats guide with a
good record for bones, permit, tarpon and redfish. Like
the other good guides, he is booked solid for months, so

call him well before your trip. He works the Keys December through June and guides fly fishermen in Montana July through November. What a life.

☆ **AUTHOR'S PICK** - **Brian Yates, ☎** *305-745-7337.* Captain Brian is a flats guide almost exclusively devoted to fly. His clients are often repeat visitors and he is usually booked up during high season. He told me, "The flats fly-fishing experience is more like hunting than fishing – you are looking for individual fish. It is my job to put the angler in the best position to present a fly to that particular fish in the best possible manner. It can take minutes or hours to find that fish." The best anglers will get the best fish, but he encourages beginners to appreciate the beauty of a day on the flats even if they don't catch the big 'un. He is an unashamed permit fanatic.

■ OFFSHORE CHARTERS

You can expect the captains to know the best techniques and to supply all the gear and bait. While some prefer trolling with artificial lures in a large spread behind the outriggers, others insist live bait dropped back to fish and raised by huge plastic teasers is more productive. Marlin are thought to be more active feeders during the two or three days just before and after the full or new moon. Other experts feel the 12 hours just before a major cold front moves through are the magic moments.

Fishcheck Charters, *Garrison Bight Marina,* **☎** *305-295-0484 or 305-304-390, fishcheck@aol.com, www.fishcheckcharters.com.* The custom 37-foot *Fishcheck* covers all the best fishing waters from Key West to the Dry Tortugas. Captain Steve Luoma has been fishing the Keys since 1963. Call to see if he can fit you in. He groups individual anglers into full charters if necessary.

☆ **AUTHOR'S PICK** - **Lucky Fleet,** *Land's End Marina by Turtle Kraals,* **☎** *305-294-7988, 800-292-3096, fishinginfo@luckyfleet.com,* consists of four boats covering backcountry fly-fishing and trips offshore.

Gulfstream III *with Captain Walter Kirschner,* ☎ *305-296-8494, $35/7-hour trip (plus $3 for bait and tackle).* They offer night fishing in the summer.

■ PARTY BOATS

Greyhound V, *Garrison Bight Marina,* ☎ *305-296-5139, $35 half-day.* Captain John Battillo runs the 65-foot air-conditioned party boat to the reefs for bottom fishing.

Tortuga, *Conch Harbor, 951 Caroline Street,* ☎ *305-293-1189.* The *Tortuga* is a 45-foot party boat with the latest fish-finding electronics.

Bridge & Shore Fishing

Since the island is intensely developed, opportunities for fishing from the shore are very limited. If you like to wet a line but don't have the wherewithal to hire one of the charter boats or backcountry guides, I suggest driving east on the Overseas Highway a few miles to some of the bridge fishing hot spots described in previous chapters.

Scuba Diving

While enjoying the plastic tourist town delights of Key West it is hard to believe that some of the best diving in North America is just a short boat ride away. The reefs near Key West are rich and vast. If you can endure a longer ride, the reefs west of Key West off the Marquesas and Dry Tortugas are the least visited and best developed in the Keys. Unfortunately, the vast numbers of tourists attracted to Key West means that the majority of the dive operators are running cattle boats designed to get a large load of tourists to the nearest acceptable reefs, in the water for two tanks and back to the dock as quick as possible in order to pick up another load. If you are a beginning diver, you will probably be satisfied with almost any of these operators. However, if you have been diving awhile and want to see more developed, offshore reefs, be selective in your choice of guide. That said, numerous operators in Key West are devoted to giving their customers good value – trips to the best reefs in comfortable and uncrowded conditions. Be sure the other people on your trip are of a similar experience level to yourself and that the operator is going to the types of reefs or wrecks you want to see.

There are wonderful reefs quite close to Key West – **the Sambos, Dry Rocks** and **Sand Key** – but liveaboards and some of the faster boats take divers to more distant reefs near the Dry Tortugas. Wreck dives on the *Cayman Salvor* and *Joe's Tug* are popular destinations close to Key West. The Spanish galleon *Atocha*, source for most of the amazing treasure on display at Mel Fisher's museum (see page 31), is open to divers. It's not much more than some piles of rock and coral on a bed of sand, but the mystique and romance are thick.

■ DIVE SHOPS & CHARTERS

In general, dive trips in the Keys start at around $60 for a two-tank excursion. The price usually includes tanks, weight belts and soft drinks. Smaller boats and boats going to more distant sites may cost more.

Blue Water Charters, *Galleon Marina Slip #2,* ☎ *305-304-8888, 866-304-8666, www.bluewatercharters-keywest.com*, specializes in customized half- and full-day private dive charters to remote sites.

Dive Key West, *3128 N. Roosevelt Blvd., Key West,* ☎ *305-296-3823, 800-426-0707, www.divekeywest.com*, is the largest dive operator in the area. Their half-day dives start at $59 without equipment.

Dry Tortugas Live Aboard, *Oceanside Marina on Stock Island,* ☎ *305-744-9928, www.drytortugasdiving. com*, has a four-day trip to the Dry Tortugas starting at $1,000 per person, including all meals, drinks, accommodations and tanks. Nitrox is available at an extra charge.

Sea-Clusive Charters, *Oceanside Marina on Stock Island,* ☎ *305-872-3940, seaclusiveKW@aol.com, www. seaclusive.com*, offers all-inclusive overnight trips along the Keys or to the secluded Dry Tortugas. Day-trips to Looe Key or remote locations in the Marquesas are also available.

☆ **AUTHOR'S PICK** - Southpoint Divers, ☎ *305-292-9778, 800-891-DIVE; fax 305-296-6888, southpoint@aol.*

com, www.southpointdivers.com, keeps its boats at the Hyatt. Voted No.1 dive shop in Key West in the People's Choice Awards, and voted the highest rated dive shop in Key West two years in a row by Rodales *Scuba Diving Magazine*, Southpoint is Key West's premier dive center.

Spearfishing Charters, *17195 Kingfish Lane West, Sugarloaf Key,* ☎ *305-872-3940, www.spearfishing-charters.com*, offers excursions aimed primarily at divers interested in spearfishing. It has half- and full-day trips, as well as liveaboard options to the Dry Tortugas and Marquesas.

Snorkeling

There are no good, land-accessible snorkeling spots in Key West. But there are many, many great shallow reefs just offshore and snorkelers are well served by a variety of dive tour operators (see above, *Dive Shops & Charters*). Be sure you go on a snorkelers-only boat so you don't end up in deep water with the scuba divers.

One of the more interesting snorkeling sites, called **The Lake**, is west of Key West near the Marquesas. It is a sandy area with some coral and turtle grass and a large variety of interesting sea creatures swimming by. **Fort Jefferson** in the Dry Tortugas has excellent snorkeling not far from shore. If you circle the sea wall around the fort you will see amazing numbers of colorful reef fish and by venturing just a bit farther out west of the fort you will find yourself in a field of coral heads populated by lobsters, sea turtles, moray eels and all the usual coral reef curiosities and monstrosities. Most of the operators taking people to Fort Jefferson provide snorkeling equipment and showers/changing rooms (see *Boat Tours*, page 223). This is definitely a good snorkeling trip.

Watersports

The possibilities for fun on the water are just as good in Key West as in the rest of the Keys. There are a couple of good beaches (see above) and plenty of diving and fishing charter operators. Catamarans, Jet Skis and kayaks are here for the asking.

■ **OUTFITTERS**

Land's End Boat Rentals, ☎ *305-294-6447, behind the Half Shell Raw Bar on Margaret Street*, rents Jet Skis, small fishing boats, runabouts and day sailors. Sailboats start at $50/hour, basic fishing boats at $85 and Jet Skis at an outrageous $150/hour (Jet Skis rent for from $25/hour everywhere else in the Keys). There is a two-hour minimum rental.

Sebago Watersports, *Key West Bright, Ocean Reef Resort, Sunset Pier,* ☎ *305-294-5687, www.KeyWestSebago. com.* Sebago sales booths can be found all over the more touristy areas of Key West. In addition to their cruises (see *Boat Tours*), they rent kayaks, personal watercraft and all types of water toys. Parasail adventures start at $38 and reef snorkeling trips are $33.

■ In the Air

Aerial Tours & Seaplane Rides

Key West serves as the base for trips to the Marquesas and Dry Tortugas, places not reachable by land. Because of their relative inaccessibility, these keys are some of the most undisturbed and interesting of any in the chain. A variety of aerial outfitters operate out of Key West. Some tours are simply aerial sightseeing and others are in seaplanes that actually land near Fort Jefferson in the Dry Tortugas, allowing you to get out, tour the fort and snorkel, birdwatch or beachcomb.

■ **OUTFITTERS**

Sebago Parasail, *Key West Bright, Ocean Reef Resort Sunset Pier,* ☎ *305-292-2411, www.KeyWestSebago.com.* Sebago's sales booths seem to be everywhere in Key West. From mild to wild, their rides (flights?) for one or two people are billed as "truly unforgettable." Prices are from $45 for one person and $75 for two.

☆ **AUTHOR'S PICK** - **Seaplanes of Key West**, *Key West International Airport,* ☎ *305-294-0709, 800-950-2FLY, fax 305-296-4141, www.seaplanesofkeywest.com.* Seaplanes of Key West offers the quickest way (about a half-hour) to cover the 70 miles to the Dry Tortugas, allowing you to spend almost an entire day enjoying this remote and historic area. This has to be one of the very best adventures in the Keys. The plane cruises at 500 feet, so you get a wonderful view of the flats, channels and tidal sands around the Marquesas and other keys on the way out to Fort Jefferson. The pilots bank low over wrecks, pods of dolphins, swarming sharks, floating turtles and other attractions; the water is shallow almost all the way so there is plenty to see. The last time I took the flight I saw hundreds of turtles. If you are lucky, Mel Fisher's treasure salvage boat will be busy sucking up emeralds and gold doubloons from the sands near the Marquesas. If you are a photographer, try to get either the front or back seats for unobstructed shots. A polarizing filter will get rid of the reflection from the water's surface. Rates are $159 per person for a half-day trip, $305 for a full day and $329 gets you an overnight camping stay. Each passenger is given a small ice-filled cooler with a selection of drinks. If you are camping, bring all your own gear and bring back everything with you when you leave. Check for weight restrictions. Be sure to ask your tour operator if the park is open for camping before you finalize your plans. Problems with bathroom facilities closed the island to campers for part of 2003.

Island Aeroplane Tours, *Key West International Airport,* ☎ *305-294-TOUR*. If the idea of a biplane ride over and around Key West appeals to you, this is your chance. Biplanes fly slower than most aircraft and allow plenty of time to see the reefs, wrecks and Old Town of Key West. Plus, you get to ride up front (the pilot sits in the back). The antique plane holds two passengers. Call ahead for prices. Aerobatic rides in their Pitts S-2C offer cartwheels, barrel rolls and other wild aerial gyrations. Lessons are available.

Island City Flying Service, *Key West International Airport,* ☎ *305-296-5422*. Island City's Cessna 172 is really the best way to see the sights from on high due to the wing being on the top and not obstructing your view.

For photographers, this is the best way to go. Bring lots of film and a medium-length telephoto lens. Prices start at $140 per hour.

Aerial view of Fort Jefferson.

Where to Stay

Your choice ranges from near-flophouses to luxury B&Bs, with everything in-between. You can find chains like Days Inn and Doubletree and some of the quaintest, restored 19th-century homes imaginable. Prices are higher than anywhere else in the Keys – you won't find much for under $100.

HOTEL SELECTION

Select your hotel based on the type of activities you are interested in. Old Town and most of the action is on the west end of the island, while the best beach is more to the east. Hotels near the airport are good for beach activities, but are far from most entertainment and restaurants. True, you can rent a scooter or bike but you'll need to scoot or bike back and forth through the more boring parts of the island during the day perhaps more than you like. If you select a place to sleep in or near Old Town you can do without a bike or scooter and walk almost everywhere.

■ Ratings & Prices

All the room prices in this book are for two people staying in a double room during high season. Taxes and meals are not included unless so mentioned. Hotels and lodges marked "Author's Choice" are my personal favorites, offering top quality lodging and services but, more importantly, something of particular interest or charm.

ACCOMMODATIONS PRICE CHART

$	Under $100
$$	$100-200
$$$	$200-300
$$$$	Over $300

■ Hotels & Resorts

Alexander's Guest House, *1118 Flemming Street*, ☎ *305-294-9919, 800-654-9919, www.alexghouse.com*, *$$$*. This is the nicest of the open-minded guesthouses in Key West. The pool and nearby decks are clothing optional.

Ambrosia House B&B, *615 Fleming Street*, ☎ *305-296-9838, 800-535-9838, fax 305-296-2425, ambrosia@bellsouth.net, www. ambrosiakeywest.com, $$$$*. Although I don't believe any actual ambrosia is served, this is a real tasty accommodation right in the middle of Old Town Key West. Several period homes have been carefully restored and converted into lovely rooms with kitchens, decks and all the expected amenities. No pets.

Atlantic Shores Resort, *510 South Street*, ☎ *305-296-2491, 800-598-6988, $$*. The clothing-optional pool defines the liberal gay clientele. The bar is popular and there is definitely a scene to be made, with a cross-section of visitors and locals of all persuasions. The Shores is a 72-room, Art deco-style waterfront resort. The rooms are reasonably up-to-date, although some are small. It's located at the quiet end of Duval Street only a short walk from most places of interest and nightlife.

Banana Bay Resort, *2319 N. Roosevelt Blvd.*, ☎ *305-296-6925, 800-226-2621, www.bananabay.com, $$$*. Located on the north side of the island away from the action of Duval Street but close to shopping centers, Banana Bay is a large, all-adult resort. The rooms are motel-style, large and well furnished; some have kitchens. There is a sandy beach facing the quiet Gulf. Continental breakfast is served by the large pool. There are docking facilities and several backcountry fishing guides operate from the hotel dock. But check around, as you may be able to find something just as comfortable for a similar price closer to Old Town. No pets allowed.

Banyan Resort, *323 Whitehead Street*, ☎ *305-296-7786, 800-853-9937, KWFBroker@aol.com, www.banyanresort.com, $$$$*, consists of several restored Key West homes, some of which are on the National Register of Historic Places. A few are condos or timeshares, but most are rented on a nightly basis. The grounds are well landscaped with tropical plants and, of course, banyan trees. No pets.

Big Ruby's Guesthouse, *409 Applerouth Lane*, ☎ *305-296-2323, www.bigrubys.com, $$$*. This open-minded guesthouse has plenty of Key West charm and a couple of fun dogs hanging around. Pet-friendly. The rooms are agreeably modern but retain some Key West atmosphere. The lagoon-style pool has overhanging palms and a five-person Jacuzzi. Big Ruby also has hotels in Quepos, Costa Rica and Mediterranean, France. They are a member of the World's Foremost Gay and Lesbian Hotels.

Blue Parrot Inn B&B, *916 Elizabeth Street*, ☎ *305-296-0033, 800-231-2473, fax 305-296-5697, www.blueparrotinn.com, bluparotin@aol.com, $$-$$$*. Built in 1884, the Blue Parrot has been lovingly and authentically restored and features nine unique units. The wonderful buffet breakfast is served poolside. There is no extra charge for the cats you'll see running around, but you can't bring your own pets. Check out their website for a complete cat genealogy. The location is in Old Town and close to the action, yet private and quiet. An adult-only policy ensures a peaceful stay. Rooms start around $100, which is not bad at all for Key West.

Center Court Bed & Breakfast, *915 Center Street*, ☎ *305-296-9292, 800-797-8787, www.centercourtkw.com, $$$$*. Award-winning restoration makes the atmosphere of Center Court very Key Westy. Some of the rooms are in their own, free-standing cottages with kitchens and hot tubs. Pet-friendly!

Chelsea House Key West B&B, *707 Truman Avenue*, ☎ *305-296-2211, 800-845-8859, fax 305-296-4822, www.chelsea-housekw.com, $$$*. Pet-friendly Chelsea House is an old, historic sea captain's home with pool and well-kept gardens.

Coconut Beach Resort, *1500 Albert Street*, ☎ *305-294-0057, 800-835-0055, fax 305-294-5066, www.coconutbeachresort.com, $$$$*. Coconut Beach is an attractively remodeled Victorian-style building with one- and two-bedroom, king and queen suites, most with kitchens. The pool is almost surrounded by lush vegetation and is overlooked by white verandas. There is a small sandy beach and a Jacuzzi. Nicely located near the quiet end of Duval Street, it has the great restaurant Louie's Backyard right next door.

Conch House Heritage Inn, *625 Truman Avenue*, ☎ *305-293-0020, 800-207-5806, www.conchhouse.com, $$$*. Built in the late 1800s and listed on the National Register of Historic Places, the Conch House was "restored to its original elegance" in 1993. Some rooms are in the main house and others are in a poolside cottage and cabana. The grounds feature a pool surrounded by tropical plants. No children or pets.

Coral Tree Inn & Oasis Guesthouse, *822 Flemming Street*, ☎ *305-296-2131, 800-362-7477, www.coraltreeinn.com, $$$*. Open-minded establishments across the street from each other, the Coral Tree and Oasis are comprised of several remodeled Key West-style homes grouped around a clothing-optional pool. Some of the rooms have been recently modernized.

Crowne Plaza La Concha, *430 Duval Street*, ☎ *305-296-2991, 800-745-2191, fax 305-294-3283, www.laconchakeywest.com, $$$$*. One of the top properties in the Keys, La Concha has been host to numerous celebrities and artists. Remarkably restored to modernity, the building is listed on the National Register of Historic Places. The 150 rooms and 10 suites are smartly appointed and seem to have everything you might need, including data ports. Their website is well designed and informative, and even has a web cam and virtual tour of the property. Puzzlingly, it offers no way to contact the hotel directly by e-mail.

Cuban Club Suites, *1102 Duval Street,* ☎ *305-296-0465, 800-432-4849, www.keywestcubanclub.com, $$$$.* These privately owned condominiums are rented on a nightly basis. The Club consists of luxurious suites of rooms on the second floor, set over tourist shops on the ground floor. Dog friendly! If you have a view of Duval Street you can scope out the action from the privacy of your own room.

Curry Mansion Inn, *511 Caroline Street,* ☎ *305-294-4093, 800-253-3466, fax 305-294-4093, www.currymansion.com, $$$$.* The Curry Mansion is situated in a building that used to be the home of the Currys, one of Florida's founding families. The rooms are actually next door to the mansion, by a lovely pool. This is one of the nicest accommodations in Key West and is relatively small and quiet. The location is convenient to all the tourist activities downtown. No pets are allowed.

Cypress House Historic Inn B&B, *601 Caroline Street,* ☎ *305-294-6969, 800-525-2488, fax 305-296-117, www.cypresshousekw. com, $$$.* On the National Register of Historic Places, the Cypress House claims to be the oldest B&B in Key West. You can hear the whole story from your window as the Conch Train passes by and slows down for the tourists. No pets or kids.

☆ **AUTHOR'S PICK** - **Dewey House**, *506 South Street,* ☎ *305-296-6577, 800-354-4455, www.oldtownresorts.com, $$$$.* Dewey House is one of the well-run Southernmost Old Town Resorts and is a luxurious B&B in a classic old Key West home loaded with history. It is set right on a natural sandy beach and conveniently located at the very end of Duval Street. The pool is next door at the Southernmost On the Beach and there is a heated dipping pool just outside the library on the patio. Rooms are large and elegantly furnished. Breakfasts feature fresh tropical fruits and pastries. Complimentary afternoon tea is served in the library. No children or pets are allowed to disturb the peaceful setting. All rooms are non-smoking.

SOUTHERNMOST HOTEL & RESORTS

A group of four old Key West properties (Southernmost Hotel, La Mer Hotel, Southernmost On The Beach and Dewey House) have been carefully restored as luxury hotels and B&Bs. Southernmost Hotel and Resorts, ☎ 800-354-4455, owns and manages the four properties. All four are directly at the end of Duval Street and all but Southernmost Hotel are on the water with a small beach. Dewey House and La Mer Hotel are restored historic homes. Southernmost Hotel and Southernmost On The Beach are both classic old Keys motels remodeled and transformed into luxury hotels. Rooms in all properties are modern and meticulously maintained. Furnishings are luxurious and new. Towels and pillows are fluffy and and the bathrooms contain a plethora of luxury toiletries.

Douglas House, *419 Amelia Street*, ☎ *305-294-5269, 800-833-0372, www.douglashouse.com*, *$$$*. Douglas House is actually several houses with individual rooms and suites in each. Swimming pools and a hot tub for relaxation are on site. It's pet-friendly, but no kids are allowed.

Duval House, *815 Duval Street*, ☎ *305-294-1666, 800-223-8825, duvalhs@attglobal.net, www.duvalhousekeywest.com*, *$$$$*. Conveniently located on Duval Street, this property offers a quiet oasis within its calm interior gardens. Some of the rooms are completely self-sufficient, with kitchens and all the amenities for a lengthy stay.

Eaton Lodge, *511 Easton Street*, ☎ *305-292-2170, 800-294-2170, www.eatonlodge.com*, *$$$*. Restored with an eye to historic detail, Eaton Lodge has old Key West character and charm. No pets or smoking are allowed.

Eden House, *1015 Fleming Street*, ☎ *305-296-6868, 800-533-5397, www.edenhouse.com*, *$$$$*. This place used to be aimed at low-end travelers; now, it is targeting the high end of the tourist trade. Some of the rooms are basic (shower down the hall), but most are elegant. Some have full kitchens. No pets allowed, but kids are okay.

Equator Resort, *818 Flemming Street*, ☎ *305-294-7775, 800-278-4552, www.equatorresort.com*, *$$$*. This all-new "resort for men" has all the mod cons and its own Mediterranean charm. The management is open-minded, offering a clothing-optional pool and large, communal hut tub.

The Gardens Hotel, *526 Angela Street*, ☎ *305-294-2661, 800-526-2664, kwgard@travelbase.com, www.gardenshotel.com*, *$$$$*. Quiet and elegant enough to cater to celebrities, The Gardens is set in beautiful grounds with pool and hot tub. A recipient of Condé Nast's Worlds Top 100 Best Places to Stay Award, the 17 rooms, suites and cottage are truly comfortable, featuring Bahamian-style furnishings, luxurious bedding, verandas and original artwork by Key West artists. Built in the 1800s, the main building is listed on the National Register of Historic Places. This is a fine example of well-restored Key West architecture.

Grand Key Resort, *3990 S. Roosevelt Blvd.,* ☎ *305-293-1818, 888-310-1540, fax 305-296-6962, www.grandkeyresort.com*, *$$$$*. On the quiet side (comparatively, even though near the airport) of Key West, the all-new Grand Key is crammed in-between a couple of condo developments. Try to get a room at the top if you can so you can see something besides other buildings. No pets.

Heron House, *512 Simonton Street*, ☎ *305-294-9227, 888-861-9066, HeronKYW@aol.com, www.heronhouse.com*, *$$$$*. Heron House is physically one block away from Duval Street, but miles away in atmosphere, with the quiet ambiance of Old Key West. It is small and luxurious, right in the middle of the fun, yet quiet. The atmosphere is one of intimacy and luxury, with wicker patio furniture, orchids and tropical pool. The 23 rooms and suites, located in three buildings, are all different, but each has a balconies and deck. The management reports that repeat visitors reserve most of their rooms, so book early. No kids.

Hilton Resort & Marina, *245 Front Street*, ☎ *305-294-4000, 800-445-8667, fax 305-294-4086, www.keywestresort.Hilton.com*, *$$$$*. Located right in the middle of the action by Mallory Square, the Hilton has all the usual good qualities you've come to expect from the hotel chain. You can't go wrong with a Hilton, but you do miss out on the Keys charm by staying in a chain. That said, you just can't beat the location of this one, and many of the rooms have truly awesome sunset views out over the harbor.

Key West

Holiday Inn Beachside, *3841 N. Roosevelt Blvd.*, ☎ *305-294-2571, www.holiday-inn.com / keywest-beach, $$$.* Even though it has been recently rebuilt, it's still a Holiday Inn. Now it has watersports offerings and tennis courts.

☆ **AUTHOR'S PICK** - **Hyatt Key West Resort**, *601 Front Street*, ☎ *305-296-9900, 800-844-0454, fax 305-292-1038, www.keywest. hyatt.com, $$$$.* This is one of the finest properties in Key West and is in a location convenient to all the nightlife and fun. It offers rooms and suites, a pool, restaurants and docking at its marina.

Hostelling International Key West, *718 South Street*, ☎ *305-296-5719, www.keywesthostel.com, $.* Be sure to reserve in advance if you want to stay at this hostel. Dorm rooms are air-conditioned, clean and comfortable, starting at $20. There are laundry and kitchen facilities. The hostel is conveniently located near Old Town.

Island City House Hotel, *411 William Street*, ☎ *305-294-5702, 800-634-8230, www.islandcityhouse.com, $$$.* These two 19th-century homes are set around a pool and hot tub. They feature suites, some with kitchens. No pets allowed, but kids are okay.

☆ **AUTHOR'S PICK** - **La Mer B&B**, *504 South Street*, ☎ *305-296-6577, 800-354-4455, www.oldtownresorts.com, $$$$.* Part of the Southernmost Old Town Resorts group of lovingly restored old Key West properties, La Mer's small, quaint house sits right on a natural sand beach. The luxurious property was completely renovated in 2003. All rooms are tastefully furnished and are reserved strictly for non-smokers. The pool next door at Southernmost On the Beach is available for guest use. Fresh fruit and pastry breakfast as well as complimentary afternoon tea is served next door in the library of Dewey House, a history-filled home (see above). The ambiance is definitely historic old Key West. No children or pets are allowed.

☆ **AUTHOR'S PICK** - **Marquesa Hotel**, *600 Fleming Street*, ☎ *305-292-1919, 800-869-4631, fax 305-294-2121, www. marquesa.com, $$$$.* The Marquesa is an ambiance-heavy grouping of adjacent 19th-century Key West-style Greek revival homes that form one charming small hotel. The location is quiet, yet close to the action of Duval Street. The sound of burbling water from garden fountains fills the air. The restored old homes surround two pools, with grounds landscaped by the renowned landscape architect Raymond Jungles. The main building is listed on the National Register of Historic Places. The 27 rooms and suites are elegantly furnished and the service is impeccable. Guests are welcomed with a complimentary glass of wine. Every time I returned to my room after an excursion, I found the ice bucket filled, room spruced up and used towels replaced. My only complaint was the lack of fridge and coffee-maker in the room. Breakfast, served by the pool with morning paper, is a very civilized practice. Of course, the staff can arrange for your participation in all of the usual Keys activities. The adjacent Marquesa Café (dinner only) offers by far the finest dining experience in town. Owner Carol Wrightman says if you can't get a reservation to eat at the Café, have the meal served in your room or enjoy it poolside. Luminaries such as Mr. & Mrs. Richard Gere, Joseph Heller, Lennox Lewis, E.L. Doctorow and Annie Proulx are frequent guests. That should give you a hint of the quality of the Marquesa. Zagat rates it as the 17th-best hotel in the US. Children under 16 are discouraged.

Ocean Key Resort, *Zero Duval Street*, ☎ *305-296-7701, 800-328-9815, fax 305-292-7685, www.oceankey.com, $$$$.* Right in the middle of the action with extensive, luxury suites that have kitchens and balconies overlooking Mallory Square and Duval Street. The rooms just about live up to the views, being among the best in town. If you walk down Duval Street towards the harbor, turn left at the end, and follow the harbor admiring the sunset and exotic humanity, you can't miss the five-story white buildings with blue roof overlooking everything. If you keep the windows in your room open all the weirdness and warmth of Key West is right there. But you're safe in your Ocean Key Resort room swathed in luxury. No pets.

The Palms, *820 White Street*, ☎ *305-294-3146, 800-558-9374; fax 305-294-8463, palmskw@bellsouth.net, www.palmshotel-keywest.com, $$$.* A combination of National Register of Historic Places charm and new construction, The Palms has a great pool and especially good breakfast. Kids and pets stay free.

Pearl's Rainbow, *525 United Street*, ☎ *305-292-1450, 800-749-6696, $$$.* Pearl's caters exclusively to the lesbian market and does not allow men, kids or pets on the premises. They have two clothing-optional pools and two hot tubs. The 38 rooms and suites, set in five historic buildings (the main building was originally a cigar factory), are clean and nicely decorated.

Pier House Resort & Caribbean Spa, *One Duval Street*, ☎ *305-296-4600, 800-327-8340, fax 305-296-7568, www. pierhouse.com, $$$$*. A rare private beach and perhaps the most sought-after sunset views in Key West (from the bar, no less) make the Pier House world famous. The location is right at the most popular end of Duval Street, on the Bay, at the edge of Old Town. The newly renovated resort has 142 rooms and suites, most with private patios or balconies, tropically inspired ambiance and furnishings, pool, gardens, spa with five treatment rooms and exercise room and, of course, watersports. The rooms are large and suitably designed for the upscale clientele who are able to pay the price for luxury and location. No pets are allowed.

Radisson Key West, *3820 North Roosevelt Blvd.*, ☎ *305-294-5511, 800-333-3333, fax 305-296-1939, www.radisson. com/keywestfl, $$$$*. The Radisson is on the east end of the island a bit away from the action. It is a large hotel (145 rooms) with all the usual Radisson comforts. The website does not allow you to contact the hotel directly by e-mail, but do check it out to learn about what this standard Radisson offers.

Red Rooster Inn B&B, *709 Truman Avenue*, ☎ *305-296-6558, 800-845-0825, fax 305-296-4822, www.redroosterinn.com, $$*. Pleasant, small and economical, the Red Rooster is for adults and pets only. Murder, drug deals, prostitution are all part of the legend from long ago. It was built in 1905 as a private home, but was chopped up into several small apartments during the Depression. Through the 60s and 70s it was the Cinderella Motel, renting mostly to Coast Guard and military personnel. The wearing of clothes in the garden and around the pool is not considered mandatory.

Sheraton Suites Key West, *2001 South Roosevelt Blvd.*, ☎ *305-292-9800, 800-45-BEACH, fax 305-294-6009, www. sheratonkeywest.com, $$$$*. All accommodations are suites, complete with coffee-makers and hot tubs. There is a big pool. One of the nice benefits for guests is the complimentary shuttle transportation around town. You'll need this, since the hotel itself is located away from the action by the airport, across the street from the beach.

Simonton Court Historic Inn B&B, *320 Simonton Street*, ☎ *305-294-6386, 800-944-2687, fax 305-293-8446, simontoncourt@aol.com, www.simontoncourt.com, $$$$*. The rooms are strewn with antiques and the atmosphere is luxurious. Some units have full kitchens. No pets, no kids.

Southernmost Hotel, *1319 Duval Street*, ☎ *305-296-5611, 800-354-4455, www.oldtownresorts.com, $$$*. This 127-room Southernmost is the flagship property of the Southernmost Old Town Resort Group (see page 240). The rooms are luxuriously renovated motel-style, overlook two pools and a Tiki bar, and are set across the street from a natural sand beach open to hotel guests. The location is convenient to the action at the quiet end of Duval Street. The property is dripping with old Key West atmosphere.

☆ **AUTHOR'S PICK** - **Southernmost on the Beach**, *508 South Street*, ☎ *305-296-6577, 800-354-4455, www.oldtownresorts.com, $$$*. Right next to a natural sandy beach and convenient to the action at the quiet end of Duval Street, the Southernmost on the Beach is a deluxe 47-room property that's been recently restored. The rooms look out over the beach to the Atlantic. The large pool and pier seem to be out to sea, you're so close to the ocean. Rooms are motel-style, but very well decorated. This property presents good value for a Key West waterfront hotel with probably the best and quietest beach in town.

Sunrise Suites Resort, *3685 Seaside Drive*, ☎ *305-296-6661, 888-723-5200, fax 305-296-6968, www.sunrisekeywest.com, $$$$*. These condos near the airport are rented on a nightly basis. All have kitchens and are furnished like regular homes. Some units have good views.

Sunset Key Guest Cottages, *245 Front Street*, ☎ *305-292-5300, 888-477-7786, fax 305-292-5395, www.sunsetkeycottages.Hilton.com, $$$$*. This is part of the Hilton chain and, like all Hiltons, can be counted on to offer modest luxury and quality. You must take a launch to get to the private island, which is directly across from the action on Mallory Square. All rooms are freestanding cottages. The on-site Latitudes restaurant is justly known for wonderful food and service, and you can even request a private chef who comes to your room and prepares an elegant meal for you and your guests. Quite spiffy service. No pets allowed.

Weatherstation Inn, *57 Front Street*, ☎ *305-294-7277, 800-815-2707, weathersta@aol.com, www.weatherstationinn.com, $$$$*. Discreet luxury hidden just two blocks from Duval Street makes the Weatherstation Inn one of the handful of finest accommodations in Key West. It is located on the grounds of the old Navy Yard in a neighborhood of old Key West homes all restored in period style. It's just down the street from Truman's Little White House and only a couple of blocks from Duval Street. The rooms are quaint in a Caribbean plantation style. No pets.

Wyndham Casa Marina, *1500 Reynolds Street*, ☎ *305-296-3535, 800-626-0777, wcmbh@wyndham.com, www.casamarina-keywest.com, $$$$*. The oldest and largest resort in Key West, the Wyndham Casa Marina Resort is a deluxe resort built in 1921. All watersports are catered for at its own marina and private beach. Other facilities and eminities include tennis courts, a fitness center, room service and organized activities for kids. No pets allowed.

Wyndham's Reach Resort, ☎ *305-296-5000, 800-874-4118, fax 305-296-9960, wombh@wyndham.com, www.reachresort.com, $$$$*. The Wyndham offers a beach, pool and the football-themed Don Shula Steakhouse. No pets are allowed. The property is right in the middle of Old Town.

■ Camping

 Boyd's Campground, *6401 Maloney Avenue, Stock Island*, ☎ *305-294-1465, fax 305-293-9301*. Boyd's has all the usual campground features – pool, games, showers, dock and boat ramp. It's just outside noisy Key West. Some pets are allowed; call for restrictions. They have 203 RV and tent sites. Most have full hook-ups.

Jabour's Trailer Court & Camping, *223 Elizabeth Street*, ☎ *305-294-5723, fax 305-296-7969, www.kwcamp.com*. RVs and tenters will find bare-bones amenities at this facility that's close to town near the charter docks. Strict pet rules allow some small pets.

■ Vacation Rentals

 It is possible to rent vacation homes with character, but pricing and availability may force you to choose a condo in a good location and comfort over merely charm.

Compass Realty Sales and Rentals, ☎ *305-292-1881*

Rent Key West Vacations, ☎ *305-294-0990, 800-833-7368*

Where to Eat

All tourist towns have innumerable eateries – some terrible and some great. Key West is no different. Many of the restaurants aim to separate tourists from their dollars as quickly as possible, providing the least possible service and quality in return. If you walk down Duval Street and pick a restaurant at random, you have about a 50% chance of getting a memorable meal. But be aware that the more expensive places are not necessarily better. Below, I try to give a selection of the best eateries in all price ranges. The locals usually know which places are tourist traps and which offer good food and value; ask the hotel staff where *they* go to eat. And try some of the cheap restaurants I list here. I don't think you will be disappointed. If you want fine dining, Key West has wonderful, innovative chefs using local seafood in interesting ways.

> **AUTHOR TIDBIT:** Be sure to make a reservation at the better restaurants as they can fill up quickly even in the low season. If I set out for a good meal without a reservation, I carry a list of three or more places I want to visit in case my first choice is full.

The price symbols for each listing consider the average cost of main courses listed on the menu.

Key West

RESTAURANT PRICE CHART

$	Under $8
$$	$8-12
$$$	$12-20
$$$$	Over $20

■ Recommendations

A&B Lobster House, *700 Front Street*, ☎ *305-294-5880, www.aandblobsterhouse.com*, *$$*. Upstairs from Alonzo's Raw Bar, the A&B has a great view to complement its tasty seafood dishes such as lobster Newburg, salmon and blackened grouper. They offer both Maine and Florida lobster. Cigars and fine cognacs are on offer in the smoking lounge. Open daily for dinner only.

Alonzo's Oyster House, *700 Front Street*, ☎ *305-294-5880, $$*. Downstairs from the A&B Lobster House, Alonzo's has oysters, conch fritters, stone crabs and Florida lobsters. You can actually get fresh local shrimp here; many Keys restaurants offer only frozen shrimp trucked in by the big, national restaurant supply companies. Open for lunch and dinner every day.

Antonia's, *615 Duval Street*, ☎ *305-294-6565, www.antonias-keywest.com*, *$$$*. Everybody on the island says this elegant Northern Italian restaurant is one of the best. Its food selections include veal, seafood pastas and good desserts, along with a very good wine list. Open for dinner every evening at 6 pm.

Blue Heaven, *729 Thomas Street*, ☎ *305-296-8666, $$*. This old, ex-whorehouse where Hemingway came for cockfights now offers jerk chicken, carrot curry soup, mango chutney, bakery goods and more. It's all Caribbean-style. The floor is dirt and chickens scurry around under your feet. The food is consistently good and "homemade." Open for breakfast, lunch and dinner.

Café Marquesa, *600 Fleming Street at the Marquesa Hotel*, ☎ *305-292-1244, www.cafemarquesa.com*, *$$$$*. Serving dinner every evening, the Marquesa is one of the best upscale dining choices in town. Diners enjoy the food in a quiet room on the corner of Fleming and Simonton streets. The wine list is appropriately appreciative of the revolution in new world wines and still has a good selection of European standards – including my favorite from Spain, Ribera del Duero. Of course, seafood is prominent on the menu and is prepared in novel ways. The presentation is superb. The dessert menu is simply awesome. I recently sampled their Napoleon with Key lime cream and fresh berries and it was superb! If you're tired of the Duval Street swill and would like a quiet bar and a shaken cocktail, the bar here is a pleasant change with a serene atmosphere. You don't need to dress up to go to the Café Marquesa (in Key West, people wear a tie only to attend a funeral or church). That said, white pants or even a white suit would not be out of place! Open for dinner every evening at 6 pm.

Café Solé, *1029 Southard Street at Frances*, ☎ *305-294-0230*, *www.cafesole.com*, *$$$$*. People's Choice award winner, young chef John Correa creates selections such as mutton snapper in pesto and champagne, yellowtail in a beurre blanc of lobster, hog snapper with red pepper zabaglione, duck a l'orange, bouillabaise, and more. All are superb. Hog snapper is probably the best eating fish in the sea, and the café gets theirs from divers (hog snappers are not line-caught). Café Solé is small, intimate and open for dinner every night. The last time I was there, diners were entertained by a classical guitarist and the fattest orange cat I have ever seen. They are open for lunch and dinner every day.

Camille's Restaurant, *703½ Duval Street*, ☎ *305-296-4811*, *www.camilleskeywest.com*, *$$*. A small place with big breakfasts, Camille's offers a new menu at every lunch and dinner, with items such as roasted garlic soup and rack of lamb. Happy hour is from 4 to 6 pm. Open every day for breakfast, lunch and dinner.

El Siboney, *900 Catherine Street*, ☎ *305-296-4184, $*. When you get tired of tourist food and paying through the nose for it, head to family-run El Siboney for big platters of Cuban-American food at reasonable prices. It is a bit off the beaten path and serves no margaritas or other tourist drinks. Perhaps this is why locals pack the place. Expect meat or seafood stews served with fried plantains and piles of rice and beans. One recent lunch for me included garlic bread, rice and beans, fried plantains, potatoes and a stew of "chicken fricassée," as they called it. Along with two huge glasses of iced tea, this cost a mere $6.50. I did not manage to get through the whole pile and decided I should have a more modest lunch in the future. They are open Monday through Saturday for lunch and dinner. No credit cards.

Johnson's Café, *306 Petronia Street/801 Thomas Street*, ☎ *305-292-2286, $*. "Did you bring your appetite? We don't play. We don't put nuttin' small outa here!" This was how I was greeted by an elderly black fellow when I walked up on the old board front porch and approached the window to place my order. Johnson's is a favorite of Key West construction workers and cabbies who come for the best fish sandwiches and conch fritters on earth. "Good food, low prices" is their motto. The fish sandwich is at least a foot long and is served on Cuban bread with several hot fish fillets, lettuce, tomato and little plastic cups on the side with lime juice and hot, hot, hot sauce. Eating an entire sandwich is possible only for the most robust among us. The conch fritters are more conch than fritter and are served wrapped in paper, hot and smoking, fresh from the fryer. There is no point in eating a conch fritter made anywhere else. The café consists of only a small window on the porch with two picnic tables. It looks as if you're eating at someone's house – and you are. Open for lunch and dinner every day.

Louie's Backyard, *700 Waddell Street*, ☎ *305-294-1061, www. louiesbackyard.com, $$$$*. Jimmy Buffett used to play here for drinks, or so the stories go. Lunch and dinner are served every day, and there's live music (not Jimmy) on weekend nights in their upscale Afterdeck bar. Most locals can't afford to eat here, but would like to (they drink at the bar instead).

Mangoes Restaurant & Catering, *700 Duval Street*, ☎ *305-292-4606, www.mangoeskeywest.com, $$$*. Chef Paul Orchard prepares "Floribbean" fine dining with guava-barbecued prawns, yellowtail in passion fruit beurre blanc, and other unusual combinations. Cheeses are a specialty and their mozzarella is "homemade" and, although not from buffalo milk, it is excellent. Just as in France, pets are allowed in the outdoor dining area. The waitstaff is well trained and does much more than simply spew margaritas out of a plastic hose. My dream is to have my own pastry chef. The pastry chef at Mangoes does wonders with local fruits. Their wonderful vanilla ice cream is made on-site. Almost every bottle of wine on the list is from California, and there are some good offerings for under $30. Wines by the glass are overpriced, starting at $6.50. The people-watching tables have a great view of the sideshow on Duval Street. Open for lunch and dinner everyday.

Meteor Smokehouse, *404 Southard Street*, ☎ *305-294-5602*, *$$*. GREAT RIBS! This is one of my favorite places to eat in town. Not many BBQ joints offer both wet and dry types. Both are excellent and you can order a sampler, which includes both styles. They have three different types of sauce, so you can experiment. The Green Parrot next door is a very hip musician's hangout. The Smokehouse is open for lunch and dinner every day until 2 am. Blues music wafts through the air, along with the wonderful smell of hickory smoke.

Nasty Burger, *308 Petronia Street*, *no phone*, *$*. Nasty burgers are served from a little shack at seemingly whimsical times. The place has no name, just a small menu tacked up to the side of the door. The menu includes only nasty burgers, which are thick, juicy, greasy and good. Locals seem to know when the place is open, but it can be closed for months at a time. My recommendation is to simply walk by from time to time and you may get lucky and find it open for business. If it's not, just go next door to Johnson's Café, which has equally soulful food (see listing above).

Pepe's Café, *806 Caroline Street*, ☎ *305-294-7192*, *$$*. The oldest (1909) restaurant in Key West is a funky shack-type place. Steak smothered in pork chops is a signature dish. "Interesting" burgers and a few seafood items grace the menu. The margaritas are excellent, made from limes, tequila and Triple Sec, instead of from dubious powders and bottled mixes that you'll see in most Keys bars. Breakfast is renowned. Open every morning at 7:30.

Seven Fish, *632 Olivia Street*, ☎ *305-296-2777*, *www.7fish.com*, *$$$*. This small eatery specializes in – surprise, surprise – fish prepared in interesting ways. Grab one of the coveted seats at the bar and have a chat with the bartender while you eat. Steaks and daily fish specials shine.

> ## FISHY STORIES
>
> The story I heard about how Seven Fish got its name is as follows: When the previous tenant, a rough Mexican bar, vacated the premises, the only things remaining were a painting of seven fish and two bullet holes in the window (from the inside, going out). Both the painting and the bullet holes remain. Ask to see them.

The selection of wines by the glass is good. The last time I was here, they only had two fish on the menu: grouper and tuna. The grouper, not line-caught, was excellent and served in a light curry sauce. The tuna was offered both lightly seared and raw. Another dish was gnocchi in a Gorgonzola cheese sauce. Seven Fish is a little bit cheaper than the other *in* places, and it is really only *in* with the locals. With a plain appearance and a location a little off the beaten path, the emphasis is on good food. Their tag line is: Simple. Good. Food. They are open every day for dinner except Tuesdays.

Square One Restaurant, *1075 Duval Street,* ☎ *305-296-4300, www.squareonerestaurant.com, $$$*. This is an excellent dinner choice with piano entertainment in casually elegant surroundings. Filet mignon, braised chops and scallops on spinach in light mustard sauce are typical menu entries. Square One is located in a little shopping arcade, Duval Square, just off the street. They have a few al fresco tables and are open for dinner only, every night. For a refreshing change from the norm, the margaritas are quite good.

Turtle Kraals Waterfront Seafood Grill & Bar, *231 Margaret Street at Land's End Marina,* ☎ *305-294-2640, www.turtlekraals. com, $$*. The food is a fusion of Southwestern and tropical, with such oddities as grouper-papaya quesadillas. The beer selection is very good, but wines tend to be of the jug variety. Open every morning at 7:30.

■ The Best of the Rest

Alice's At La-Te-Da, *1125 Duval Street,* ☎ *305-296-6706, www.lateda.com/Alices, $$$*. The strangely named but well regarded upscale dining spot serves unusual omelets, as well as lamb and other dishes. Open for breakfast, lunch and dinner every day.

B.O.'S Fish Wagon, *801 Caroline Street*, ☎ *305-294-9272*, *$*, has big, big, juicy fish sandwiches served with squid or onion rings and beer. The ambiance is fishy, with nets on the wall and plastic fishing floats dotted around. Open daily for lunch and dinner.

Bagatelle, *115 Duval Street*, ☎ *305-296-6609*, *www.bagatelle-keywest.com*, *$$$*. Set in what is reputed to have been an old sea captain's house, the Bagatelle is drenched in faux Key West charm. Make a reservation for dinner since they are almost always crowded. "Ah!" you say. "A crowded restaurant is usually a good bet." The food is quite good (Key West pricey), but the real selling point is being able to watch the action on Duval Street from the balconies. You just can't beat this people-watching perch. Anyone casually strolling down Duval Street looking for a place to eat and rest their feet instantly sees that the Bagatelle is the perfect spot. Open for lunch and dinner every day.

Banana Café, *1211 Duval Street*, *www.banana-café.com*, ☎ *305-294-7227*, *$$$*. The menu includes crêpes, duck and other French classics mixed in with some innovative seafood concoctions. Breakfast, lunch and dinner are served every night. Jazz bands play on some week nights.

Café Des Artistes, *1007 Simonton Street*, ☎ *305-294-7100*, *$$$$*. This is the real thing if you're looking for contemporary, *Gourmet Magazine* fine dining. The seafood is elegantly and imaginatively prepared and presented, while the wine list is probably the best in town, focusing heavily on French and California reds. Open for dinner every night at 6 pm.

Chico's Cantina, *5230 U.S. Highway 1, Stock Island*, ☎ *305-296-4714*, *www.chicoscantina.com*, *$$*. Here you'll find wonderful Mexican food prepared with care and using only fresh ingredients. The salsa is superb, with sufficient cilantro to give it that real *auténtico* flavor. Open every day for lunch and dinner.

Commodore Steakhouse, *700 Front Street*, ☎ *305-294-9191*, *$$$*. This upscale steakhouse features white linen tablecloths and wood paneling. My personal favorite is the New York strip Roquefort, but then I'm a freak for stinky cheese. Dinner only, every night.

Conch Republic Seafood, *631 Greene Street*, ☎ *305-294-4403*, *www.conchrepublicseafood.com*, *$$*. The big bar, made to look old (but quite new), catchy name, live music and aquarium invite diners to enjoy the regular old Keys seafood and steaks. At least the shrimp is fresh and not the frozen variety. They have a very good selection of rum, but offer only a few tired wine selections. Open every day for lunch and dinner.

Crabby Bill's, *511 Greene Street*, ☎ *305-292-0802*, *$$*. Is Crabby Bill's different from Crabby Dick's (below)? Other than the name, you would be hard pressed to differentiate after a couple of their margaritas. They open early in the morning for thirsty tourists and the noise level slowly rises all day. The action tapers off sometime in the wee hours. The food is surprisingly good for such a tourist-oriented place. The menu has mostly seafood with lots of crab and fried food.

Crabby Dick's, *712 Duval Street*, ☎ *305-294-7229*, *www. crabbydickskeywest.com*, *$$*. Owned (and given the unfortunate name) by two guys named Dick. Crab and the usual Keys seafood are menu features. They are open every day for lunch and dinner. Their happy hour runs from 4 until 7 – one hour longer than most Key West bars. Much of the seafood seems to have been frozen, which is okay in Oklahoma but is unforgivable in the Keys. I personally love catfish, but what's it doing on a seafood restaurant's menu in Key West?

Croissants De France, *816 Duval Street*, ☎ *305-294-2624*, *$$*. Although handy for a morning cup of excellent coffee, I find it hard to enjoy a cup of Joe that cost close to $5. Come with a full wallet if you want to sample one of their delicious pastries along with your espresso, cappuccino, latte, frapuccino, café au lait, café con leche or....

Damn Good Food To Go, *700 Front Street*, ☎ *305-294-0011*, *$*. I guess it's hard to make your mark in the food business in Key West, but a catchy name helps. This is all that's really notable about the place. And the fact that you can call them up from your hotel for a late night grouper Reuben sandwich.

Dennis Pharmacy Restaurant, *1229 Simonton Street*, ☎ *305-294-1577*, *$*. Jimmy Buffett reportedly ate his cheeseburger in the paradise of this straight-ahead, counter-style restaurant.

Fish sandwiches, cheeseburgers, steaks and a few Cuban items sprinkle the menu. Open daily for breakfast, lunch and dinner.

Duffy's, *1007 Simonton Street*, ☎ *305-296-4900*, *$$*. Get a seat near the window so you'll have something to do while waiting for the food and drinks. Lobster, steak and prime rib are features.

El Mesón De Pepe, *410 Wall Street*, *www.elmesondepepe.com*, ☎ *305-295-2620*, *$$*. This faux-Cuban place has live Latin bands every night, and its waterfront location means people pack in here. *Mesón* actually means something like funky old bar in Spanish, but the ambiance here is more yuppie young tourist. Open every day for lunch and dinner from 11 am.

Half Shell Raw Bar, *Margaret and Caroline streets*, ☎ *305-294-7496*, *www.halfshellrawbar.com*, *$$*. With oysters Rockefeller, buffalo shrimp, and the usual Keys seafood items, this raw bar and regular ol' seafood joint serves food family style at long tables overlooking the Gulf. The walls are covered with license plates from all over. The food is good, simply prepared and served on paper plates. Although the Half Shell is usually packed with tourists, somehow I am just not fond of the place. Unless you eat a bunch of fries or order something breaded and greasy, you have to spend well over $20 to fill up on seafood. The portions are not huge and customers are expected to fill up on slaw, and side dishes. I've always imagined that there is a huge factory somewhere in Key West that supplies all the bars with pre-mixed margaritas made from lemon-flavored powder and tap water with a bit of cheap tequila thrown in. That's what the bar seems to be serving here. I suggest sticking to beer or handmade rum drinks. Don't linger – you'll be asked to move right along after your meal. Open for lunch and dinner every day.

Harpoon Harry's, *832 Caroline Street*, ☎ *305-294-8744*, *$*. Diner-style, with cheesy knick-knacks hanging everywhere, Harpoon Harry's serves meatloaf, pork chops, sandwiches and the regular breakfast things. They are open only for breakfast and lunch.

Hyatt Paradise Key West Hotel, *601 Front Street*, ☎ *305-296-9900*, *www.keywest.hyatt.com*, *$$$$*. A ferry ride takes you to New York Chef Paul's sophisticated dining experience with macadamia nut-encrusted grouper and mango-mint mojo –

whatever that is. This is high-design dining with tastes that amuse all of your senses.

Iguana Café, *425 Greene Street*, ☎ *305-296-6420*, *$$*. Open around the clock, this is *the* place to come if you want to try alligator burger, chowder, fritters or alligator tail steaks.

Jamaican Me Hungry/Coco Palms, *300 Front Street*, ☎ *305-296-0046*, *$*. Open for lunch and dinner every day, this place serves jerked chicken more or less the way would expect to find it in Jamaica.

Jose's Cantina, *800 White Street*, ☎ *305-296-4366*, *$*. If only the food in Cuba were this good! Jose's serves breakfast, lunch and dinner every day.

Kelly's Caribbean Bar & Grill, *301 Whitehead Street*, ☎ *305-293-8484*, *www.kellyskeywest.com*, *$$$*. Owned by obscure TV actress Kelly McGillis and located in what used to Pan American Airways offices, the bar and grill carry an airplane theme. Very good draft beers are brewed on site, but the food is the same old Keys stuff like shrimp, yellowtail and fish sandwiches. This place is noted for its coconut shrimp and Key lime pie. The building next door, a beautiful old white house with outdoor piano, is also owned by McGillis.

Kyushu, *921 Truman Avenue*, ☎ *305-294-2995*, *$$*. Japanese food is served on low tables (take off your shoes and sit on the floor) with emphasis on sashimi, sushi and tempura. Open for lunch and dinner every day.

La Concha at the Holiday Inn, *430 Duval Street*, ☎ *305-296-2991*, *www.laconchakeywest.com*, *$$$$*. This is not your typical Holiday Inn. Although it is overpriced (everything is in Key West except the sunshine), La Concha puts you right in the middle of the tourist action. Tennessee Williams and Hemingway both stayed here (so the stories go). They open for breakfast at 7 and have a full menu with the expected seafood slant. Steaks, chicken, fish and pasta are all available prepared in unsurprising ways.

Latitudes Beach Café, *245 Front Street, Sunset Key*, ☎ *305-292-5394*, *$$$*. Latitudes is located on Sunset Key, a small island near the harbor accessible only by a five-minute boat ride. You must make reservations and show up on time for the boat or *you* *go hungry!* Just kidding. Pick up the boat at the Hilton marina at 245 Front Street. They are open every day for all three meals.

Mangia Mangia, *900 Southard Street*, ☎ *305-294-2469*, *$$*. Despite the name, this place serves German (as well Italian favorites) dishes like schnitzel and spätzel. The standard seafood fare is also available. Fresh pasta, classic marinara sauce and conch minestrone combine in a Key West-Italian fusion. Mangi Mangia won the Wine Spectator's Award of Excellence. Its wine list is wonderful, and you can find a decent wine for under $20 or explore some unusual, more costly Chiantis.

Margaritaville Café, *500 Duval Street*, ☎ *305-292-1435*, *$$$*. With the Jimmy Buffet-inspired name, everyone seems to think they need to sample this touristy watering hole. Drinks are mediocre – stick to beer. It is unlikely that the live entertainment will be someone you've heard before or would like to hear again, but I guess you have to check it out anyway. And the food? Margaritaville is not about the food.

Martha's, *5 Roosevelt Blvd.*, ☎ *305-294-3466*, *$$$*. Set right by Key West International Airport next to Benihana's, Martha's has grouper, lobster tails, yellowtail, prime rib and steaks. Open for dinner every day.

Michael's Restaurant, *532 Margaret Street*, ☎ *305-295-1300*, *www.michaelskeywest.com*, *$$$*. Every night Michael's serves up some of the best steaks in the Keys, with obligatory seafood also on the menu. The desserts are good. The bar follows the trendy martini craze, offering a wide variety of vodkas (whatever happened to gin as a martini ingredient?) accompanied by a choice of olives stuffed with interesting things. Try not to fill up on olives before your dinner arrives. Michael's offers one of the better wine lists in town.

Nicola Seafood, *601 Front Street*, ☎ *305-296-9900, ext. 54*, *$$$*. Set inside the Hyatt hotel, Nicola's is open for breakfast, lunch and dinner. Caribbean-influenced seafood and steaks are featured. Try the sweet potato-crusted yellowtail while watching the sunset.

Origami, *1075 Duval Street*, ☎ *305-294-0092*, *$$*. Sushi, sashimi, baked fish and shellfish in cheese sauce are typical offerings at Origami. You can eat at the bar. Dress is smart casual. They are open for dinner every day.

Key West

Our Place, *1900 Flagler Street*, ☎ *305-292-4002*, *$*. Good, filling food at good prices is what Our Place is all about. Taxi drivers are supposed to know where to get good food and they congregate here along with other locals until 3 am.

Paradise Café, *1000 Eaton Street*, ☎ *305-296-5001*, *$*. Enormous sandwiches are the hook here and, although they are huge, they are made for people who will probably never return. The size is the gimmick – not the quality. This is a lunch-only place and is closed on Sundays.

Perry's, *3800 North Roosevelt Blvd.*, ☎ *305-294-8472*. Skip it. There are too many great places to eat in town to bother with this chain. Shoney's would be a better choice, and I don't say that lightly.

Rusty Anchor, *5510 3rd Avenue, Stock Island*, ☎ *305-294-5369*, *www.rustyanchorseafood.com*, *$$*. Much of the fresh seafood served in local restaurants is supplied by the commercial seafood market located at the back of the Rusty Anchor. That means the fish here should be fresh. Anchors, buoys and a great stuffed marlin supply nautical ambiance. Closed on Sundays.

Nightlife

If you want to have a big night out, Key West was designed for you. Just walk along Duval Street or stroll down some of the side streets and listen for music that suits you. There are hundreds of bars and clubs here, and almost all of them fall into the category of what I have to call "tourist bars." This is partly because they are usually packed with tourists, but also because the proprietors realize their patrons are just there for one night and will probably never come again, so the emphasis is on separating tourists from their dollars with the minimum of fuss.

> **WARNING:** Police often stop cars just outside town on the Overseas Highway on weekends, checking for inebriated drivers as they leave Key West.

The flood of in-and-out tourists means the bars don't have to make a real effort to do a fantastic job – their customers are probably never coming back anyway. Most Key West bars have those hoses with multiple buttons on the business end that allow bartenders to serve up coke, sprite, water, soda water or beer without changing hands. In Key West, the hoses also serve premixed margaritas, which tend to be served in plastic cups to minimize the fuss and muss associated with real glasses. Unless I am sure the bar makes their own drinks from fresh ingredients (no powdered mixes, please) I stick to bottled beer or call drinks. Of course, I don't go to fast-food joints either, so maybe I'm a little weird in this regard (so says my wife, anyway). You may be quite happy with the swill. Just keep in mind that you can get good drinks for the same price if you know where to go.

Partly due to the captive audience, the quality of live entertainment in Key West is also poor. It costs so much to stay in Key West that most regional bands cannot afford to play for the $100 to $200 most bars pay, and sleep and eat too. As a consequence, beginners and mediocre locals are the mainstay for bar entertainment. A few places have good bands and a few places serve great, handmade drinks. A very few do both. My "Author Picks," below, reflect this. But keep in mind I'm a middle-aged old fogey. Many people enjoy spending time in an alcoholic fuzz in a loud, crowded bar and don't really care if the drinks are made from a mix as long as they are cheap and don't make them sick. Such people will have a great time in Key West.

ENTERTAINMENT WORTH WAITING FOR

While being a quintessential tourist bar, **Sloppy Joe's** has the best entertainment in the Keys. If **Pete and Wayne** are on stage, you must see them. These guys serve up the most childish adult comedy entertainment imaginable, but they are not for the timid. The show starts at an early 5:30 and ends early at about 10 pm, so you can still go on to a late dinner or to yet another party spot. Other, more raucous bands come on after that and play until the wee hours. Sloppy Joe's serves good, honest drinks and the place is always packed.

AUTHOR NOTE: Many of the watering holes are also restaurants. If they are a serious eating place, I've reviewed them in the *Where to Eat* section.

Most of the bigger-name bars on Duval Street have a cover charge in the evenings or on weekends.

801 Bourbon Bar, *801 Duval Street,* ☎ *305-294-4737, www. 801bourbon.com*. The 801 offers gay entertainment. The nightly drag show is a real hoot and fun no matter what your lifestyle.

☆ **AUTHOR'S PICK** - **Afterdeck Bar**, *700 Waddell Street in Louie's Backyard,* ☎ *305-294-1061*. Jimmy Buffett used to play here for drinks, or so the stories go. Louies is a good restaurant and the bar on the waterside deck is a popular local and tourist hangout with live music on weekend nights.

Atlantic Shores Pool Bar, *510 South Street,* ☎ *305-296-2491*. The clothing-optional pool tends to define this gay bar that's popular with locals.

Bourbon Street Pub, *703 Duval Street,* ☎ *305-296-1992*. Happy hour runs from noon until 8 pm in this entertaining gay bar. The very latest in dance craze sounds are pumped out through huge speakers. Stage entertainment runs from comedians to loud bands and dancing men wearing pretty dresses. Lots of fun for all.

Bull & Whistle Entertainment Complex, *224 Duval Street,* ☎ *305-296-4565*. The Bull has live music in the garden, a pool and a good view of the action on Duval from its second floor. There is nude dining on the roof. You can't get anymore Key West than this without ending up in jail.

Captain Tony's, *428 Green Street,* ☎ *305-294-1838*. This was the original Sloppy Joe's – the one where Hemingway did his drinking.

RAISING THE RENT

The story is that bar owner Sloppy Joe Russell got mad at the landlord for raising the rent and moved the whole bar down the street to its present location in the middle of the night. Supposedly, this was well after Papa gave up on Key West for the fleshpots of Havana.

Many, many places in the Keys like to say that Jimmy Buffett ate/drank/smoked pot/slept at their place. Captain Tony's has its "Buffett was here" claim too. The walls are "decorated" with underwear. One of them are supposed to have been Jimmy's. Try to guess which pair while enjoying mediocre drinks and mediocre live music.

Funky Old Town Bar.

Diva's, *711 Duval Street*, ☎ *305-292-8500*. This mostly gay dance club starts happening sometime after 11 pm. Don't miss the queen show (drag, that is).

Fat Tuesday Key West, *305 Duval Street*, ☎ *305-296-9373*. Fat Tuesday's draws a very touristy, young crowd hot to do Jell-O shots. Drunk and shouting college kids are great if you're one of them. Management doesn't seem to throw people out for passing out under the table.

Finnegan's Wake, *320 Grinnell Street,* ☎ *305-293-0222, www. keywestirish.com.* This is the usual Irish pub with Guinness and a dartboard. They are open for lunch, dinner and drinking until 4 am. You even get to hear Irish music from live musicians on weekend nights.

☆ **AUTHOR'S PICK** - Green Parrot, *601 Whitehead Street,* ☎ *305-294-6133, www.greenparrot.com.* You can almost always find some of the better bands playing at the Green Parrot. Pool table, dartboards and good drinks make this a worthwhile stop for the evening. If you get hungry, go next door for wonderful ribs and BBQ at the Meteor Smokehouse. The place is a musicians' hang-out after midnight and is very, very hip among the hip.

Hard Rock Café, *313 Duval Street,* ☎ *305-293-0230, www.hard-rockcafe.com.* Just like at McDonald's, you always know just what to expect at a Hard Rock Café, no matter where you are. They are all the same tourist trap, but that doesn't mean you shouldn't enjoy them. Relax and be the tourist you know you are. You can always just go get the T-shirt and get out again unless you like the cookie-cutter, shlocky, plastic decorating clutter and mediocre food and drink. The lines can be long just to get in. Ordering is another nightmare, but you can say you've been, right? And you'll have the T-shirt to prove it.

Hog's Breath Saloon, *400 Front Street,* ☎ *305-296-4222, www. hogsbreath.com.* A crowded tourist bar, the Hog's Breath is open from 11 am every day. There are live music acts through the afternoon and into the evenings on weekends. Bikini and wet T-shirt contests round out the flavor of this popular place. This is not a place for serious eating, but you can munch on one of their popular (but dry) fish sandwiches. The drinks are served in the usual plastic cups.

Jimmy Buffett's Margaritaville Café, *500 Duval Street,* ☎ *305-292-1435, www.margaritaville.com.* The T-shirts are better than the food and drinks, but few people come here to eat. This is *the* place to go for close-up views of clueless tourists. It's loud, crowded and serves lousy, overpriced drinks and food, but has a name that tourists can't resist. Locals would die before being seen in here. Open from just before noon every day and has live entertainment. If you've read this far in the book you know there are some really great places to eat and drink in Key West – this is not one of them. If you must, run in, buy a T-shirt for the kids back home, and go eat and drink someplace more salubrious.

Mulcahy's Tavern, *509½ Duval Street,* ☎ *305-295-8796.* The Irish flavor at Mulcahy's runs to Guinness and the occasional Irish folk group. The entertainment is often pretty poor, but the Guinness is fine.

Pier House, *One Duval Street,* ☎ *305-296-4600, www.pierhouse. com.* This is touted as the place from which to watch the sunset, but get here plenty early or you will be straining your neck to see a glimpse of the sky over the heads of those near the bar. If you start drinking early enough, you may even believe you have seen the famous "green flash" that is sometimes seen when the sun's fading light is filtered through the sea just as the sun drops below the horizon. Seeing the green flash is the height of Keys hipness. To have seen it at the Pier House is as hip as it gets.

PT'S Late Night Bar & Grill, *902 Caroline Street,* ☎ *305-296-4245, www.turtlekraals.com.* Locals come for the food, pool tables and late-night drinking. Bands occasionally play here on weekends. A full menu of good food and large portions is available 24 hours a day, and the beer selection is excellent. If you're out real late and want something good and filling, this is the place.

Rick's, *200-300 Block of Duval Street,* ☎ *305-294-3765, www. rickskeywest.com.* Rick's offers terrible drinks, live bands, karaoke and adult entertainment all in a complex of four bars. Ever popular, it keeps on rockin' until 4 am.

Schooner Wharf Bar, *202 William Street,* ☎ *305-292-9520, www.schoonerwharf.com.* The Schooner has a nice raw bar with good bands that play blues, jazz and island music. Dogs are welcome in this local hangout named for the *Western Union* schooner that is usually parked right in front (it does sunset cruises and charters).

☆ **AUTHOR'S PICK** - **Sloppy Joe's**, *201 Duval Street,* ☎ *305-294-5717, www.sloppyjoes.com.* Loud, crowded and probably the most touristy spot in the Keys, Sloppy Joe's makes much of the fact that Hemingway used to drink here – it just didn't happen to be *this* Sloppy Joe's, but who cares? Hemingway really did his drinking at what is now called Captain Tony's at 428 Greene Street (see above). The bar is rowdy and fun, but you have to pay a cover charge on the weekends. Wacky entertainers Pete & Wayne are a hilarious comedy duo that are the usual opening act starting at 5:30 (www.peteandwayne.com). This is outrageous adult comedy – not for the kiddies and not to be missed. They love to get the audience involved and will tease people unmercifully if they sense weakness. Don't sit up front! If I come to Key West and fail to see Pete & Wayne, I feel my trip was not a complete success. The drinks, served in plastic cups to avoid trouble from rowdy guests and work for the dishwashers, are honest and not overly expensive. Still, I stick to bottled beer when I come here. Don't let them fool you – their specialty beers are made by Coors. Although one of the worst tourist traps, its popularity means it can afford good entertainers. Look for Barry Cuda, too.

Stick & Stein Sports Rock Café, *2922 N. Roosevelt Blvd.,* ☎ *305-296-3352*. Pool and game tables, seemingly hundreds of big, blaring TVs and all the usual sports bar stuff make this a regular sports bar. Bring earplugs or simply drink a lot to get in the mood.

Turtle Kraals Waterfront Bar, *231 Margaret Street at Land's End Marina,* ☎ *305-294-2640, www.turtlekraals.com*. The beer selection is very good but the margaritas are just okay. They have live bands when the season is high and things are rockin'.

Virgilio's, *524 Duval Street,* ☎ *305-296-8118*. An upscale martini bar, Virgilio's specializes in sophisticated, handmade drinks like Gibsons, Manhattans and a dozen or more types of martinis. They tend to have small local combos playing unobtrusive instrumental sounds. If you find yourself a bit tired of wet T-shirt contests, dwarf tossing and drag queen shows, Virgilio's is a pleasant oasis.

Wax, *422 Applerouth Lane,* ☎ *305-304-6988*. Wax is a hip spot for the late-20s/early-30s, mostly local crowd who come to dance, dance, dance to the sounds of house, trance and regular dance music. No sandals or T-shirts – hip sophistication is the deal here. Whatever you do, do not order a margarita here – it's not cool; apple martinis (yuck!) are.

Everglades National Park

Everglades National Park

Close to Miami yet far away in time, Everglades National Park has wildlife galore. Crocodiles, alligators, panthers, bears and terrible snakes share the same marshy spaces with brilliantly plumed birds, exotic sea life and the stark beauty of saw grass and cypress hammocks.

The park was established in 1947 primarily to preserve the "river of grass." This shallow "river" is a vast swamp extending from Okeechobee to the Keys, from just outside Miami to the Gulf coast. It is the breeding grounds for most of the marine species that make Florida so popular with nature lovers and outdoorsfolk.

Due to its proximity to the urban sprawl created by millions of Miami and South Florida residents' with pollution-emitting cars and homes, it is at risk of becoming a memory of wildlife, rather than a sanctuary. Big business wants to develop it or use its water. Conservationists of several persuasions argue over whether the area should be left as is, reformed by man into what it used to be, or preserved as a park for camera-toting tourist hordes. Politics on a national level intrude as Big Sugar pours hundreds of millions into promoting their interest in the area: use the water for growing cane and worry about the pesticide and fertilizer runoff at some date in the future. Me? I just want to be able to go there and soak up the sounds and sights of relatively undisturbed nature: the wind blowing almost silently across miles of saw grass, the screech of hawks and the grunts of gators.

Can these interests coexist? Decades of "water management" have changed the course of the river of grass probably forever, drying out hatcheries for snapper, redfish, mullet and shrimp and reducing the take of commercial fishermen and recreational anglers alike. Attempts to alleviate some of the problems we've created for the Everglades are frequently blocked by big business and development interests. We should be gloriously thrilled that the existing parks were created at all. We should support and enjoy them responsibly. Preservation and research face off against "use" by hunters, airboat operators, swamp buggy tourism and cattle grazing – activities currently allowed in adjacent Big Cypress Swamp.

Covering almost all of the bottom tip of Florida and reaching well out into Florida Bay and the Gulf of Mexico, Everglades National Park is one of America's favorite parks, seeing hundreds of thousands of visitors every year. They come to view wildlife on land and in the marine environments. The park contains temperate and tropical climates that support pinelands, hardwood hammocks, mangrove swamps, miles of saw grass and turtle grass, as well as sand flats.

NOTED STATUS

Everglades National Park is designated a World Heritage Site, an International Biosphere Reserve and a Wetland of International Importance.

At a Glance

LARGEST TOWN: Homestead, population 33,727

ELEVATION: 10 feet

AREA: 2,354 square miles

COUNTY: Monroe, Collier

MAJOR ROUTES: Overseas Highway (US 1); Tamiami Trail

NEAREST AIRPORTS: Marathon (66 miles); Miami International (25 miles); Naples (37 miles)

ZIP CODES: 33030; 34138

AVERAGE TEMPERATURE: January 66°; August 81.5°

PRECIPITATION: January 2.3 inches; August 8.7 inches

History

Even as the plume hunters blasted the few remaining exotic birds, people were thinking about the need for their protection. In 1928, Ernest Coe, a landscape architect, began his efforts to convince Congress to set aside large parts of the Everglades as a park. In 1934, Congress officially established the basis for a park to be formed, but it took until 1947 before the park was officially opened. Harry Truman officiated at the formal opening ceremony at Flamingo. Nearby Big Cypress National Preserve was set aside in 1974 after a battle against a huge jetport outside Miami. For his efforts, Ernest Coe has been dubbed the "Father of the Everglades" and had a visitor center named after him. Since the park was first established it has expanded from the original 460,000 acres to cover 1.5 million acres.

Marjory Stoneman Douglas, author of *River of Grass,* was influential in publicizing the plight of the area and building support for the park. Her book still influences conservationists and supports them in their continuing efforts to protect more areas of the Everglades.

Everglades National Park

Geology & Terrain

Everglades National Park is about as flat as any place can get. Most of it is at sea level and nowhere does the elevation rise more than a few feet. Before modern drainage systems changed things, the Everglades was mostly an enormous sheet of water moving very slowly south from the Lake Okeechobee area. Even now, during rainy season, the park can be almost 93% water. Saw grass is able to live in a partially submerged habitat and thrives over much of what is now the park. This sea of grass is dotted with clumps, or hammocks, of pine, cypress or gumbo-limbo trees. Where the broad expanse of the Everglades meets the coast of Florida Bay, it is ringed with dense mangroves forming an almost impenetrable barrier to the interior. Ten Thousand Islands near Chokoloskee is a labyrinth of narrow channels winding through the mangroves.

Just under the shallow water and muck is what remains of an ancient coral reef. Eons ago, a living reef grew to be one of the largest on earth just under the surface of the ocean. When the ocean receded due to glacial expansion in the first ice age, the reef died as it was exposed to air. As the glaciers melted, the water rose over the reefs once again. A series of glacial expansions and contractions resulted in a huge dead reef that is now the bedrock of South Florida.

THE EFFECTS OF HURRICANE ANDREW

Hurricane Andrew blew through the Everglades and South Florida in August 1992. Parts of the park suffered extensive damage and the main visitor center was almost completely destroyed. All of the facilities have now been rebuilt or replaced. Some damage to vegetation can still be seen, but most of the worst hit areas have now grown up enough so that few visitors would know of the damaged that occurred.

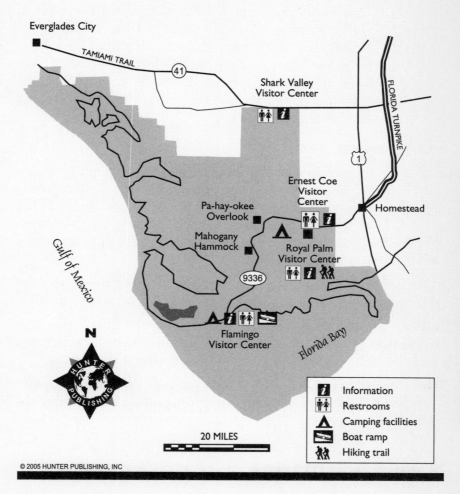

Everglades National Park

■ Everglades Ecosystems

Coastal Marsh

 The coastal marsh is where the inland areas of saw grass meet the mangroves, where freshwater meets salt. Only a few inches of elevation separate the two ecosystems. The marshes are dotted with small holes slightly deeper than the surrounding area, giving habitat to fish, frogs, alligators, and are a source of water during dry spells.

Hardwood Hammocks

Hammocks are small groves of trees dotted about the river of grass. The word "hammock" comes from a West Indian word meaning "shady place" and that's exactly what they are. Most hammocks cover less than a couple of acres and are home to a variety of wildlife. Hammocks are usually made up of mahogany, cypress, gumbo-limbo, tamarind, slash pine (technically not a hardwood) and royal palm trees.

Mangroves

With a bit of practice you can discern three types of mangroves – black, red and white – as you travel through the park. Mangroves reproduce mostly by dropping long "roots" through the air to the mud below, or by letting the roots drop off to float away and possibly take root in shallow oyster bars or mud flats, thus starting a new mangrove island.

Red mangroves, sometimes known as "walking trees," are the ones along the edge of the water that drop aerial roots and shed sprouts that float away to form new mangrove colonies.

Black mangroves tend to be a bit taller than red mangroves and grow behind them, farther away from the water's edge.

White mangroves are even taller than red or black mangroves. They are a variety of buttonwood and usually grow behind the other two mangroves. They tolerate saltwater, but rarely send down aerial roots.

Marine & Estuarine

As water runs off the Everglades, silt and sand form huge areas of turtle grass and sand flats. The hard bottom supports small corals. Mangroves border the edges, making a rich spawning ground for many sport and commercial fish species, as well as a mating area for both crocodiles and manatees. Most of Florida Bay is quite shallow with insufficient influence from tidal action to flush detritus from the ecosystem. Only the occasional strong hurricane adequately scours silt from the Bay.

Pineland

Slash pines establish themselves wherever the elevation is a little higher than the surrounding swamps. The pines need a relatively dry soil. The roots they send into cracks in the underlying limestone suck nutrients out of small pockets of sediment. Fires regularly rage through the pinelands, but the trees have developed a thick bark that protects them from scorching.

Cypress Zones

Cypress tends to grow where pockets of sediment form in shallow pits and holes found in saw grass areas. Dwarf varieties grow in brackish water, while the taller cypress need freshwater. These dryer areas were home to early Native Americans who spent months at a time in temporary camps living off the oyster beds just offshore. Huge mounds, some as high as 20 feet, were formed as the natives discarded the oyster shells. These mounds can still be found today, and some include stone or shell artifacts.

Coastal Prairie

Coastal prairie zones are drier than most of the saw grass areas and can serve as a transition between the inland swamps and slightly more elevated areas in back of the mangroves. The salt-tolerant species such as cactus, yucca and grasses thrive in prairie zones.

Freshwater Sloughs & Freshwater Marl Prairie

Freshwater sloughs, the wettest parts of the Everglades, are basically very shallow, wide rivers flowing slowly through a network of depressions and, possibly, old riverbeds. Shark River Slough is one of the largest of these and it can be 40 miles wide after heavy rains. In the dry season, the underlying marl is sometimes exposed, revealing a series of small channels and sinkholes.

Everglades National Park

Visitor Information

■ Open Hours

 The park is open 24 hours a day, all year long. The Shark Valley entrance is open daily, 8:30 am to 6 pm. The obscure Chekika entrance is open Monday-Friday, 8 am to 5 pm and 8 am to 6 pm on Saturday and Sunday. You can access general park information by calling ☎ *305-242-7700*. Ernest C Coe is the park's main point of entry.

■ Visitor Centers

At the main entrance to the park is the **Ernest F. Coe Visitor Center**, *open daily, 8 am-5 pm,* ☎ *305-242-7700.*

The **Royal Palm Visitor Center**, *also open daily, 8 am-4:15 pm,* ☎ *305-242-7700*, is s nice place to cool off, grab a soda from the drink machine (a bargain at 75¢) and browse the good selection of books about Florida and the Everglades, including childrens' books. You can pick up some modest souvenirs at the center. There are restrooms. Ranger-led walks usually run daily; call ahead for details and schedules. The center is six miles from the park entrance.

The **Shark Valley Visitor Center,** ☎ *305-221-8455,* is where tram tours of the Shark Valley area begin. The trams have open sides, but are shaded and are a comfortable way to see the saw grass marshes and wildlife. The two-hour trips leave every hour on the hour. The price is $9.50 and reservations area good idea in the winter.

At Everglades City, right by the start of Ten Thousand Islands, is the **Gulf Coast Visitor Center**, *open daily, 8:30 am-5 pm,* ☎ *239-695-3311*. This is the place to pick up maps and check on upcoming ranger-led events. Boat tours through Ten Thousand Islands usually leave every hour on the hour. Boat tours through Ten Thousand Islands usually leave every 30 minutes; rates are $16 adults; $8 children. No reservations.

■ Getting Here

The park is within easy driving distance of Miami and Fort Myers, so day-trips are practical. To get the full Everglades experience, stay in one of the motels that have sprung up around park entrances, in the park itself at a campground, or at the park's motel at Flamingo. Shark Valley and the western visitors centers are reached from the Tamiami Trail, either from the Miami or Fort Myers end. The Tamiami Trail (Highway 41) runs from Miami along the northern border of the park and passes right by Shark Valley Visitors Center. Highway 9336 heads from Everglades City, near Homestead, into the heart of the park, leading to Royal Palm Visitors Center. It ends 40 miles later at remote Flamingo, where the Flamingo Visitors Center on Florida Bay has a modest motel, restaurants, a marina and campgrounds. There are interpretive centers and trails along the spectacular drive through the park.

■ Getting Around

Highways

The one major road (Highway 9336) through the park runs from Florida City to Flamingo. The funky town of Chokoloskee is inside the park and reached by a short drive from Everglades City. Other than that, getting around the park is done on foot, by canoe or kayak or on the tram that runs from Shark Valley Visitors Center to the observation tower. This lack of access is what preserves the area so, rather than frustration that so much of the park is inaccessible, visitors should feel jubilation that so much of the park is close to pristine.

Airports

Miami, Ft. Lauderdale and Fort Myers are the closest airports with commercial service. Homestead has a small local airport accessible to private charter jets, but it does not have rental car agencies.

■ Information Sources

Websites

 www.nps.gov/ever/welcome2.htm has just about everything you might need to know about visiting the park.

Books

A Canoeing and Kayaking Guide to the Streams of Florida: Volume II Central and South, by Lou Glaros and Doug Sphar, Menasha Ridge Press, 1985, ISBN 0897320670. $13.95

The Best in Tent Camping: Florida: A Guide for Campers Who Hate RVs, Concrete Slabs, and Loud Portable Stereos, Johnny Molloy, Menasha Ridge Press, 2000, ISBN 0897322738. $14.95

Everglades River of Grass, Marjory Stoneman Douglas, Henry Holt & Company, Inc., 1997, ISBN 0030289505. $16.95

Boat & Canoe Camping in the Everglades Backcountry, D. Kalma, Florida Flair Books, 1988, ISBN 096132368X.

A Paddler's Guide To Everglades National Park, J. Molloy, University Press of Florida, 2000, ISBN 0813017874. $16.95

Everglades Wildguide, J.C. George, US Government Printing Office, 1988, ISBN 0160034205. $8.

Maps & Charts

The following NOAA Nautical Charts are $17.75 each.

- No. 11430 ... Lostman's River to Wiggins Pass (Stock #2120)
- No. 11432 ... Shark River to Lostman's River (Stock #2130)
- No. 11433 ... Whitewater Bay (Stock #2140)
- Topographic Map - Everglades National Park (#2058), $9.95

Downloadable maps are available at **www.nps.gov/ever/pphtml/maps.html**.

▪ When to Come

 The best time to visit the Everglades is in the winter; summer brings heat and rain, as well as fiercer mosquitoes. The South Florida climate can be hot even in December, but is reasonably mild from late October until early March. Summer weather can be humid and very hot, but the stout among us will don hats, spray on plenty of bug repellent and go for it. Afternoon rains occur almost daily in summer, providing relief from the heat. Of course, winter is the busiest time and you may need to reserve well in advance for lodging or camping sites. Many of the tours and ranger-led activities operate only during winter.

▪ Special Concerns

Accessibility

 A surprising amount of the park and its facilities are wheelchair-accessible. The visitor centers, boat tours from Flamingo, Shark Valley tram tour and all of the major trails are suitable for wheelchairs. The campgrounds at Flamingo, Long Pine Key and Chekika are also accessible to those in wheelchairs. The Pearl Bay primitive wilderness campsite is handicapped-accessible.

Pets

Pets are not allowed on any of the trails or anywhere besides campgrounds, parking lots and at the Flamingo Lodge. They must not be left unattended.

Sightseeing

▪ Suggested Itineraries

Driving down from Miami to enjoy the park and back again in the same day is doable and enjoyable. From Miami, Homestead is only (depending on traffic) an hour or so south, and Flamingo is 1½ hours. Some of the nicest trails are close to the park entrance.

If You Have One Day

You could make a quick stop at the park entrance, Ernest F. Coe Visitor Center, but there's not much there. Better to go 10 miles farther to the **Royal Palm Visitor Center** and browse through the books a little before setting out on the best trail in the park: the **Anhinga Trail**. This trail starts out right by the visitor center and is wide, comfortable and filled with sights and sounds. The gators make a real racket and the ponds are brimming with fish. Birds flit about and after a short walk away from the center you feel like you could have gone back 100 years in time. Check and see if there are any ranger-led activities you want to join. The **Gumbo-Limbo Trail** also starts close to the center.

You could blast on down to Flamingo and take one of the **boat tours** that leaves from the Flamingo Marina or walk the **Snake Bight Trail** before heading back. After you leave the park, stop for refreshments at the **Robert Is Here Fruit Stand**, *19200 SW 344th Street, ☎ 305-246-1592, www.robertishere.com.*

If You Have Three Days

The drive from the park entrance towards Flamingo passes almost all the best trails in the park. Some are not much more than a place to park and view wildlife, but many are longer. Stop at several of them on your way to the lodge at Flamingo (**Flamingo Lodge, Marina & Outpost Resort**, ☎ *941-695-3101, 800-600-3813, fax 941-695-3921, www.flamingolodge.com*). The **Royal Palm Visitor Center** is the place to find out about any upcoming ranger-led activities. The **Anhinga Trail** starts just past the visitor center building and is one of the best trails in the park. After checking into the lodge, head out on one of the boat trips through the backcountry or out into Florida Bay for a good introduction to the region. Book your trip at the Flamingo Marina upon arrival.

> **AUTHOR TIDBIT:** As soon as you check in, you should make reservations at the restaurant as it is small and fills up quickly in the evening.

There is no other place to eat unless you drive
back to Homestead.

Early morning and dusk are often the best times for wildlife
viewing and I suggest getting up as early as you can on Day Two,
grabbing a quick cup of coffee and walking over to the **Eco Pond**
for a slow circuit around the water's edge. Note: Watch for gators
on the path.

If you have the energy and brought your mosquito repellent, the
Bayshore Loop (two miles) is a nice walk along the shoreline
just up from the mangroves. If you are a big hiker, you might try
an early start (things can get hot later in the day) on the **Coastal
Prairie Trail** (15 miles). Both trails start at the end of the campground. The rest of the day can be spent driving on the road back
towards the park entrance, stopping at any of the trails along the
way that catch your interest.

If you are staying in Flamingo you will probably want to set aside
most of Day Three to drive over to the **Shark Valley tram** for a
view of another part of the park. If it's hot in the afternoon, head
back to the lodge for an air-conditioned nap before setting out
again just before dark for yet another walk.

If you don't have to get back to Miami immediately, renting a
kayak for a trip on your own or guided through the mangroves
and a little of the backcountry is the best way to immerse yourself in the beauty of the unspoiled Everglades. Arrange this at
the Flamingo Marina.

If You Have a Week

7 DAYS A week allows you to explore all the main parts of the
park. Stay at **Flamingo Lodge**, ☎ *941-695-3101, 800-
600-3813, fax 941-695-3921, www.flamingolodge.com,*
for four nights and then drive over to Everglades City or
Chokoloskee for the last three nights. Stop at the **Shark Valley
Visitor Center**, ☎ 305-221- 8455, for a tram ride through park.
An interesting side trip involves leaving the Tamiami Trail and
taking the gravel **Loop Road** that heads off at Forty Mile Bend.

Backcountry camping trips can take as little as a day or two but,
with a week, another option is to go on one of the guided
backcountry **canoe** or **boat tours** that leave from Chokoloskee

Everglades National Park

and end up in Flamingo. These trips are completely guided and supply just about everything you'll need other than hat and bug spray (you'll definitely need these two items). There are no trails in the western part of the park, but a boat tour through the Ten Thousand Islands is an unforgettable way to see the area. Book with **Everglades National Park Boat Tours**, *Everglades City,* ☎ *941-695-2591.*

A 'gator drifts lazily in the water.

Adventures

■ On Foot

Everglades National Park has 156 miles of canoe and nature trails. Some of the best ones are wheelchair-accessible. You don't have to be in particularly good shape to enjoy yourself and see much of the wildlife typical in the area. If you like to hike into the backcountry and camp far from civilization, there are 47 wilderness campsites. Most of the hiking trails are accessed from the road that runs from the Ernest F. Coe entrance to Flamingo, with Bobcat, Otter Cave and the Tram Road located in the park's Shark Valley area. There are no hiking trails in the west end of the park.

I describe the trails in the order you would encounter them as you drive through the park, starting from the Ernest F. Coe Visitor Center with the Shark Valley Trails at the end. For details and schedules of ranger-led walks and other activities, contact the visitor centers directly.

Exploring the park is easy if you stick to the maintained trails and viewing platforms. Off-trail treks can be inhospitable due to heat, sharp saw grass, bugs and muck. Hiking and wading off of the main trails is allowed, except in closed areas.

> **WARNING:** If you choose to wander off the designated trails, watch your step! Holes and sharp rocks are hidden under shallow water and vegetation. Snakes and other nasties lurk in palmettos and bushes. Stout boots are recommended.

CLOSED AREAS

Of course, some areas are closed to the public; most are marked with signs. All of the keys and beaches in Florida Bay are closed to protect rookeries, with the exceptions of Carl Ross Key, Little Rabbit Key, North West Key and Bradley Key. In northeast Florida Bay, Little Madiera Bay, Taylor River, East Creek, Mud Creek, Mud Bay, Davis Creek, Joe Bay and Snag Bay are closed. Rogers Bay Rookery, Indian Key Rookery and Cuthbert Lakes are also closed. Landing on Pavilion Key is allowed only on its northernmost point.

Anhinga Trail

The half-mile trail goes comfortably for a half-hour or so through seemingly unspoiled Taylor Slough and takes visitors close to turtles, dozens of huffing and chuffing alligators, rabbits, herons, egrets and anhingas. The trail is wide and paved, with long boardwalks through saw grass and over ponds teeming with fish.

Everglades National Park

This is one of the finest wildlife-viewing experiences in the US. If you don't have time to get deeply into the park, you should at least stop here for an hour or so. You can't fail to get some good pictures and, if you have a zoom lens, you will get some great ones. The trail begins just past the Royal Palm Visitor Center, six miles from the park entrance. Wheelchair-accessible.

Gumbo-Limbo Trail

The half-mile Gumbo-Limbo Trail also begins just past the Royal Palm Visitor Center. It passes through what was once a dense hardwood hammock. In 1992 Hurricane Andrew did some serious damage to the hammock, but it is now recovering nicely. Wild coffee, gumbo-limbo and orchids are easily spotted. You can also see orchids and royal palms. Wheelchair-accessible.

SPOTTING A GUMBO-LIMBO

You can tell the gumbo-limbo tree by its bright red bark that earns it the nickname of "tourist tree" because it resembles peeling, sunburned skin.

Pa-hay-okee Overlook Trail

This quarter-mile boardwalk leads to a wooded viewing platform with a good view over the "sea of grass." Huge cypress trees shade parts of the walk; look for emerging cypress "knees" at the base of the big trees. And keep your eyes peeled for evil-looking vultures, red-shouldered hawks and red-winged blackbirds. Wheelchair-accessible.

Mahogany Hammock Trail

This half-mile boardwalk trail sets off through the sea of grass and leads to a hardwood hammock, where it loops around. Check out the poisonwood tree on the right side as you head out toward the hammock. Of course, you will find mahogany trees too. In fact, the largest mahogany in the US is here. Look for liguus tree snails and golden orb weaver spiders. Mahogany Hammock was damaged by Hurricane Andrew. Wheelchair-accessible.

West Lake Trail

A half-mile boardwalk takes you through a mangrove swamp at the edge of a large lake. Air plants and magnificent groups of nesting birds are seen, along with all four types of mangrove. Mangroves provide some limited protection from hurricanes and this trail suffered less from Hurricane Andrew than other parts of the park. Wheelchair-accessible.

Bayshore Loop

This two-mile loop trail begins at the Flamingo campground, runs along the shore and heads back inland as it returns to the campground. This can be a very peaceful walk in the early morning. Look for wading birds, air plants and the occasional deer. You may be able to discern the remnants of a 19th-century fishing village by the water.

Snake Bight Trail

A little over three miles long, round-trip, Snake Bight Trail passes through a hardwood hammock and has a boardwalk at its end. The "Bight" in the trail name refers to a geographical feature rather than a "bite." While snakes are undoubtedly present, the danger of being bitten is no greater here than in other areas of the park. The trail is famous for birds. Expect sightings of anhingas, white-eyed vireos and palm warblers. Blue herons and white ibis are spotted near the end of the trail, at the edge of the shore overlooking Florida Bay. Rowdy Bend Trail intersects Snake Bight Trail about half-way along.

Rowdy Bend Trail

This 2½-mile route passes along an old roadbed through coastal salt prairie. Gumbo-limbo, palm and other Spanish moss-draped trees shade parts of the walk.

Coastal Prairie Trail

This is one of the longest trails in the park (7½ miles, one way) and its distant reaches are not visited nearly as much as the more convenient trails closer to the park entrance. For this reason, you are likely to see a little more wildlife. The trail follows an old road that passed by a couple of small fishing settlements and

Everglades National Park

farms from the 1800s. Buttonwoods, mangroves, grasses and small succulents are seen, along with deer. In the very unlikely event that you see a panther, this is where it could happen. Birders like the trail for the numerous wading birds seen at the edges of Florida Bay.

■ On Wheels

Cycling Trails

 The few biking trails are nice ones. You can head along the main road towards Flamingo, stopping at the overlooks and exploring trails on foot. The Shark Valley tram road, Old Ingraham Highway, Long Pine Key Nature Trail, Snake Bight and Rowdy Bend trails also allow bikes.

■ OUTFITTERS

North American Canoe Tours, *Everglades City in the Ivey House,* ☎ *239-695-3299, fax 239-695-4155, www. evergladesadventures.com.* NACT rents canoes, kayaks, bicycles and all sorts of camping equipment. They have half-, full-day and overnight tours with naturalist guides. Two-day trips start around $500.

Everglades International Hostel & Tours, *20 SW 2nd Ave., Florida City,* ☎ *305-248-1122, 800-372-3874, fax 305-245-7622, gladeshostel@hotmail.com, www. evergladeshostel.com,* rents canoes and bicycles with drop-off and pick-up service. They also offer guided canoe, biking or hiking tours from $50 for a long half-day.

■ On Horseback

 Anyone interested in riding a horse in the park must first get a permit. Contact the chief ranger's office, ☎ *305-242-7700,* for more information.

■ On Water

 Exploring Everglades canals and the Ten Thousands Island by kayak, small boat or canoe is one of the most interesting things you can do in the park. You need to get away from the boat docks and back in the mangroves for the best views of wildlife and to get a feel for what the watery wilderness is really like. Fortunately, you can do this in relative comfort.

> **AUTHOR NOTE:** Motorized personal watercraft, such as JetSkis, are prohibited in all areas of the park.

Airboat Rides

Airboats are flat-bottomed, blunt-nosed boats similar to john boats and are powered by airplane engines with huge propellers facing the rear. The propellers are (usually) covered by screens to minimize the chopping off of arms, etc. Bench seats are provided and the operator sits up high just in front of the engine. As you might imagine, these are very loud trips. I suggest bringing earplugs or screwing up small pieces of tissue to put (gently) into your ears. Because of their very shallow draft and high speed, this type of boat can zoom through very shallow water and even scoot over small islands and sand bars. They are a very good, but ecologically unsound, way to move through the sawgrass swamps of the 'Glades. You can get far out into the wilderness quickly, but the noise and commotion caused by your passage means much wildlife will head for distant parts long before you get close. Smashing down grasses, small trees and bulling through and over hammocks and small islands does significant damage. How can anything this noisy be a good way to see nature or contribute to its preservation?

Although I personally disapprove of them, airboat rides are popular tourist activities and hundreds of operators can be found here. Call ahead for prices and reservations.

■ OUTFITTERS

Everglades Private Airboat Tours, ☎ *941-695-4637*

Gator Park, ☎ *800-559-2255*

Speedy Johnson's Fun Cruise, ☎ *941-695-4448*

Everglades National Park

Boating

The full-service **Flamingo Marina**, ☎ *239-695-3101, 800-600-3813*, has slips and hookups for over 50 boats. There is a small shop with a very limited supply of expensive groceries, fuel service and a good boat ramp. The channel leading into the marina can handle boats with up to four-foot draft. Houseboat, canoe and kayak rentals are available. Canoes rent for $12 per hour, kayaks $11. Two-night houseboat rentals start at $475.

There are **boat ramps** at the marina in Flamingo, West Lake, Everglades City, Chokoloskee next to Outdoor Resorts and on Highway 41 near Ochopee and Little Blackwater Sound on Key Largo.

Fishing

Fishing in and around Everglades National Park is excellent in both fresh- and saltwater, although some areas are off-limits to all anglers. Non-residents need separate fishing license for salt- or freshwater fishing. You'll see some ponds loaded with bass, bluegill and other introduced species like tilapia. Fish seemed to be packed in like sardines in a can. This is what most of the Everglades waters were like before modern use of surface water dried up the grass and large nearby urban populations brought fishing pressure and pollution.

Most of the fishing is flats or backcountry fishing in Florida Bay and in and around Ten Thousand Islands. Guides with small skiffs can take two anglers out into the wilderness hoping to hook up with tarpon, snook, redfish, snapper and spotted sea trout. Such guides usually provide everything you need, including all poles and tackle, bait, license and cold drinks.

■ OUTFITTERS

Captain John Griffiths, *Flamingo,* ☎ *305-248-9470, www.captainjohngriffiths.com*. Captain Griffiths is a licensed and insured National Park Guide and certified by the US Coast Guard. He can tell you about the wildlife you encounter, as well as put fish on your hook. Prices start at $325 for a half-day.

Captain Bobby Hackney, *Flamingo,* ☎ *305-394-0087*. One of the more active captains in the park, Captain

Bobby has been fishing here for more than 30 years.
Rates start at $325 for a half-day.

Canoeing & Kayaking

Traveling by canoe or kayak is the very best way to see the park,
most of which is covered with narrow channels that wind their
way through even the most remote areas. Some trails are
marked with white markers and some are marked with the traditional nautical green (leaving) and red (returning) marker posts.
Just remember "red, right, return" meaning that if you keep the
red markers on your right side you will be heading back to the beginning of the channel.

Flamingo Area Paddling Trails

> **AUTHOR NOTE:** There is a $3 launch charge
> for non-motorized watercraft in the Flamingo
> area.

The **Nine Mile Pond Trail** covers 5.2 miles and passes through
a broad expanse of saw grass marsh dotted with a few groups of
mangroves. Alligators and wading birds are the most likely wildlife encounter, but you are also in good territory for alligators,
blue herons, turtles, ibis, bromeliads and orchids. Numbered
white poles mark the route.

The two-mile **Noble Hammock Trail** leads through mangrove
tunnels and ponds. It is protected from the wind and there is little current. Lots of birds are seen along the route, including blue
herons, ibis and other wading birds. Bromeliads, paurotis palms
and several types of mangrove are present. There are alligators
galore.

"Hell to get into and hell to get out of" is what early settlers said
about Hell's Bay. The well-marked **Hells Bay Trail** runs three
miles through mangroves and over small ponds. This was once a
prime spot for alligator and plume hunters, although a few never
returned from their trip. Fishing can be quite good.

> **AUTHOR TIDBIT:** Tides and wind can make
> your journey by kayak or canoe much longer
> and more difficult than you might expect.

Everglades National Park

Florida Bay stretches out for miles and is easily accessible from Flamingo. There are literally thousands of small keys to visit in this mostly shallow area, so you can enjoy the sea life on the turtle grass and sand flats. The wind can be very strong; be sure you don't get too far downwind of your starting point. Landing is prohibited on most of the keys in the area.

Bear Lake Canal is a 1.6-mile abandoned canal shaded in many places by overhanging trees leading to Bear Lake. From the lake, you can go another 11 miles to Cape Sable or connect with the Mud Lake Canoe Trail or the Buttonwood Canal. The very straight canal can get quite shallow. The last time I was here, the markers were obscured or missing and I was unable to travel the whole route due to lack of water.

Mud Lake is a good birding spot with anhingas, ibis and many other wading species. The 6.8-mile trail connects with the Buttonwood Canal, Coot Bay and Bear Lake Canoe Trail.

The 7.7-mile West Lake Trail crosses over some large lakes and through narrow connecting mangrove channels. There are plenty of crocs and 'gators to be seen, along with ducks, anhingas and ibis. Since much of the route is exposed, winds can make this a difficult trip. Look for gigantic bromeliads. There is a large pavilion where you can get out of the sun and stretch your legs a bit.

Two miles across Chokoloskee Bay through a marked channel is **Sandfly Island**, a Calusa Indian shell mound. The mound has evidence of an abandoned homestead where early settlers grew tomatoes and had a small store. A one-mile trail leads around the island, where raccoons, turtles, crabs and lots of birds are the only inhabitants.

> **AUTHOR TIDBIT:** The dock on Sandfly Island can be difficult to use since it is high and the surrounding water is very shallow. If you decide to make a circuit of the island, realize there is a very shallow oyster bar off the north end. Currents can be strong and heavy wind may make the trip impractical.

Chokoloskee Area Paddling Trails

AUTHOR NOTE: There is no launch fee for non-motorized watercraft in the Gulf area.

The **Chokoloskee Bay Loop** follows a marked channel 2½ miles through the flats and oyster bars of Chokoloskee Bay. Some great smaller channels lead through numerous mangrove keys. Poke your nose in and you may be surprised that you can actually penetrate some of them to small interior lakes. This area is one of the best in which to see manatees. If the wind is up, you may want to select a more protected trail.

Just west of the H.P. Williams Roadside Park on Tamiami Trail (Highway 41) is the start of the eight-mile **Turner River Trail**, which ends up in Chokoloskee Bay near Everglades City. The trail begins in cypress forest, passes through open prairie marsh, and finishes in dense mangrove swamp. Watch out for airboats roaring around and spoiling things.

Halfway Creek and Turner River Loop. This route starts just behind the ranger station and heads along the shoreline. It loops through mangroves and returns to Chokoloskee Bay not far from where it begins. Most of it passes through a mangrove tunnel, which is fun but does limit viewing wildlife or anything other than dense mangroves with oysters clinging to their roots. There are lots of air plants, bromeliads and a few orchids. Portions of the trail pass through Big Cypress National Preserve.

Shark River Area Paddling Trails

The 99-mile **Wilderness Waterway** is an adventurous paddling trip that takes at least nine days to paddle, although you can zoom through it in a motorized craft in just one very long day. This is absolutely the very best way to experience the Everglades. The trails are well marked and there are covered campsites along the route. If you are not a very experienced wilderness paddler and self-sufficient camper, come with one of the outfitters listed below. On your own, come well equipped. A hundred years ago most travelers who set out to cross the Everglades simply never returned. Be sure you have a backcountry camping permit, obtained in person from a visitor's center or ranger station. Costs are $10 per day, plus $2 per person, per night. Charts

Everglades National Park

of the area are a must; even though the trail is marked, there are so many twists, turns, and alternate channels that it is quite possible to get lost. There are many places where low overhanging trees make passage impossible for anything other than a canoe, kayak or alligator.

> **AUTHOR TIDBIT:** Large parts of the waterway pass through open water (Whitewater Bay), where stiff winds can make paddling strenuous. Mosquitoes, heat and intense sun make the trip extremely challenging during summer months.

The Waterway starts out near Everglades City and ends up near Flamingo. Outfitters arrange for drop-off and pick-up at either end. This is a demanding but very rewarding expedition.

■ OUTFITTERS

Kayaks rent from $35 per day. Boat tours start at $25.

Florida Bay Outfitters, *MM 104, Key Largo,* ☎ *305-451-3018, www.KayakFloridaKeys.com*, offers three-hour kayak tours and rentals deliver you to the back side of the park from their Key Largo base. They can also arrange guided multi-day trips through some of the park's less-traveled areas.

Everglades National Park Boat Tours, *Everglades City,* ☎ *941-695-2591.*

Majestic Everglades Excursions, *Everglades City,* ☎ *941-695-2777.*

■ In the Air

 Views of Florida Bay and the Ten Thousand Islands area are a spectacular photo opportunity.

■ OUTFITTERS

Wings 10,000 Islands Aero-Tours, *Everglades Airport, Route 29, Everglades City,* ☎ *239-695-3296.* Starting at $75, Wings takes visitors on low-flying trips over the Ten Thousand Islands area and Florida Bay.

Where to Stay

■ Ratings & Prices

 All prices are for two people staying in a double room during high season. Taxes and meals are not included unless so mentioned. Hotels and lodges marked "Author Picks" are my personal favorites, offering top-quality lodging and services but, more importantly, something of particular interest or charm.

ACCOMMODATIONS PRICE CHART	
$	Under $100
$$	$100-200
$$$	$200-300
$$$$	Over $300

■ Hotels & Resorts

The only hotel actually inside the park is the **Flamingo Lodge** on Florida Bay at the end of the long road from Homestead. It is an older hotel, but is very conveniently located for enjoying the bottom end of the park on Florida Bay. Several trails start within a short walking distance of the lodge and a variety of backcountry and Florida Bay fishing and wildlife tours leave from the marina next door. There is a large campground near the lodge.

Plenty of hotels can be found just outside the park entrance in Homestead and there are a few near the west end of the park in and around Chokoloskee. Staying in Homestead allows you to explore the eastern end of the park without having to drive too far.

Inside the Park

Flamingo Lodge, Marina & Outpost Resort, ☎ *941-695-3101, 800-600-3813, fax 941-695-3921, www.flamingolodge.com, $$*, is in need of some tender loving care. It is, however, clean and comes with working air-conditioning and a pool. The staff is friendly and pets are allowed. Accommodations include regular motel-style rooms as well as cottages, and some units have kitchen facilities. All the rooms are located right on the bay with handy access to park facilities and services.

Best Western Gateway to the Keys, *411 S Krome Avenue*, ☎ *305 246-5100, $$*. This is the last motel before you hit before the long road going through the swamp to the Keys. It is a typical Best Western, with clean rooms, coffee makers, iron and ironing board and the usual free breakfast offered in the lobby each morning. Local calls are free. No pets.

Everglades Int'l Hostel, Inc., *20 SW 2nd Avenue, Florida City,* ☎ *305-248-1122, $*. The hostel offers dormitories and private rooms. They also offer bike and canoe rentals. Dorm beds start at $13.

Grove Inn Country Guest House, *22540 S.W. 177 Avenue, Redlands,* ☎ *305-247-6572, 877-247-6572, www.groveinn.com, $$*. Pet-friendly Grove Inn is a B&B in a lovely setting near Homestead. The location is handy to Everglades National Park and the Upper Keys. It's quiet and in the same neighborhood as the nation's most successful orchid and tropical plant nurseries, several of which are open to the public. Breakfasts are included in the price and feature local fruits and produce from the owners' garden.

Hampton Inn, *124 E Palm Drive, Florida City,* ☎ *305-247-8833, 800-426-7866, fax 305-247-6456, www.hamptoninnfloridacity. com, FCMIA@hcifl.com, $$*. Here you get the usual Hampton quality and cleanliness with T-1 Internet access in all rooms. It's located at the very end of the Florida Turnpike and is convenient to Everglades National Park, Biscayne Bay and Key Largo.

Redland Hotel, *5 South Flagler Avenue, Homestead,* ☎ *305 246-1904, 800-595-190, www.redlandhotel.com*. Definitely not a chain-style hotel, the Redland has plenty of atmosphere and style. Rex & Katy Oleson and Jerry & Nancy Gust are the proprietors. Built in 1904, the historic Redland Hotel was Homestead's first hotel, first mercantile store, first US Post Office, first library and first boarding house. This is an interesting alternative to the chain motels that line US 1 near the entrance to the park.

Barron River Resort, *Everglades City,* ☎ *239-695-3591, 800-535-4961, fax 239-695-3331, suzgrif@evergladespark.com, www.*

evergladespark.com, *$$*. Barron River is owned by brothers Don and Larry Harmon. It offers basic motel-style rooms. Pets are allowed for an extra charge of $10 per night for each.

Captain's Table Hotel, *Everglades City*, ☎ *941-695-4211, 800-741-6430, fax 941-695-2633, www.capttable.com*, *$$*. Captain's has basic hotel rooms, junior suites and villas at a variety of price ranges. There's a restaurant and conference facilities, as well as a boat ramp and slips.

Everglades City Motel, *Everglades City*, ☎ *239-695-4224, 800-695-8353, fax 239-695-2557, evergcitymotes@aol.com*, *$-$$*. The motel rooms here are basic, but clean and air-conditioned.

Everglades Rod and Gun Resort Lodge, *P.O. Box 190, Everglades City*, ☎ *941-695-2101*, *$$*. Even though it is a bit run-down, this is a real classic from Old Florida days. Presidents and celebrities still trickle in from time to time – John Wayne slept here. Pets are allowed.

Ivey House B&B, *Everglades City*, ☎ *239-695-3299, www.iveyhouse.com*, *$$*. They have a nice pool and a variety of rooms at various prices. The restaurant serves some of the better food in the area.

Everglades Spa & Lodge, *201 West Broadway, Everglades City*, ☎ *941-695-3151, 888-431-1977, fax 239-695-3335, www.banksoftheeverglades.com*, *$$*. Located in the landmark Bank of Everglades building, this full-of-charm hotel is convenient to the west side of the Everglades National Park. It still looks like a turn-of-the-century bank, but everything has been modernized with care. All rooms are non-smoking. Their "funcierge" service can help arrange all the activities you might be interested in.

■ Camping

 There are two campgrounds and 48 backcountry campsites in the park. Charges at either campground are $14 per night during winter; sites are offered free of charge June through August. Reservations can be made through the **National Park Reservation Service** at ☎ *800-365-2267, 301-722-1257, reservations.nps.gov*. Pets on leashes are allowed. There are no RV hookups in the park.

The park's large campground at Flamingo is right on Florida Bay, close to the park's marina and right by some of best hiking and paddling trails. Sites in Loop A are closer to the showers. The whole campground is fairly open, but even so the breeze does not blow away the mosquitoes – bring plenty of repellent. Pack in all the food you need as the Restaurant at Flamingo Lodge is small, not particularly wonderful and can get full early. The marina's small grocery/bait store has a very limited, high-priced selection of goods. Reservations are essential.

Although not quite as exciting as the area around Flamingo, the **Long Pine Key Campground** is perhaps a bit nicer. There are plenty of pine trees, so it seems cool and slightly private. You'll need reservations during winter.

For those with energy for **backcountry camping**, the heart of the Everglades is open to you. The park's 48 sites, accessible by land and water, vary in what they offer. Some have chemical toilets, others have covered eating areas and some have docks. You can check them out on the park's website, www.nps.gov/ever/visit/backcoun.htm, which shows the facilities offered at each. Permits are needed and, starting at $10, vary in cost depending on the number of people and length of stay. There are limits on the total number of campers permitted at any one time and the permits are offered on a first-come, first-serve basis. A call to the park, ☎ 305-242-7700, will get you a map and a Wilderness Trip Planner. During peak season, November through April, there are limits on the amount of time you may stay at any one campsite.

Several camping & RV facilities are found near the various park entrances.

City of Florida City Camp Site and RV Park, *601 NW 3rd Ave, Florida City, FL 33034*, ☎ *305-248-7889*. Tent and RV sites, some with hookups. There are laundry facilities, picnic tables and a playground.

Goldcoaster Mobile Home & RV Park, *34850 SW 187 Ave, Homestead, FL 33034*, ☎ *305-248-5462*. RVs only from $40 per night. Book well in advance.

Southern Comfort RV Resort Inc., *345 East Palm Drive, Florida City, FL, 33034*, ☎ *305-248-6909*, has 350 full hookup sites for RVs only. There's also a Tiki bar, pool and laundry.

Chokoloskee Island Park, *P.O. Box 430, Chokoloskee, FL 34138*, ☎ *941-695-2414, www.Chokoloskee.com*, has a good marina, a laundromat and RV hookups.

Glades Haven Recreational Resort, *Everglades City across from the visitor center, 800 S.E. Copeland Ave./Rte. 29*, ☎ *941-695-2746, fax 941-695-3954*. Glades Haven offers 60 full RV hookups for $30/day. There is a marina, convenience store and deli. They have tent sites from $12/ day.

Outdoor Resort at Chokoloskee Island, *Highway 29 South, Chokoloskee, FL 34139*, ☎ *941-695-2881, fax 941-695-3338*. The "resort" has motel rooms, 283 RV sites, a full marina with boat ramp and three tennis courts. Some pets are allowed.

Where to Eat

Unfortunately, the one restaurant in the park is small and not particularly noteworthy. If you don't bring your own food or can't reserve a table at the restaurant at Flamingo Lodge, you'll have to drive all the way back to Homestead (about 50 miles) for a bite.

The price symbols for each listing consider the average cost of main courses listed on the menu.

RESTAURANT PRICE CHART
$ . . . . Under $8
$$ $8-12
$$$ $12-20
$$$$ . . . . Over $20

Robert Is Here Fruit Stand, *19200 SW 344th Street*, ☎ *305-246-1592, www.robertishere.com*. As you head to the park, you'll see what appears to be a cheesy fruit stand. Don't be fooled. Robert's is actually a WONDERFUL fruit stand. They have a titanic selection of interesting, fresh fruits and make the best fruit smoothies in the land. You can't miss the place. I like to stop here

Everglades National Park

on my way in and out of the 'glades. Go ahead and ruin your lunch here with a smoothie.

Flamingo Lodge Restaurant, *Flamingo Lodge Highway*, ☎ *941-695-3101, 800-600-3813, fax 941-695-3921, $$$.* This restaurant is small and gets busy at times, as there is no other place to eat nearby. The food is mediocre and the prices are similar to those of a nice restaurant in a big city. A typical entrée of fish or chicken with plain salad, potato, steamed vegetables and a glass of wine costs about $25. Be sure to make reservations – if you miss out on this, you'll have to drive all the way back to Homestead for food.

Redland Rib House, *Coconut Palm & Krome Avenue, Homestead,* ☎ *305-246-8866, $$.* A good rib joint. You can wear flip-flops and get BBQ sauce and grease all over your shirt – no problem!

Rosarita's, *a couple of blocks off Highway 1 on the road to the park's main entrance, $$.* Mexican, *muy autentico.* Humble but good, this is a real find. Along with the usual tacos and burritos, look for beef tongue on the menu. My mother recommends the green chile enchiladas.

Index

Index